INVESTMENT
WISDOM
—— FOR THE ——
DIGITAL AGE

DR HARRY LIEM

To my wife and best friend Vivian and my children
Alyssa and Julian for their love and understanding.
May they have a bright future.

To my colleagues at Mercer, especially Simon Eagleton,
Deb Clarke and Rich Nuzum, for their support and
encouragement for this book project.

To the CFA Institute, notably Phil Graham
and Rebecca Fender, for contributing to a book that
benefits the wider industry.

To Aristotle for a life of learning and teaching.

ACKNOWLEDGMENTS

I am grateful to all of those who contributed their time, effort and expertise to help produce this book.

Development of this publication was in particular sponsored and encouraged by Simon Eagleton, Senior Partner and Mercer's Institutional Wealth Leader for the Pacific region, and Phil Graham, Presidents Council Representative for the CFA Institute covering the Asia Pacific North and Oceania region.

I wish also to thank Rich Nuzum as President of our global Wealth Business and Deb Clarke as our Global Head of Investment Research for making this book update once again a global initiative and for the final endorsement of the project. This only happens once every 12 years!

I would also like to express thanks to my companions at Mercer's Global Strategic Research Committee, especially Nick White as our Global Head of Strategic Research, for many years of always stimulating conversations and out-of-the-box thinking. Thanks also go to Tracey Hayward, Yumeko Sahely and Natalie Truong at Mercer for internal and external distribution and marketing assistance, Maan Beydoun for compliance and Rachel Finlayson, Alyson Portlock and Michael Hanrahan for assisting with the publication and book launch.

We wish to thank Rebecca Fender, Head of the Future of Finance Initiative at the CFA Institute, and the many external participants and firms who reviewed draft manuscripts in the preparation of this book. Particular acknowledgments go to them for their valuable insights, detailed critiques, assistance, and constant support throughout the development of this publication.

Most importantly, thanks to my wife Vivian and my children Alyssa and Julian, who put up with a string of lost weekends and odd working hours.

Praise for *2020 Vision: Investment Wisdom for Tomorrow*

What will the investment world look like in 10 years' time? What would it be like to ask some of the greatest minds in the world what they think? In 2007, we interviewed 12 of the world's prominent investment and academic experts on this question, in the prequel to *Investment Wisdom for the Digital Age.*

2020 Vision: Investment Wisdom for Tomorrow was issued as a limited print edition for Mercer colleagues, clients and institutional investors, and has featured in publications such as *Pensions and Investments, Financial Times, Financial Standard, Forbes Magazine, Institutional Alternative Investment, The Australian, The Hedge Fund Journal, Investment and Technology* and *Scoop Business New Zealand.*

'Dear Harry; congratulations on your wonderful book and thanks for including me as part of it. It's a wonderful compendium of great thoughts of exceptional people which will serve as an important contribution to our industry. I'm honoured to be included. Thank you.'
Ray Dalio, co-CIO and former CEO, Bridgewater

'Your book is great, though you've given away too many secrets!'
Dr Clifford S. Asness, Founding and Managing Principal,
AQR Capital Management

'Just a short note to say congratulations on your book, a fantastic effort. I look forward in the future to be able to quote many "pearls of wisdom" from your various publications, no doubt on the drawing board as we speak.'
Andrew Howard, former CIO, Mercer, Melbourne

'Terrific! Kudos, Harry! The 2020 book is creating quite a stir here in the States.'
Bruce Lee, Principal, Mercer, New York

Disclaimer

CONTENTS

Foreword **1**
Introduction **3**
Preface **7**
The interviews **11**

Part I: The new investment environment 13

Chapter 1   Megatrends **15**
Chapter 2   A brave new world **29**

Part II: The Digital World 45

Chapter 3   Humans versus machines **47**
Chapter 4   Rethinking the alpha bet **63**
Chapter 5   Investment firms in the Digital Age **79**

Part III: East versus West 91

Chapter 6   The road less travelled **93**
Chapter 7   Crossroads **105**

Part IV: Alternative investments 115

Chapter 8   Alternative investments of the future   **117**
Chapter 9   Private investigations **135**

Part V: A better tomorrow 147

Chapter 10   Building a sustainable world: opportunities in real estate
             and infrastructure **149**
Chapter 11   Alpha in responsible investments   **173**

Part VI: Long-term investing 185

Chapter 12   Investment beliefs for the future   **187**
Chapter 13   Views from the ivory tower **203**

Summary **219**
Evolutionary dynamics in the Digital Age **227**
Afterword **233**
About the author **235**

FOREWORD

In this book, Harry Liem presents investment insights and wisdom gathered from interviews with leading practitioners and academic experts to investigate how the investment industry will evolve and whether traditional investment wisdom remains relevant in the Digital Age.

Wisdom, sapience, or sagacity is the ability to think and act using knowledge, experience, understanding, common sense and insight. Many of the interviewed participants are at later stages of their careers and have lived through multiple market cycles. For many this is a way of giving back to the industry before they retire.

A strong theme of institutional investment is the search for alpha or outperformance. At the same time, it seems that much of what has been marketed as alpha is being defined away as factor based or replicable, therefore beta. Institutional investors have long battled against the erosion of alpha as their ideas and processes are taken up by competitors. The best of them are constantly searching for new ideas and new sources of information, and ways to collect and process it faster to establish or maintain their advantage.

How will the search for investment opportunities be impacted by the rise in artificial intelligence and machine learning? Will investing in the future be an art, science or skill? How do we create a future that is sustainable for shareholders and broader society? Without giving away any spoilers, we believe this book will assist investors to appreciate where our industry is headed.

Simon Eagleton
Business Leader Institutional Wealth for the Pacific region
Sydney

INTRODUCTION

As the investment industry has developed, it has tended toward greater specialisation and complexity, and the role of the CFA Institute as a professional body is to help weave together the pieces so that rigorous thinking can be applied across the financial ecosystem. This book demonstrates the value of bringing together wisdom from leading practitioners and academics, and it reminds us of the importance of connecting theory with experience.

In the Future of Finance initiative, we aim to shape a more trust-worthy, forward-thinking investment profession that better serves society. We found in *Future State of the Investment Profession* that only 11% of investment leaders describe the impact of the investment industry today as very positive, but 51% expect it could be very positive contingent on stronger principles.

Successful investment professionals learn from the past and have an insatiable curiosity. The interviews here will provide helpful perspective, but readers should not expect it will give them all the answers. Instead, this volume will be most useful if it prompts readers to question their assumptions about investing and to envision an industry that serves its enduring purpose – to contribute to society through increases in societal wealth and wellbeing – while it adapts through innovation.

Nearly 50% of core investment professionals, such as analysts, portfolio managers, and wealth managers, expect these roles to be significantly different or even non-existent in the next five to 10 years, so adaptability is essential.

A Digital Age of disruption requires greater learning and deepening of skills to stay competitive. This book is a great resource for those who want to thrive in the investment profession of the future.

Rebecca Fender, CFA
Head of the Future of Finance initiative
CFA Institute
Charlottesville, Virginia

'Existence is beyond the power of words to define.'
Lao-Tzu

'We are what we think.
With our thoughts, we make the world.'
Buddha

'Any path to knowledge is a path to God – or Reality,
whichever word one prefers to use.'
Arthur C. Clarke

PREFACE
The challenges of the digital future

In 2007, I asked 12 investment and academic experts whether investing is an art, science or skill, and what this meant for how people should invest.[1]

- If investing is mostly art, then you want to put your money with a virtuoso with talent who dares to act differently, like George Soros who stood against the Bank of England in 1992.

- If it is science, then you want to hire the manager with PhDs, access to data, and algorithms, like Jim Simons at Renaissance.

- If it is skill, you want somebody with practical, hands-on experience and tools, like Warren Buffett at Berkshire Hathaway.

In the short run, participants correctly anticipated the Global Financial Crisis and the corresponding shakeout and subsequent decline in alpha within the hedge fund industry. In the long run, the book highlighted that the upcoming 'great divide' and paradigm shift as skill (or alpha generation) was expected to become increasingly separated from risk premia exposure (or beta replication). While the prediction was made early in 2007, a decade later this has come to pass with an explosion in ETFs and alternative risk premia and indexing products. But what does the future hold for investment manager skill now, as we enter the Digital Age? How rewarding will risk premia remain? And what sort of investments can we expect in the future?

To an algorithm engaged in investing, human biases that create many of the risk premia and anomalies in the investment markets simply would not exist. Yet, humans can be creative in ways that are rare, as are algorithms that can perform human tasks without being explicitly programmed to do so. Machines can process huge sets of data in an unbiased manner. What then makes investment skills valuable in the future?

---

1   Refer to *2020 Vision: Investment Wisdom for Tomorrow*, Mercer, 2007.

Some might argue we have never seen more rapid and far-reaching technological changes than in the last few years, and with so much uncertainty about the future, any prediction would be futile. While forecasting the future is inherently difficult, it's worth remembering technological breakthroughs are not something new to our generation. The world was in a similar flux after the transistor was developed in 1948.[2] The following astonishing prediction was made in 1954, and could conceivably reflect the world as it will come to pass:

> *'Whenever a baby is born anywhere in the world, he is given at birth a telephone number for life. As soon as he can talk, he is given a watch-like device with ten little buttons on one side and a screen on the other. When he wishes to talk with anyone in the world, he will pull out the device and punch on the keys the number. Then, turning the device over, he will hear the voice of his friend and see his face on the screen, in colour and in three dimensions. If he does not see him and hear him, he will know that his friend is dead.'*

Harold S. Osborne, former Chief Engineer of AT&T

Is humanity and technology becoming so blended together that chips in the brain and 3D-printed organs will one day be considered a normal part of life? And if we were to become no longer totally human, but not totally digital either, would that make us a new species – *Homo Digitalis*? Are we going to take over evolution and decide for ourselves how we want to change? Today's rapid developments in technology are by no means new, but represent a confluence of long-running technological evolutions:

- *Computing power.* Moore's Law (1965) suggests that the number of transistors in an integrated circuit doubles about every two years. Since the 1970s this has approximately occurred. IBM's world-class Summit supercomputer can crunch through 200 quadrillion mathematical calculations each second, a speed called 200 petaflops. That is as fast as each of the planet's 7.6 billion people doing 26 million calculations per second on a hand calculator. The drawback is that Summit is as big as two tennis courts and needs 9,216 processors boosted with 27,648 graphics chips.

---

2   The transistor is the key active component in modern electronics. Many consider it to be the greatest invention of the 20th century. The vast majority of transistors are produced in integrated circuits, often referred to as ICs, microchips or simply chips.

- *Data storage cost.* Similar to Moore's Law for transistors, over the last 30 years, the space per unit cost has doubled roughly every 14 months. In 1981 a gigabyte of storage cost $300,000. Today the price is below $0.10. This has led to the storage of more 'Big Data', but also more noise.

- *Algorithm complexity.* Modern thinking on artificial intelligence can be traced back to 1950s. Advances in artificial intelligence from adopting practical techniques from statistics, computer science, mathematics and engineering have matured and amalgamated into powerful new algorithms.

In addition, the following prescient forecast of how our present-day society conceivably operates was made over 40 years ago:

> '*Today we live in a society in which spurious realities are manufactured by the media, by governments, by big corporations, by religious groups, political groups ... So I ask, in my writing, what is real? Because unceasingly, we are bombarded with pseudo-realities manufactured by very sophisticated people, using very sophisticated electronic mechanisms. I do not distrust their motives; I distrust their power. They have a lot of it. And it is an astonishing power: that of creating whole universes, universes of the mind. I ought to know. I do the same thing.*'
> Philip K. Dick (1928–1982).[3]

As a science fiction writer, Philip K. Dick captured the 'fake news' movement of the 21st century well. The impact of fake news has become more instant and widespread with the opening of the internet in the 1990s. 'Deepfake' takes this even further as it uses artificial intelligence to create events and videos that never happened.[4]

We live in a world where news through technology becomes progressively personalised, with content adapted to reader preferences. The capacity to mislead is enhanced by the widespread use of social media and media bots. In the United States, two-thirds of Americans rely on social media to receive news and mainly read headlines.[5]

---

3   Philip K. Dick was an American science fiction writer. His novels have been adapted into movies like *Blade Runner* (1982), *Total Recall* (1990 and 2012), *Minority Report* (2002) and *The Man in the High Castle* (2015).
4   Refer to a convincing fake Obama speech at https://www.youtube.com/watch?v=cQ54GDm1eL0.
5   https://www.reuters.com/article/us-usa-internet-socialmedia/two-thirds-of-american-adults-get-news-from-social-media-survey-idUSKCN1BJ2A8.

This book seeks to improve our understanding of a future where man will co-invest with increasingly intelligent machines.

At the same time, we are now at a crossroads in history in terms of global economics, politics and philosophy, where decisions and mega-trends will no longer just impact us, but generations to come, with a rise in populism and de-globalisation. A decade of quantitative easing (QE) and record low interest rates has fuelled rising capital markets, a wider wealth disparity, as well as rising debt levels and reduced effectiveness of central bank policy. Demographics are becoming more important at a time when population growth in emerging markets and ageing in developed markets is straining financial and environmental resources.

There are moments in our lives when we find ourselves at a cross-roads, afraid, confused, without a roadmap. When faced with the unknown, most of us prefer to turn around and go back. When faced with what is easy and what is right, most of us prefer what is easy. Yet, some of us prefer to create a roadmap and forge ahead. A generation of influential thinkers in finance is nearing retirement, and this may in some cases be a final chance to pass on their wisdom to the next generation of investors and provide them with a framework for understanding our changing world and our own role in it. Which is why I decided an update of my original book was not only desirable, but a necessity.

Harry Liem
Sydney, August 2019

THE INTERVIEWS

'If I have seen further it is by standing on the shoulders of giants.'
Isaac Newton (1643–1727)

We conducted interviews with some of the world's leading academic and industry experts and asked them to share their views on a wide universe of asset classes, and think on a global dimension about where they feel the opportunities lie in the coming years. All have had long and outstanding careers and remain actively involved in the industry.

In part I, we investigate **the new investment environment**. Deb Clarke, Mercer's Global Head of Investment Research, will lead us through global megatrends impacting investors. Deb is followed by Ben Inker, Head of Asset Allocation, GMO, who discusses the long unwinding road in a 'brave new world'.

Part II sets out **the Digital World**. In 'Humans versus machines', Dr Anthony Ledford, Man AHL's Chief Scientist and Academic Liaison based at the Man Research Laboratory at Oxford, provides us with a better understanding of the Digital World and machine learning. In 'Rethinking the alpha bet', Dr Stan Beckers, Fellow at the London Business School, examines the implications of the Digital World on alpha, beta and cost. Finally, Julia Hobart, Partner, Oliver Wyman, in 'Investment firms in the Digital Age', examines how fund managers are impacted by trends in technology and diversity.

Part III takes us to the **East versus West debate**. In 'The road less travelled', Dr Mark Mobius, Chairman of Mobius Capital Partners, former chairman of Templeton Emerging Markets Group, discusses emerging markets and the battle of the giants as China is challenging the US global hegemony. Ray Dalio, former CEO of Bridgewater, then examines the crossroads for humanity in terms of economics, politics and philosophy, and the potential for conflict.

Part IV examines the opportunities in **alternative investments**. In 'Alternative investments of the future', Dr Keith Black, Managing

Director, Curriculum and Exams, Chartered Alternative Investment Association, examines some of the more exotic opportunities. He is followed by 'Private investigations' by Dr Ludovic Phalippou, Professor of Financial Economics at the University of Oxford and former Head of Private Markets Research for the BlackRock Investment Institute, who revisits some of the popular myths surrounding private equity.

Part V, **a better tomorrow**, is about building a sustainable future. In 'Building a sustainable world: opportunities in real estate and infrastructure', James McKellar and Sherena Hussain, Professor and Assistant Professor at the Brookfield Centre in Real Estate and Infrastructure, York University, Canada, examine the impact of demographics and building sustainable real estate and infrastructure for future generations. Subsequently, Dr Rob Bauer, Professor of Finance at Maastricht University, discusses the merits of 'Alpha in responsible investments' and optimising investment and social objectives.

Part VI discusses **long-term investing**. Dr Cliff Asness, Founder, Managing Principal, and Chief Investment Officer, AQR, reviews 'Investment beliefs for the future'. He is followed in 'Views from the ivory tower' by Dr Stephen Brown, Emeritus Professor at NYU, Professor at Monash Business School, and Executive Editor of *Financial Analysts Journal*, who surveys trends in academia.

The interviews are followed by a summary looking at some of the themes that have emerged from our interviews and aiming to provide an understanding of the future of investing as viewed by our participants.

Having introduced our topics and participants, it's time to meet our first interviewees in Part I: The new investment environment.

THE NEW INVESTMENT ENVIRONMENT

— CHAPTER 1 —
MEGATRENDS

An interview with Deb Clarke on megatrends shaping our future

'Prediction is very difficult, especially if it is about the future.'
Niels Bohr (1885–1962)

The coming decade will be dominated by the upcoming collision between demographics, technology and debt. This trilemma has lasting implications for investors, and will likely create a shift in world order.

In terms of *demographics*, the world population is expected to reach 8.5 billion by 2030.[1] The United Nations forecasts 1 billion additional city dwellers by 2030, led by Asia and Africa. The competition for energy sources with the newly developing nations will become a major issue in the near future as protectionism, nationalism and populism fan de-globalisation and climate change impacts the environment.[2] By 2030 China will be the world's largest economy, and emerging markets will account for two-thirds of global growth.[3]

From a *technology* perspective, the Fourth Industrial Revolution blurs the lines between the physical, digital and biological spheres.[4]

---

1 'Population 2030: Demographic challenges and opportunities for sustainable development planning', United Nations, 2015.
2 https://www.un.org/sustainabledevelopment/sustainable-development-goals/.
3 https://enterprise.press/wp-content/uploads/2018/10/HSBC-The-World-in-2030-Report.pdf.
4 https://www.weforum.org/agenda/2016/01/the-fourth-industrial-revolution-what-it-means-and-how-to-respond/.

The possibilities of billions of people connected by mobile devices – with unprecedented processing power, storage capacity and access to information – are unlimited. At the same time, those without the necessary resources and education – from poorer rural areas or countries – could be left behind in the technology race, further widening the income disparity, both within and across countries.

From a *debt* perspective, QE together with easy monetary policy, has facilitated the continuing rise in global debt. Ten years after the Global Financial Crisis, debt remains at historic highs, with China on its way to equalling Japan in terms of total debt to GDP.

The trilemma in creating a sustainable future

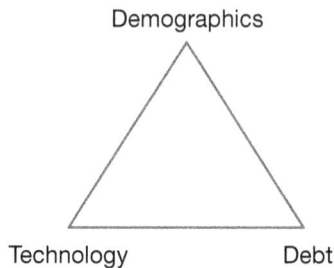

Demographics

Technology   Debt

Introducing Deb Clarke

Deb is Mercer's Global Head of Investment Research, which includes responsibility for manager research and strategic research. Based in London, Deb manages a group of over 100 asset class specialists across Diversifying Alternatives, Fixed Income and Equities. She also oversees the teams responsible for Strategic Asset Allocation, Dynamic Asset Allocation, Strategic Research and Responsible Investing. These teams work together to support a full range of client solutions from Advisory to Fiduciary Management.

Deb was previously the Global Leader of Mercer's Equity Boutique, specialising in researching global and global emerging market equity managers. Deb is Chairman of Mercer's Global Policy Committee and a member of the Mainstream Assets Global Investment Committee.

Deb has been named as one of the 100 most influential women in European finance by *Financial News* and received the *2016 Distinguished Woman Investment Professional of the Year* Award in Chicago.

Deb joined Mercer in November 2005 from Watson Wyatt, where she was a Senior Investment Consultant advising a range of clients and researching Asian and emerging market equity managers. Prior to this, Deb was a fund manager for 20 years, most recently working for Friends Ivory & Sime as Head of Equities.

Deb holds a bachelor's degree (honours) in business studies from Plymouth University, UK. She is an Associate of the Society of Investment Professionals, UK.

Deb, many thanks for participating in our book. What do you consider to be the most important global megatrends affecting investors today?

In terms of *demographics*, we have a changing environment with ageing populations in several parts of the world. As a result, healthcare systems and needs – for example, transportation – and consumption patterns are changing; most economies are not suited or prepared for those changes. More of our GDP and wealth will need to be invested in looking after that ageing population. It would be encouraging to think we would see a return to old-fashioned values of families looking after each other; whether that will actually occur I don't know. Another aspect of demographics is people looking to live even longer than the current life expectancies. If we could indeed live to the age of 150, 200 or even longer, using stem cell technology and replacing parts of our bodies, that brings challenges. Do people really want to live that long? What about the social impact? Many elderly people are very lonely. How do we ensure they lead fulfilling lives for that many years? These are some of the demographic and related social challenges.

On the *economic* side, we've been in a prolonged period where we've manufactured lots of 'stuff' and had relatively strong GDP around the world. We could now be in for a sustained period of low growth, inflation and interest rates, alongside increased trade tensions. We have had quantitative easing for 10 years and arguably markets resisting reality. That reality could be challenging in terms of how we cope with several years or even decades of lower returns. This could be the time we see a return to investing in order to create long-term wealth and not just investing to beat a benchmark. We are all going to have to adjust our thinking about what investing means, why people are investing, what is their time frame, and realistically what the returns are likely to be.

If I have $100 as I get closer to retirement, I may want that to go to $102 or $103. I don't really care what the index does as an individual because that is not relevant to my needs. But I do care whether my $100 becomes $80 as I can then no longer fund my social care or other needs. So those are the big economic and investment trends.

Overlaying that is the whole *climate change* debate. What are we doing living in a world that we appear to be destroying? There is clear evidence of the connection between climate and its impact on the world. It is driving investment in new technology, like batteries, and encouraging changes in behaviour. Climate change will impact how we live, how we eat, the agriculture we produce, and much more, and we will have to adapt. As individuals assume more responsibility for their investments, they are challenging how their money is being invested. Not necessarily through impact investing, but at least making sure their money is invested in a sustainable way. To some degree sustainable investing is built on common sense. Why invest in a company that destroys the planet and our social fabric and doesn't have good governance? That makes no sense. So ESG (environmental, social and governance) to me is, to a large degree, common sense, and companies need to demonstrate that they are focused on improving in all areas of ESG.

Technology is another megatrend where we're seeing big changes. I have children now who are telling me they are doing jobs collecting data on things that I would never have even expected. You have AI, DNA sequencing, robotics, blockchain technology. We don't really know the impact, apart from that they could all be transformational, like steam engines, telephones, cars and mass production. When I started work in 1983 we didn't have computers. When I say that to younger people, they look at me like I landed from Mars! Yet we got things done. We all need to adapt, and continuous learning is an important component of that.

What do you see as the major trends among institutional investors?

One major trend for institutional investors we're seeing at an accelerating pace is *the move from DB (defined benefit) paternalistic plans to DC (defined contribution) plans*, which means individuals are taking more responsibility. Even with DC plans there is a question about how much companies should be doing. Should there be a greater focus on Master Trusts or combined industry plans? Is it really a company's responsibility to provide retirement savings? I think there is some merit; for example, it provides loyalty, but it is also potentially an expensive by-product for your company.

Increased allocation to alternatives is another trend that's here to stay and absolutely key in generating long-term returns and providing portfolio diversity. Looking at asset allocation trends around the globe, we see a trend away from public to private assets and other diversifying alternatives. We also observe many private companies coming to the public markets later than they have historically, and some long-only asset managers wanting to make investments in these companies before they come to market.

Globalisation has been a strong trend, and at the margin we are seeing a movement towards more local or emerging markets, as some economies develop and become mainstream; for example, Brazil or Mexico. Perhaps going forward, institutional investors will use a mix of local and global mandates, rather than using all global portfolios.

Institutional investors are seeing the trend of *technology* manifest itself in many ways; employing data science to 1) find a competitive advantage in terms of using data more efficiently, and also 2) to make better decisions are just two. As an example, one large asset manager has hired people from the sporting world to use data to analyse when people make the best decisions. Is it after eating or having coffee? After they've been given a certain amount or type of information, or information presented in a certain format? We have long known that the way information is presented can have implications on decisions, but now we have the data to confirm those views. Investing in a competitive world is all about finding small edges.

ESG considerations have always been present during my career, and ESG has a firm foundation in many forms of equities; for example, long-only, long-term, benchmark unaware and private market investments such as infrastructure. What you're seeing now is the broadening of ESG considerations into other investment areas, which are playing catch-up from a lower base. Many asset managers want to increase their ESG credentials, and we need to avoid greenwashing and see a genuine commitment to ESG considerations at the individual strategy level.

Ethics and diversity are also becoming more important. Is there a culture of ethical behaviour, supported at the business level and demonstrated by senior management? Does the business embrace diversity and inclusion – not just in policies but through its actions and embracing that diversity for the benefit of clients? It is imperative to create a sustainable business, and it is encouraging that industry bodies such as the CFA have this at the heart of their programs.

The investment landscape is changing for the whole community, for asset managers, asset owners and consultants as well; it is an industry that is likely to be disrupted in the next 10 years. The underlying need is to deliver a client's objectives in a cost-effective manner. This is being delivered by an industry facing headwinds of a lack of trust, lower returns for operators and lower fees.

We have spoken about major trends – are these discussions fairly common across regions, or are there any region-particular issues that stand out?

The direction is similar for most regions outside of the developing markets. The one that stands out perhaps is the US. It is relatively siloed when looking at returns; equities for example are still focused on large, mid, and small caps and value versus growth. That is relatively narrow, and much of the rest of the world has moved more towards a broader range of factors and an increased focus on outcome/solutions-based approaches with more manager flexibility.

Also, in a period of low returns, regional currency and interest rates will matter more, so currency hedging could become a more important element of returns. For example, if you get higher interest rates in the US than Europe or Japan, that may impact your hedging decision as a US investor.

In terms of investment research, which areas do you think institutional investors should focus on?

Investors need a clear roadmap to their destination – their ultimate objective. Most investors consider this to be set by the strategic asset allocation. I actually think it is a bit deeper than that. It starts with having a set of beliefs and a series of signposts. That leads to your governance structure, strategic allocation, return expectations, risk and liquidity tolerance, timeframe and so on – a beliefs and outcomes-based approach that will become increasingly bespoke and individualised.

While strategic asset allocation remains important, manager selection will have a role to play in the environment we expect to unfold. New asset classes are constantly emerging, like secure finance and multi-asset credit, where manager selection is key. Manager selection is also critical in private markets, where you are committing your capital for a long period with the expectation of higher returns.

Other areas where institutional investors need to pay attention are risk management, being aware of non-financial risks as well as financial risks, and the costs associated with investing throughout the process – these demand transparency.

What do you see as the hallmark of a successful long-term institutional investor?

By definition that would be the patience to stay the course! I'm a big believer in a couple of things. First is the time horizon for long-term investors like DB plans. We don't have to go as far as the Church of England buying a piece of land and holding it for 300 years, but be prepared to be brave and contrarian. Don't follow the herd. Know your own roadmap.

Second, have clarity and the right governance structure for you so that you can implement your decisions. That is the key. So set out your beliefs and governance, and then have the patience to do what you need to do.

There's an interesting angle if you take it from an asset manager perspective: the hallmark would be about knowing what you're good at and sticking to it. If you look at the investment industry, many asset managers have profitable books of business but where demand for those products is declining. They need to realign their business, but are unlikely to develop solutions that have the same level of capacity; they are in an awful pinch. Capacity is often one of the biggest challenges and tensions asset managers face – at what point does their success risk being diminished by their desire to have larger assets under management?

Where do you think AI and Big Data can be most useful in the investment decision-making process from an asset owner perspective?

From a DC plan perspective I would say it would be in the area of data analytics and robo-advice. It should help answer questions like:

- 'Who within my population is matching the required contributions needed to achieve their outcomes?'
- 'Who is patiently sitting in the default fund?'
- 'Who is reacting to short-term market performance, and should we try to discourage that behaviour?'

These are interesting aspects from a monitoring and behavioural perspective, where AI and Big Data can help. We could have personalised robo-advice/videos that could say: 'Would you like to top up your pension this month? Here is the benefit in 20 years' time if you do, or you may need to do this in order to achieve your goals.' There is always the challenge of advice not being personalised, but new technologies are likely to create an environment where that challenge will diminish.

And from an asset manager perspective?

In terms of Big Data, asset managers are considering Big Data as an alpha source or research advantage. I think that both have yet to be proven as a replacement for underlying analysis. Everybody is scrambling for new ideas, using new data. An example often quoted is using a drone to collect information from car parks about how many cars are parked at certain times of day – it's not clear to me how useful this information is or how predictive it is. It becomes old hat very quickly. I believe there will be a trend back towards creating genuine long-term wealth using fundamental analysis, incorporating technology to assist in sifting information for those data points that are important to that asset manager's process rather than trading on the latest information craze. I would call that a trend towards 'genuine investing'. People want to invest, not trade their money. They also want to know how their investment is helping not only themselves, but the whole of society.

In terms of AI, I have met asset managers who are now using machine learning to understand that if a stock reacts in a particular way in certain market circumstances, can it learn how the stock might react next time? So learning applications may well become something people want to use to give confidence; for example, if there is a huge standard deviation event.

Can you comment on any interesting trends you see in the manager research field?

Clients are asking us to look at the total portfolio in a more holistic way. So the traditional asset class boundaries are increasingly overlapping or dispersing. Strategies may no longer fit into a single box, an example being an options strategy.

The second thing clients are asking us to look at are strategies where the manager has more freedom. So we need to help them understand how they can measure the performance of those strategies. It is unlikely to be a standard market benchmark but rather a benchmark aligned to their own objectives (say, cash or CPI plus) or a competitive peer group benchmark; for example, the top 10 value managers.

So I think it is about taking a slightly more holistic view of the world. It is no longer about new products but about what problem any product is trying to solve. There is a real genuine end-client need and that is important to remember.

In which asset classes are investors most and least likely to find alpha, whether through managers or direct investment?

It's fair to say we don't see alpha in all universes.

We've always said that it's hard to achieve alpha in US large caps. Having said that, there are some really good US large cap managers, but not many.

In areas like developing countries, small caps and credit, you can make a difference as a manager. Those are not controversial. You can improve your return/risk profile provided you have the right governance and execution structures.

One of the other trends on the equity side is a move to highly concentrated 10- to 15-stock portfolios. That is fine, provided the person buying them knows what they are buying into! You can have a passive core and a series of these satellites which are benchmark unaware.

We also believe there are value and alpha opportunities across areas like infrastructure, whether direct or indirect. That fits nicely into the income requirements – increasingly important to asset owners – and 'doing good' for the community at the same time.

Can you comment on any interesting asset classes or products that investors could take note of?

In terms of regions, China and emerging markets would be interesting. For frontier markets you really need to have the governance, and any investment needs be a meaningful part of your portfolio to have an impact.

Thematic funds – which we believe have the potential to be interesting in order to capture the opportunities from the long-term changes we have referenced elsewhere – have struggled to gain traction. It is an area we will continue to do work in and look for suitable strategies.

In fixed income, clients are looking for mandates and strategies that give the asset manager freedom to access a broad range of opportunities. Return expectations from government bonds remain low, so we continue to develop new areas such as multi-asset credit and secured finance – the latter tapping into interesting opportunities that suit investors prepared to tolerate illiquidity, scarcity and complexity.

On East versus West, where would you invest your marginal $1?

I have to be honest – I would probably give my $1 to China, but it doesn't come without political risk. I have a view, probably non-consensus, that China is no longer the copier of IP as much as people think it is. They have competitive advantages in some areas; for example, green energy. The number of graduates that come out of universities and now want to go and work in the East is incredible. If you can overcome the politics, I would put my money on China.

In the institutional world, there is currently a lot of focus on ESG. What are your thoughts on how institutional investors can best align shareholders and stakeholders?

Yes, there is a lot of focus on ESG, but you have to be careful it's not just 'greenwashing', and that it genuinely reflects better alignment. Asset owners need to hold asset managers to account. It's all well to say they vote, but how do they vote? Do they just follow a third-party provider, or do they think and act like active owners? We have to appreciate that it does potentially raise the cost for asset managers, but to me it is integral to investing and your responsibility as an active owner.

Manager reporting needs to improve. Asset managers can produce reports that talk about carbon emission avoidance or carbon footprint reduction, but these are baby steps. You need much deeper inroads into how you measure and understand the broader impact of your investments on society. To me there is no doubt that ESG has nothing to do with broad exclusions, but everything to do with how the companies we invest in impact the real world. Asset owners are stewards of client capital and need to engage as such.

So, 'E', 'S' or 'G': which one is most important?

If you had to pin me down, I would say 'G' is most important, as, by implication, it automatically includes the 'E' and the 'S'. If a company has good governance, the 'E' and the 'S' should come naturally.

With the trend towards more private market investing, how can investors best add value in private markets?

There is a lot of capital which has been committed to private markets in recent years, and that is likely to increase over the next 10 years. If you think about what you're doing, you are investing with a time period of at least 10 years in companies which have the ability to add value, in many cases by rolling up their sleeves and changing the underlying business – so it's less reliant on beta and less correlated to other investments in your portfolio. But you do need to think differently to invest in private markets. Yes, dry powder is near record levels currently and valuation multiples are high, but there are also a lot of opportunities. I really don't know what's going to happen in 10 years' time, so you need to have a long-term perspective and build a program that creates a diversity of vintage years. I think an interesting aspect is, where are you taking the money from? Both public and private markets may be highly valued. Or are you taking it from cash? What is the opportunity cost? It takes a high degree of governance to build an effective private markets program.

I think you are saying: market timing is just as hard in private as in public markets?

Exactly; in fact, it may be more difficult. Investing in private markets is a journey. It takes a period of time to get invested, and in the end you want vintage-year diversification. Private market timing is almost impossible; you need to build up a program.

There was an article from the Boston College Center for Retirement Research which showed defined benefit-funds outperform defined-contribution 401(K) funds.[5] What can DC plans learn from DB plans and vice versa?

That is a really tough one. You have more pairs of eyes on a DB plan, a clear direction of travel, and generally the support of a covenant. You also know DC plans are typically structured around available products which fit a particular cost constraint.

---

5   Munnell, A., Soto, M., Linbby, J., and Prinzivalli, J., 'Investment Returns: Defined Benefit vs 401(K) Plans', 2006, Boston College Center for Retirement Research. https://crr.bc.edu/briefs/investment-returns-defined-benefit-vs-401k/. Half the participants in 401(K) plans did not diversify and held either all shares or no shares at all. In addition, fund size had a positive impact on the performance of defined-benefit plans. Large plans hire better managers and spread fees over a larger base.

So you're not comparing like with like, you're comparing something that is deeply embedded and has the security of a covenant to an individual who doesn't necessarily understand the importance of the decisions they make. If you're a 25 year old in a DC plan you absolutely should have private markets, but how do you get that under daily dealing/liquidity options? So a DC allocation to alternatives is challenging. If you said to most DC participants: do you want to continue with the constrained fees or higher returns, I'm sure most would go for the latter.

So, the outcome from the article is hardly surprising as we are dealing with different stakeholders, engagement levels, time horizons and frameworks.

Do you have any thoughts on the insourcing versus outsourcing (OCIO) trends for institutional asset owners? How will this change the nature of asset consulting?

You'll see more outsourcing for asset owners as they need to focus on their core businesses. What is really important for any asset consultant is that they need to be able to deliver to client needs, whether it is DIY platforms (client does it all) or delegated (client outsources everything), and everything in between. To me, any asset consultant needs to provide that continuum in an independent way, to say to the client: 'How do you want to think about the governance of your plan and how can we help you deliver your objectives?'

What do you think will be the key differentiators for asset consultants going forward? (For example, fees, service levels, ability to customise/provide integrated services, IP generation, technology, other.)

Customisation is absolutely critical. It is important to maintain a trusted advisor status. To be an excellent consultant you need to be adaptive and open-minded. It's actually the same when you're an asset manager. There is no point in generating lots of 'product' if that's not what the client demands. It is about bespoke and customised solutions.

What keeps you busy outside of office hours?

I love crafting, so I do lots of quilting, cross stitch and crochet. I like making baby quilts; I generally make them for the babies born in my team wherever they may be, although at times I find myself with a waiting list!

I am delighted that I am soon to become a grandmother and will be able to make many more quilts!

If you hadn't been doing this, what would you have been doing?

Well, that's a funny one. When I left university, I got an offer from a big publishing company to do accountancy training. However, it would have taken me 45 minutes to drive there. Then I found a job advert for an investment analyst. I had no clue what it was, but it was only a 10-minute drive from home. And the rest is history, so to speak. Of course, I could have been a really interesting accountant!

How do you see the investment industry in 10 years' time?

I see fewer investment managers and increased consolidation. Boutique managers may struggle. The smaller ones face increased costs of regulation and compliance, which may lead to boutiques being housed within the umbrella of larger firms. The industry will be more diverse (hopefully!). Also, we'll see fewer star fund managers and more team-orientated approaches. The time is right for the culture of star fund managers to change and for cognitive diversity to be recognised as the important driver of returns I have always believed it to be. It will still be a good industry, but an industry with lower margins. There will likely be a disruptor that comes along, like 'Google Asset Management'.

Take Amazon, for example. Most of us shop on Amazon. You buy an item, they package it, they send it to you – amazingly, often the next day! For investments, we know what the need is. Based on the megatrends we talked about earlier, you need a stream of retirement income as 'the product'. Yes, there is regulation associated with the 'product' which Amazon may not want to deal with, but they could delegate that element to somebody else. And then they could send it to us as a service. So you would end up with a much more streamlined process, with far less behavioural bias and at a lower cost.

If I asked my 25 year old: who does she trust? She will say Apple, Amazon or Google. That's who young people trust. It's not names in the investment industry. The investment industry has created its own bubble which can no longer be protected. Asset owners, led by local authorities in the UK and industry funds in Australia, will continue to consolidate and pool their assets. This will create a very different industry landscape than the one we have today.

Finally – investment: art, science or skill?

I think it's a combination. I actually think skill is very rare and hard to determine in the investment industry. It's not like a footballer or musician. It's also not an exact science, as in something you can plug in and say 'here is the answer', but elements of quant thinking play a part in investing. There is also an element of art in overcoming the biases we all face when making decisions. Therefore investing has to be a combination of all three.

Thank you for your time.

Conclusions

There is a whole series of megatrends impacting investors and our personal lives, which start with the demographic and economic background, our social and environmental contracts, and the impact of technology.

The investment landscape is changing for the entire community of asset managers, asset owners and asset consultants. Investors want value for money and delivery of what is required to their satisfaction. And all of these challenges are in a world of lower trust, lower returns for operators and lower fees.

Deb considers the most important thing to be a clear roadmap to achieve specific objectives. Most investors consider this to be set by the asset allocation. However, she emphasises the importance of having a set of beliefs and signposts. The hallmark of a successful long-term institutional investor she considers to be the patience to stay the course.

Deb is a firm believer in long time horizons, the right governance structure, and less so of market timing for either public or private markets. She notes asset managers are considering Big Data as an alpha source or research advantage which she thinks is yet to be proven.

As she notes: ' … using a drone to collect information from car parks about how many cars are parked at certain times of day – it is not clear to me how useful this information is or how predictive it is.' She believes there will be a trend back towards creating genuine wealth using fundamental investing, rather than trading on the latest information craze as people want to invest, not trade their money, and want to know how their investment is helping not only themselves, but the whole of society.

— CHAPTER 2 —
A BRAVE NEW WORLD

An interview with Ben Inker
on the long, unwinding road

'Common sense is not so common.'
Voltaire (1694–1778)

The Brave New World has brought about a number of arguments for changes to portfolios typically maintained in the past by investors:

- Years of quantitative easing (QE), low interest rates and inflation have led to massive capital gains in equities and bonds. Investors are now faced with rich valuations.

- Investors are faced with an environment of low yields, where capital gains in especially bonds may be more limited as yields have turned negative in large parts of the world and effectiveness of central bank policy is increasingly diminished.

- Equity managers have increasingly relied on technology stocks[1], tax cuts and the abnormal length of the US economic cycle, while fixed-income managers have increased allocations to credit markets and absolute-return investing.

---

1 FAANG stocks (Facebook, Apple, Amazon, Netflix and Alphabet's Google) reached a combined market capitalisation of over US$3 trillion in 2018.

- To reduce volatility in returns and increase downside protection, demand for less-correlated products and private markets has increased.

A number of parallels may be observed between the late 1960s and the current environment:

- *Yield curves:* flat and periodically inverted yield curves worldwide have reduced opportunities for bond investors.

- *Geopolitical tensions:* there are concerns about populism, nationalism and protectionism, as well as concerns about a Eurozone breakup, and China's and Russia's increased global footprint.

- *The emergence of new economic powers:* from the late 1960s, Japan and Germany contributed much to global economic growth, while during recent years this role has been taken over by China and India.

On the other hand, a number of alternative products have become available for both wholesale and retail investors that have potential to add value to the performance of a traditional investment portfolio.

Pension funding crises in certain countries and the lower return outlook are causing funds across the globe to rethink their investment strategies. The major themes resulting from this rethink are a reduction in equity allocations, a move to liability-driven investment approaches in some countries (often resulting in increased fixed-income allocations) and increased interest in a range of alternative assets.

Introducing Ben Inker

Ben Inker is director of asset allocation at GMO. He is also a member of GMO's Board of Directors. Ben joined GMO in 1992 following the completion of his BA in Economics from Yale University. He is also a CFA charter holder. GMO was founded in 1977 and remains a privately held global investment management firm servicing clients in the corporate, public and endowment and foundation marketplaces. The firm's approach is based on several key underpinnings, including discipline, a value orientation, investment research and constant innovation. We will discuss with Ben some of the more important recent economic and market developments, including the trend towards alternatives.

Ben, thanks for participating in this update of the book. First of all, can you comment on the 'long, unwinding road' investors are facing? You mentioned, 'we've only started the transition from easy to hard, and that path is, almost by definition, not a pleasant one'.[2]

I have to admit, I wouldn't claim to really know what impact quantitative easing had. I have even less confidence in knowing what quantitative tightening implies. I do think the easy monetary policy era had a meaningful impact in bringing down discount rates. It strikes me there are two possibilities from here:

1. The period of easy monetary policy unwinds and the tailwinds behind all sorts of long-duration assets – such as equity, bonds and real estate – turn into headwinds.

2. The second possibility is that central banks are never able to go back to the old world. If that is true, then that's not as bad in the short or medium term, but we are then faced with a long-term difficulty. The underlying assumptions regarding portfolio returns of what a balanced portfolio can achieve would then be wrong. In such a world, a traditional portfolio would have no hope of delivering 5% above inflation in the long run. So the general rule of thumb of saving 10% of your income for retirement will not be enough, as in retirement that pot of money will not be able to sustain you.

So either the markets or investors will have to come to grips with a change. For our part we hope for possibility 1), and that interest rates are going to go back up and valuations down. For those who invest for the next 50 to 100 years, you hope valuations come back down as lower valuations support higher long-term returns. We are however trying to build portfolios that are robust to either of those two outcomes.

What do you think are the main challenges investors face today?

The debt issue is an interesting one. A lot of people think it is a profound problem. I don't know whether that is true. Every liability is somebody else's asset. The world has gradually accumulated more capital, which is an asset, which also has to be a liability (equity, debt or a residual liability). It's not immediately obvious to me that a liability structure

---

2 'Is Investing Starting to Get Difficult Again? I Hope So', Ben Inker, GMO, May 2018.

with more or less equity or debt would be magically better for the global economy at present.

It is clear that certain types of entities are weak issuers of debt. Back in 2007, the big issuer of debt was the financial services industry. They are weak borrowers, as they can be in a situation very easily where the ability to raise debt gets shut off. As they are highly leveraged, that is an issue.

There is some concern about the level of government borrowing. Governments borrowing in their own currency are different. Apart from the ability to print money, the buyers are very unlikely to go on strike, whereas with companies at some stage buyers switch to different options.

Who do you think are the weak holders in the current environment?

The closest thing we see today is the non-financial corporate sector, as globally the cost of debt is low. So it was a rational decision to take on additional debt. They are less leveraged than the financial sector, and their debt tends to be more long term. So they are not as weak as the banks were in 2007. But they are capable of going bankrupt, and presumably some will.

Where do you see vulnerabilities?

There are some real estate bubbles, like in Australia and Canada. For Australia I see a cosy oligopoly among lenders. While that is lousy for borrowers, it means less competition for loans. In the US we had thousands of banks competing for razor-thin margins at the time of the crisis. Also, apart from it being easier to regulate an oligopoly, it means there is less likely to be one big entity going under, as they are all in the same boat doing the same thing, and the government is likely to step in as they are too big to fail. The big four banks have probably managed to skew things in their favour. It is less likely one of them would have done something individually stupid. If one of them is in trouble, they are all in trouble.

Do you see any other countries with potential banking problems?

The other country where there is a potential banking problem is China. China is an area where there is a banking problem, but we do not know how this is going to play out. If nominal GDP grows at 10% to 14% for decades, it's actually pretty hard to wind up with a bad debt problem.

The ability of the economy to service that debt is high as GDP is growing so fast. GDP at 14% a year can double in five years, meaning debt as a percentage of GDP reduces even if debt is growing pretty fast. As China slows, even if it doesn't grind to a complete halt, I believe debt servicing will become an issue as it has never been before. There is more potential for things to go wrong in China.

What does that mean for Chinese bond and equity investors?

I am not a fan of Chinese bonds. As an external investor, it is not immediately obvious to me why you want to own Chinese bonds. The legal system is not in your favour as a foreign holder. There is little recourse in the legal system for the foreigner, and you will not be judged as someone they will care about. The lack of a well-defined bankruptcy code is less of an issue for equity holders as they will get wiped out anyway.

The nice thing about being an equity holder is that it's hard to differentiate between domestic and foreign equity holders anyway. To my mind, for equity holders, Chinese equities have done quite badly and are pricing in a pretty bad outcome. So you can have a bad outcome and the equities will be just fine. There aren't any good or bad assets, only assets that trade at reasonable or unreasonable prices. In China, bonds are pricing in a good outcome, stocks are pricing in a bad outcome. I think a risky asset pricing in a lot of risk is perfectly fine to hold.

Does the fact that equity investors have not made any real returns in China over the past 20 years bother you at all?[3]

Not really. China over the past 20 years is not unique. It's a bit like 1975 to 1995 in Korea where investors got close to zero real returns while the economy was growing more quickly than any economy ever had before. Or, Taiwan during its fast growth period. Japan also rather famously had a lousy return even though it outgrew other developed economies. While a country is growing fast, it invests an extraordinary amount, which is good for workers as productivity and income go up fast, but bad for capital investors as the margin of return significantly lowers. China has overinvested, so they have a lousy return on capital. On a forward-looking basis, what do we expect the return on capital

3   L'Her, J.F., Masmoudi, T. and R.K. Krishnamoorthy, 'Net Buybacks and the Seven Dwarfs', *Financial Analysts Journal*, 2018, v74(4), pp. 57–85.

to be in China? I can make the argument that at least for most entities where you can buy the equity, the return on equity looks to be okay.

Do you differentiate between NYSE ADRs and Chinese A shares in terms of equity risk premium?

The companies with US ADRs are skewed to large cap and internet, so it's a very idiosyncratic group and hard to comment on as a whole. A shares have had some impressive bubbles. But this is not one of those times when they are in a bubble.

If you had the marginal $1 to invest, would you invest it in China or the US?

The US stock market is trading at a very high premium to the rest of the world because everybody thinks it is special. Growth and profitability are at an all-time high. There is a case to be made that a big driver of the US is monopoly power and high industry concentration. The question is whether that can be sustainable. We have seen historically with monopolists that technological change can destroy them. Government policy can also break them down, or reduce their return on capital. So, we will find these monopolies will have to reduce power or else the government will need to step in. We're talking here about US companies that are global in nature as well. The internet giants are facing a lot of pressure from European governments.

The valuation and spectacular performance of the FAANGs have been likened to that of the tech stocks before the 2000 dotcom burst. However, some analysts have noted that there is a difference between these two tech classes, stating that there is plenty of room for the current tech class to grow as areas of cloud computing, social media, e-commerce, artificial intelligence, machine learning and Big Data are still being explored and developed. What is your view on this?

It is quite different from the dotcom bubble in that those companies weren't making money. Apart from Netflix, the FAANG stocks are making money. Dotcom was priced as if the future were better than the present. The FAANG companies are priced as if the future will continue to look like the present. It isn't a given though that the companies that dominate in one era will be the dominant companies in the next era as artificial intelligence takes over. For example, Kodak had a lot of valuable IP in digital photography, but didn't make much money out of it.

But to compete for new technology with, say, a Google, the barriers to entry in terms of resources and entry are nowadays quite high. For example, one interviewee, Professor Stephen Brown, acknowledged academia may no longer have the leading edge in terms of research and innovation?

Well, that is an interesting view. Nobody was better funded than Bell Labs, which spawned an extraordinary amount of tech (such as the transistor) we still use today, but were bad at capitalising on it. Another example is Xerox, which invented the personal computer in 1973, laser printers, the internet, mice, Windows. It was all created at Xerox's Palo Alto Research Center (PARC).[4] And yet, they were not the ones who made money from it. But it isn't a foregone conclusion. Any firm trying to continue their dominance into the indefinite future has the risk of being wrong, making a misstep, getting broken up or being constrained in their behaviour.

What's your view on the sustainability and market timing ability of style premia?

It strikes me as certainly reasonably intuitive that the premium, if any, that value-style investing as a technique is going to deliver, should in the end be driven by the size of the discount that value stocks trade at. And that in itself should lend it to some kind of timing.

If value stocks have a premium, it is because they are trading at too cheap a price. I have trouble imagining there wouldn't be some times when this happens. That could even survive a world where the average premium to value has fallen to zero. If there is some cyclicality then at times they can be priced to win.

Value is certainly not as well positioned now as during the internet bubble, but from a relative perspective it's probably in the 75th to 90th percentile of cheapness now. It is trading at a discount that historically has led to outperformance.

---

4   In 1979, some guys in the industry took a tour of Xerox's facility. The company management at the East Coast of the US did not care for the PARC's research results unless they were directly involved with photocopiers. One of the visitors was a young guy named Bill Gates, who rightly decided to take away as many ideas as he could. Another was a guy named Steve Jobs. Steve Jobs described the graphical user interface as 'the best thing I'd ever seen in my life'. Five years later, Apple unleashed the first Macintosh computer, and the rest is history.

Whether there is a permanent premium to value is a much harder one to solve. The basic argument why value wins is a behavioural one. While I think some of the behavioural finance people would say human beings don't change, I think human beings *do* change, and the prospect of profits is a pretty good incentive to change. We can learn to do uncomfortable things, and certainly with the rise of AI, computers won't have that issue. They don't understand what uncomfortable is.

So you are saying while premia could disappear due to changes in human behaviour or AI, their cyclicality could remain?

Exactly. For cyclicality to not remain, volatility would have to completely disappear. As long as prices remain more volatile than the underlying cashflows, the market can remain inefficient.

Certainly we don't see any evidence that our superhuman computer overlords have taken over!

I'll give you another example: small-cap stocks have not outperformed in the US since the mid-1980s. In those days, small-cap stocks were not considered institutional quality. Nowadays, most institutions have an in-built small cap bias as they assume they are inefficient. So the relative pricing (the large discount) has changed. If you pressed me to say that size will win over the next 50 to 100 years, I would say probably not.

The small effect has not worked over the past 30 years in the US, and that had nothing to do with AI but changing human behaviour, when we were initially not comfortable owning smaller stocks, but over time shifted to a small-cap bias.[5] You could even argue the same for the size of the equity risk premium. If you go back 100 years, it was not considered prudent to own equities; now it is not prudent to *not* own equities. The less equities are considered an imprudent thing to own, the smaller a return that is necessary to entice people to invest. This almost certain drop in the forward-looking equity risk premium has, ironically enough, led to a larger ex-post equity risk premium.

---

5 Ben specifically bases his views on the annualised returns from 31/12/1983 to 31/12/2018 of 10.7% per annum for the S&P 500 versus 9.0% for the Russell 2000 index. Based on the Russell 2000, size has decisively underperformed since 1984, contrary to the basic idea that there is a small-cap premium. Ben notes the Russell indices have continually existed since that time, so they are truly 'live' indices. He admits he prefers the use of live indices over academic data unless utterly necessary, as academics have less incentive to make sure the data is truly correct, and plenty of incentive to create data that comports with their theories.

Do you have any view on what constitutes the 'optimal' approach to portfolio construction for the next decade? (For example, enhanced balanced fund, risk premia fund, risk parity fund, real return fund, multi-asset fund, hedge funds.)

A lot of it is different packaging on similar products, but they do have material biases. Risk premia/risk parity funds assume certain things will be compensated in the long run. They assume the risk of those things is stable. What worries me about risk parity portfolios is that the key feature suggests a balanced exposure among asset classes but a tremendous amount of leveraged duration (both stocks and bonds).

If discount rates go up, that is one event for which risk parity funds are inherently ill prepared. Risk parity funds can't possibly deal with that, as their basic nature is leveraging small risk premia up so they return the same as equities. So it is a vulnerable asset. The only way to put together equal risk is to run a 20/80 stock/bond portfolio. But this gives you low return unless you lever it up and then you get the embedded duration again.

So you could end up with premia doing nothing but a lot of risk?

In my mind the right way to put together a portfolio is to pay attention to valuations, and maybe use some leverage at times. I have trouble with anything that is a leveraged bet that things will continue to be the way they have been forever. Risk premia and risk parity funds assume that, irrespective of what market valuations are.

Any better solutions than the original hedge funds?

Liquid alternatives have been a tremendous disappointment since the financial crisis. People misunderstand why.

Take for example an equity-neutral market portfolio which has no beta. In the absence of alpha you get cash returns. Which are very low.

Let's say you do merger arbitrage instead – you're underwriting a correlated equity risk. So you do well in good markets, but you don't do as well as a long equity portfolio.

Don't forget, equity is a long-duration asset, whereas merger arb is short duration. For long equities with a duration of 25, if the discount rate drops 2% you make a 50% gain. If on the other hand the duration is six months like in merger arb, then you make much less.

So you expect to go from, say, cash +4.5 to cash +2.5. Equities have however delivered more than cash +4.5. So people have been disappointed with hedge funds, as a lower cash yield and low duration mean a lower return. And they are confusing ex-ante and ex-post returns.

Hedge funds or liquid alts were sold as 'equity-like returns', but equity returned cash +10% to +12% in the US, so even if the hedge funds delivered cash +4.5, that will have seemed to be a disappointment. On an ex-post basis the outcome is going to be different than what you were expecting.

What is your view on alpha versus beta?

In a good environment, alpha cannot keep up with long-duration beta. If this reverses, anything is going to do better than beta. In a discount rate reversal, short duration will beat long duration. They could both underperform, but one underperforms less.

The reason equities were positively correlated with bonds before was because they react similarly to inflation risk, and in an opposite fashion to depression-type risk. They are both long-duration assets. If essentially the risk is inflationary, bonds and stocks have a positive correlation. So their correlation will depend on what the world is concerned with.

When it comes to risk premia vs traditional assets, not everything is something you should obviously get paid for. The basic risk in every risky asset is depression risk. Almost all risky activities do badly in an economic crisis. So if we have an economic crisis, alts will not do well, as they have depression risk. If discount rates go up they may do okay because inflation risk and short-duration risk do better than stocks and bonds with long duration.

You mentioned, 'our analysis of the underlying fundamentals for emerging markets, on the other hand, gives us confidence that the assumptions behind our forecasts are sound and emerging-value stocks represent the most attractive asset we can find by a large margin'.[6] What catalysts are needed for a re-rating of emerging-market equities and currencies, especially in a risk off environment?

I don't know if we are going into a risk off environment. Emerging markets have a beta of approximately 1 with developed markets, maybe slightly higher. If you have a period in which US stocks don't do much

---

6 'Emerging Markets – no Reward without Risk', Ben Inker, GMO, August 2018.

because profit margins gradually decline, then emerging markets with more sustainable growth could do just fine. When assets get cheap they become increasingly resilient to bad news. I wouldn't say emerging markets at these levels have extraordinary resilience to bad news, but it is a lot closer to it than the US is. If we had a three-year bear market, in the first year emerging markets may not outperform, but in years two and three they probably do.

Are there any particular emerging markets you favour?

No. While there are differences, what they have in common is that their valuation cycle tends to be similar across most markets. Today there is a starker gap between the US and everyone else than between emerging markets and the developed world ex-US. That said, emerging markets look pretty cheap almost everywhere.

What type of real assets do you expect to keep generating real returns in a rising inflation environment?

Equity, infrastructure and real estate have real cashflows, so those assets should be okay. There are a few issues with those that heavily rely on debt finance and their basic valuations. If inflation goes up, debt becomes more expensive and assets that are heavily leveraged, like some infrastructure and real estate assets, would be vulnerable.

Private equity is public equity + leverage, so its effective duration is even higher (2.5× public equity), so they were very big beneficiaries of falling discount rates, moreso than anybody else. I worry about private equity, about the weight of money going into it and the high fees.

What is your view on energy prices and their impact on developed and emerging markets?

We found that it's really hard to predict energy prices in the short and medium term. Not because of political issues, but because they are so volatile and news sensitive. In stocks you sort of forget the short-term news, and focus on the long run.

On the other hand, we've been managing a resource strategy over the past five to six years, and we have found value techniques work quite well in the resource sector. If you can find a company where you pay less for a barrel of oil than they can produce it for, you can do well.

Commodity stocks therefore seem to be somewhat predictable. I think that is also because value managers have no interest in them.

Are oil companies a good inflation hedge?

Well, yes if it is an oil shock, but not if inflation is, say, due to a wage crisis or tariffs – then it is less obvious. Nothing is a perfect hedge for everything.

How do you see the debate on ESG and climate change working its way through investors' portfolios? Is there any way investors can create excess return by taking positions there?

Perhaps. At the end of the day it is about being able to predict the future better than other market participants. If climate change means the world has to stop burning coal, then selling coal companies will work well. It is not certain to all market participants at this stage. Perhaps they have a dimmer view of humankind's ability to look after themselves. It is certainly good for everybody to stop smoking, but that doesn't mean investing in tobacco stocks is a stupid idea.

I don't think there is any obvious or easy way to make excess returns from climate change. For the vast majority of people who believe man-made activity is causing it, it would be strange to ignore, as it would have some impact on future cashflow-generating activities. Is the market going to figure that out? The market could get it right in the end. That is a weird and strong statement to make though.

From the standpoint of a responsible investor we similarly don't know if there is a premium or not for being responsible, but there is some cyclicality. For good governance not priced at a premium you should buy good governance. For bad governance that is oversold, that is a bit harder to defend morally. If tobacco stocks are under-owned and underpriced, a lot of people will still say, 'I'm not making money out of something that kills people'. Then it is no longer primarily an invest-ment thing.

What new research projects is the team working on? Has there been any consideration on machine learning and Big Data?

Parts of our firm are certainly looking at it. I have to say that for asset allocation there's not that much Big Data available that is useful. It's mainly for security selection. Or at least that is the stance we are taking.

Big Data is more useful for shorter time horizons, where you have to make lots of buy/sell decisions on single securities.

How do you see the investment industry evolving over the coming decade?

There is certainly a fair number of things historically done by investment firms in an active fashion which can be cheaply replicated, whether that's style premia or other things that can now be coded. I don't think it is sustainable to have a business model which assumes you get a lot of money for doing something that can be done cheaply.

I also think markets have not magically become efficient. The trouble with active management has always been about generating net of fees decent alpha. So the investment industry has to shift.[7]

What keeps you busy outside of office hours?

Other than my children? I read a lot of books … mainly children's books. [Laughs.]

Finally – investing: art, science or skill?

Outperformance could fall under art, science or skill.

- If you are paid for a unique skill, you can do things other people can't.

- It could be that in the end it is payment for work and effort; for example, distressed debt investing is very labour-intensive investing.

- It could be that you have some unique insight at a certain time, which the rest of the world has not discovered.

- It could also be the case that you are willing to take a risk that other people are not.

Any of those four are unique ways to sustain value-add. For the unique skills, you may want to have the most PhDs. You have to work on the right problems though and put in a lot of hours. If you put in the work, you deserve to win. It is important for anybody who wants to outperform

---

7   We note this is the same 'final conclusion' reached under the Berk and Green model, in which investments with active managers do not outperform passive benchmarks because of the competitive market for capital provision, combined with decreasing returns to scale in active portfolio management. Refer also Berk, J.B., and R.C. Green, 'Mutual Fund Flows and Performance in Rational Markets,' *Journal of Political Economy*, 2004, Volume 112 (6), pp. 1269–1295.

to understand what the underlying driver is of the performance and why it's sustainable. If it is mainly for effort, you must damn well put in plenty of effort!

Thank you for your time.

Conclusions

Catching up with Ben again after so many years, it was the prevalence of common sense in investing that really shone through in a world increasingly dominated by re-engineering, sophisticated product repackaging and the technology focus of the Digital Age.

Ben suggests there are two possibilities for the coming decade:

1. The period of easy monetary policy unwinds and the tailwinds behind all sorts of long-duration assets, such as equity, bonds and real estate, turn into headwinds.

2. The second possibility is that central banks are never able to go back to the old world.

He suggests either the markets or investors will have to come to grips with a change. Perhaps surprisingly, he is less concerned with a negative credit-collateral cycle like in the Global Financial Crisis, apart from the situation in China, as similar preconditions currently do not exist. Ben suggests Chinese equities have done quite badly and are pricing in a pretty bad outcome. He also questions whether the US monopoly power and high industry concentration is sustainable, and notes that companies that dominate in one era will not necessarily be the dominant companies in the next era of technology. He cites Xerox as a company that laid the groundwork for much of the technology we use today, but which failed to profit from it.

His mindset on risk premia is refreshing. He acknowledges for many risk premia the basic argument is a behavioural one: 'While I think some of the behavioural finance people would say human beings don't change, I think human beings *do* change, and the prospect of profits is a pretty good incentive to change. We can learn to do uncomfortable things, and certainly with the rise of AI, computers won't have that issue.' He also suggests that cyclicality can remain as long as volatility does not completely disappear.

He acknowledges there is a lot of different packaging on similar products. For risk parity portfolios he is worried about the tremendous amount of leveraged duration (both stocks and bonds). Leaving aside the wide return dispersion in what are supposed to be risk premia (beta?) providers, Ben notes 'In my mind the right way to put together a portfolio is to pay attention to valuations, maybe use some leverage at times. I have trouble with anything that is a leveraged bet that things will continue to be the way they have been forever. Risk premia and risk parity funds assume that irrespective of what market valuations are.'

He suggests hedge funds are another misunderstood and short-duration asset, whereby in the absence of any skill or embedded betas, you are likely to earn cash rather than the promised 'equity-like returns with lower volatility'. He notes 'in a good environment, alpha cannot keep up with long-duration beta. If this reverses, anything is going to do better than beta.'

Another area of concern for him is private equity, which he sees as public equity plus leverage, so its effective duration is even higher: 'They were very big beneficiaries of falling discount rates, moreso than anybody else. I worry about private equity, about the weight of money going into it and the high fees.'

A similar answer is found on climate change: 'I don't think there is any obvious or easy way to make excess returns from climate change … The market could get it right in the end. That is a weird and strong statement to make though. From the standpoint of a responsible investor we similarly don't know if there is a premium or not for being responsible, but there is some cyclicality.'

Back to the impact of the Digital Age, he notes that 'for asset allocation there's not that much Big Data available that is useful. It's mainly for security selection. Or at least that is the stance we are taking. Big data is more useful for shorter time horizons, where you have to make lots of buy/sell decisions on single securities.'

Finally, he notes it is important for anybody who wants to outperform to understand what the underlying driver is of the performance and why it is sustainable. As he suggests, 'if it is mainly for effort, you must damn well put in plenty of effort!'

PART II
THE DIGITAL WORLD

— CHAPTER 3 —
HUMANS VERSUS MACHINES

An interview with Anthony Ledford on understanding the Digital World

'Any teacher who can be replaced by a machine should be.'
Arthur C. Clarke (1917–2008)[1]

Financial markets do not exist in isolation, but are reflective of the societal and technological structures in which they operate. New quantitative methods and insights into machine learning have the potential to transform investment markets. To gain a deeper understanding, researchers acquire experience in fields that include mathematics, economics, computation, statistics, law, engineering and data science.

This work can shed new light on subjects that range from identifying hidden risks and uncertainties in the financial system to extracting valuable information from noisy market data.

What better way to understand the increasing interdependence between science and financial practice than to hear from the Chief Scientist at one of the largest hedge funds in the world?

---

1   Sir Arthur C. Clarke was a British science fiction writer, science writer and futurist, inventor, undersea explorer, and television series host, famous for being co-writer of the screenplay for the 1968 film *2001: A Space Odyssey*. Clarke contributed to the idea that geostationary satellites would be ideal telecommunications relays.

Introducing Anthony Ledford

Dr Anthony Ledford is Man AHL's Chief Scientist and Academic Liaison. Dr Ledford is based at the Man Research Laboratory (Oxford) and has overall responsibility for Man AHL's strategic research undertaken there.

The Oxford-Man Institute of Quantitative Finance is an inter-disciplinary research institute of the University of Oxford, England. The Institute was co-founded in June 2007 with Man Group plc. It brings together faculty, post-docs and students throughout the university inter-ested in research into the quantitative finance applications of machine learning and data analytics.[2]

Prior to joining Man AHL in 2001, Anthony lectured in Statistics at the University of Surrey. Dr Ledford read Mathematics at Cambridge University, holds a PhD from Lancaster University in the development and application of multivariate extreme value methods, and is a former winner of the Royal Statistical Society's Research Prize.

Anthony, thanks for participating in this book. First of all, can you comment on what you define as AI, machine learning and deep learning, noting that not all of our readers may have sat through your instructional videos?[3]

Of course. Although the terms *artificial intelligence* (*AI*, for short) and *machine learning* are often used interchangeably, they mean quite different things. AI is a broad catch-all term that describes the ability of a machine – usually a computer system – to act in a way that imitates intelligent human behaviour.

In contrast, *machine learning* is the study of the algorithms and methods that enable computers to solve specific tasks without being explicitly instructed how to solve these tasks, instead doing so by identify-ing persistent relevant patterns within observed data.[4]

Deep learning refers to a subset of machine learning algorithms that make use of large arrays of artificial neural networks (ANNs).[5]

---

2   Refer also http://www.oxford-man.ox.ac.uk/About-us.
3   https://www.ahl.com/insights/machine-learning.
4   This general definition of machine learning is very broad. However, within Man AHL the convention is to exclude standard statistical techniques such as linear regression. Others take a different view.
5   Artificial neural networks represent computing systems inspired by the biological neural networks that constitute animal brains. Such systems progressively improve their ability to do tasks by considering examples, generally without task-specific programming.

So why the resurgent interest in artificial intelligence, as the field has been around since the 1950s?[6]

Many practical problems that humans take for granted – such as driving a car, translating between languages or recognising faces in photos – have proven to be too complex to solve with explicitly codified computer programs. Indeed, AI researchers tried this approach for decades, but empirical research showed it is much easier to solve such problems by gathering a large number of examples (so called *training data*) and letting the relevant statistical regularities emerge from within these. For solving such problems, this *machine learning* approach has beaten – by a wide margin – the best human-engineered solutions.

Deep learning has become extremely popular since 2012, when a deep learning system for image recognition beat competing systems based on other technologies by a significant margin, but the development of artificial neural networks (ANNs) can be traced back to at least the 1940s and 1950s, as you point out.

Can you go over the concepts behind the different 'machine learning' methods?

Supervised learning is when each example in the training data has both input features (things you can observe, measure or infer) and an outcome or target. The idea is to learn the relationship between the inputs and the outcomes from the assembled training data.

For example, in the 2012 image recognition competition that kick-started all the subsequent deep learning interest, supervised learning was used on Imagenet. This is a large database of digital images where each image has been pre-labelled according to its contents (for example, bird, fish, plant).[7] Here, the inputs were the images, the outcomes or targets were the keywords describing each image, and the learning task was to develop a system to reproduce the labels for each image.

Unsupervised learning refers to when the elements of the training data do not have outcomes, and the focus is then on identifying structure

---

6   The field of artificial intelligence research was founded as an academic discipline in 1956. The earliest research into thinking machines was inspired by a confluence of ideas that became prevalent in the late 1930s, 1940s, and early 1950s. Research in neurology had shown that the brain was an electrical network of neurons that fired in all-or-nothing pulses. Alan Turing's theory of computation showed that any form of computation could be described digitally. The close relationship between these ideas suggested that it might be possible to construct an electronic brain.

7   See http://www.image-net.org/.

within the training data. One example is identifying sub-groups or clusters that exhibit similar features or behaviour, although unsupervised learning includes broader applications than just clustering.

To illustrate, referring back to the Imagenet database, if the labels describing the images are ignored, then grouping the images into separate clusters containing similar features is an unsupervised learning problem. You'd like to allocate images of birds into the same cluster, and images of fish into another, but without the labels describing the image contents you can't explicitly assess whether an image is classified correctly or incorrectly, and consequently you can't guide, or supervise, the learning process to do well. The task here becomes looking for common features within the images and clustering according to these.

Reinforcement learning is a special type of machine learning where an agent explores an environment sequentially by taking actions that generate rewards. In many cases, the reward associated with a particular action may be unclear, and all we can say is that a good or bad outcome was later obtained. Good outcomes generate positive rewards, and bad outcomes negative rewards (punishments). The idea is to maximise long-run total reward by combining exploration of the environment with exploitation of knowledge about the observed rewards.

It's worth noting that machine learning systems are not necessarily bound to just one of these fields. In particular, the combination of deep learning and reinforcement learning in *deep reinforcement learning* has produced some high-profile successes, a recent example being the AlphaGo engine which beat the world Go champion Lee Sedol.[8]

There is this whole focus on 'Big Data'. Why now (apart from the fact that there is a lot of available data now and storage capacity has increased exponentially)? What do we exactly mean when we say *Big Data*?

Unfortunately there is no widely accepted definition, but in our view, Big Data is not just 'having a lot of data'. It's more about having data from multiple sources, of various types and arising at different frequencies; for example, information from financial markets, national statistics and news, in numerical and text formats, obtained in real time, daily and monthly.

---

8   See https://en.wikipedia.org/wiki/AlphaGo.

As you know the more data/variables in any equation, the greater the chance of overfitting the conclusions?

Yes, it is important to contrast the unknowns within the model, which are sometimes called parameters, from the training data; in fact, it is useful to think of the training data as 'the knowns outside the model'. Fitting any machine learning model involves calibrating the unknowns within the model using the information conveyed by the knowns outside the model.[9] When a model with few parameters is fitted to a set of training data, then the amount of information per parameter is large compared to a model with many parameters applied to that same data. This is why simple models with few parameters can be reliably calibrated more easily than machine learning models which may have thousands or even millions of parameters. To address this issue, special techniques have been developed and are now in common use to assist fitting machine learning models.[10]

How do AI researchers prioritise the data?

This very much depends on the nature of the AI research: methodology breakthroughs typically involve demonstrating best-against-peers performance on one or more benchmark datasets.[11] As algorithms obtain ever better performance on these fixed benchmark datasets, it is legitimate to ask how effectively they will perform in real-world data applications. If they don't generalise well outside their training data, this is another example of over-fitting. In contrast, applied research often starts with a data problem, and ideally an open mind about what tools to employ to solve it.

There is no point in using a complicated machine learning model if what it discovers could just as effectively be captured using a linear regression.

The lesson is always to fit a simple model first, and then only adopt a more complicated machine learning model if the extra predictive accuracy (value) it provides is worth it. Give me the simplest model that does the job every time.

---

9 As an illustrative example, the same is true for simpler statistical models such as linear regression. The unknowns within the model are the intercept and slope parameters. The knowns outside the model are the observed data, which are known in the sense that they are given, and do not change.

10 Examples include techniques such as Dropout and Early Stopping, both of which are used to avoid overfitting in deep learning applications.

11 For example, Imagenet.

How do researchers deal with the fact that Big Data may contain a lot of fake data?

By 'fake' data I assume you mean 'data created with the deliberate intention of misinforming', as opposed to statistically 'noisy' datasets which may contain errors, missing values or other corruptions. For 'noisy' data, a suite of modelling techniques that goes by the name *Bayesian Machine Learning* is particularly robust at dealing with the statistical uncertainty implicit with such noise. Indeed this is one of the areas where we have enjoyed both collaborations with academics at the Oxford-Man Institute and applications within our systematic trading. Systematic fund managers like ourselves have been dealing with noisy data for decades, so in some sense this can be thought of as business-as-usual but using the latest cutting-edge tools. Other branches of machine learning do not naturally take account of such statistical noise, and in their basic form may fail to give appropriate results when exposed to noisy data. Such models are described as brittle rather than robust. This is a criticism often levelled against deep learning, however recent methodological breakthroughs in *Bayesian Deep Learning* have led to new machine learning techniques which at least partially address such issues.

Back to 'fake' data. This is not so relevant for market quantities such as price or volume, as there are mechanisms in place to ensure such data accurately reflect reality. It becomes more of an issue for text-based data such as news or commentary, but again most financial news reporting is of a high standard. It is also the case that opinions can be wrong without being fake. It's more of a problem in unregulated data sources such as social media, but most institutional level investment and trading is not driven by these anyway.

How do researchers deal with biases in Big Data?

'Bias' in data *is* an issue, and distinct from 'fake' or 'noisy' data. We all know the story of the AI-based recruiting tool that exhibited a strong gender preference in the candidates it put forward for interview because it had been trained on data with a gender bias. This deeply problematic outcome reflects an obvious, but important, truth: these algorithms learn whatever pattern is in the data they are trained on regardless of whether that pattern is what you *want* them to learn. Indeed removing bias in training data and developing techniques for steering machine learning algorithms to learn some things but ignore others (for example, things you already know, or that stocks tend to increase in price over time) is a key task in the applied research the machine learning team at our firm undertakes.

How do researchers deal with non-stationarity (Big Data not being stable over time)?

This is a pretty universal problem in any quantitative financial modelling so is felt more widely than just in applications of machine learning. To calibrate any model with parameters requires data, and the more data you have, the more precisely you can estimate the parameters. Precision in estimated parameters is good to have, so this suggests you should use lots of data. However, using more data typically means using data from increasingly historical periods, but that is at the risk that these data may not reflect the current world. To avoid that risk you should therefore use only the most recent data; in other words, use few data. Unfortunately these considerations pull you in opposite directions; it's a Catch-22. In practice, we tilt towards using as much data as we can and apply a penalty that discounts the impact of historical data compared to recent information.

One of the common fears about machines (and machine learning perhaps) is about algorithms working things out for themselves and becoming aware. Alan Turing[12] once famously remarked 'machines take me by surprise with great frequency', which suggests even in his time algorithms had some ability to create solutions (or algorithms) not designed by their creator. How far do you think we are from 'aware' machines?

I have been regularly surprised by algorithms since the days of my PhD deep in the last century! But, that has never meant they're about to take over the world!

Fitting a model typically relies on some optimisation algorithm. This seeks to find a set of parameters that makes some goodness-of-fit criterion as large (or small) as it can. Sometimes, the optimisation algorithm zooms in on parameters which are useless but happen to yield particularly good values of this criterion. It boils down to the computer doing

---

12 Alan Turing (1912–1954) was an English mathematician, computer scientist, logician, cryptanalyst, philosopher and theoretical biologist. In 1941, Turing and his fellow cryptanalysts set up a system for decrypting German Enigma signals. Turing is widely considered to be the father of theoretical computer science and artificial intelligence. 'Computing Machinery and Intelligence', published in 1950, is considered the seminal work on the topic of artificial intelligence.

what you asked it to rather than what you wanted it to do, an annoying type of user error that I seem to repeat regularly.

Algorithms becoming aware and 'taking over' is definitely in the domain of science fiction rather than science fact! That does not mean algorithms can't or won't exhibit destructive behaviour; however, if they do, then it won't be because they've gained consciousness, but more likely that they've stumbled on some corner-case solution of an ill-specified optimisation criterion.

Which areas of investment management have the most potential to be affected by machine learning? For example, data analysis, stock selection, asset allocation, risk premia, electronic trading, hedge funds, or other?

For machine learning to have an impact, you need a few things: ample amounts of representative data, and effects that are not easily described using simpler models. Without large amounts of data, you cannot precisely calibrate a machine learning model; you need that data to be representative so that the model learns effects that are still current, and you are just undertaking needless and pointless complications if you use a machine learning model when a simpler model will do. For numerical data this points towards the non-linear effects which are most prevalent at daily, intra-day and faster speeds, and where there is a relative abundance of data compared to slower strategies. Developing trade execution and smart order-routing algorithms is another ideal domain for the use of machine learning, and is an active area of research within our firm.

Another area where machine learning is having significant impact is in exploiting text-based data, using so-called Natural Language Processing. Although our firm and other systematic traders have been around for several decades, it is only relatively recently that such data sources have been systematically harvested and deployed within live trading.

Where do you see the main risks and opportunities for institutional investors?

The investment opportunities offered by machine learning strategies can be summarised in one word: diversification. As with the rest of quantitative investment, there are many more words for the risks.

Like anyone considering investing in a quantitative strategy, investors should have a good understanding of the range of market-data regimes used to build and test the model. Are the returns offered by the machine learning model sufficiently diversifying to their existing portfolio, or can they be adequately captured by a simpler technique? What can be expected when markets become strained; is there any reason to believe the diversification (assuming it exists) will persist? Lots of firms are exploring machine learning, so is the risk of crowding higher or lower for machine learning models than for mainstream quantitative strategies? If they have higher turnover, then what capacity do such strategies have? Should I expect them to have shorter half-lives? How much do transaction costs have to increase in order to cancel-out the alpha? Does the strategy make profits smoothly through time or in bursts? And so on.

How high do you rate the chance of large corporations with extremely deep pockets – like Alphabet – getting involved in developing machine learning applications for investment purposes and competing with other investors?[13]

It would not surprise me. In fact, it is somewhat of a surprise that it has not happened already!

A partial explanation might be the large proportion of machine learning researchers who want to work on applications involving computer vision, self-driving cars, consumer apps and seemingly anything *other* than finance.

In one sense, it would be great to see the coupling of machine learning and quantitative finance become more mainstream. This is something Man Group has been promoting since 2007 through our co-creation of the Oxford-Man Institute of Quantitative Finance (OMI) with the University of Oxford, and our ongoing financial support of the OMI's research.

Sure, there would be more competition, but there would also be a lot more research getting done and a lot more people doing it. The trick would be to remain at the forefront of that increased research activity, something we've been good at so far.

I wanted to draw your attention to a Man AHL paper written in December 2016 called 'Man vs Machine: Comparing Discretionary and Systematic Hedge Fund Performance'[14]**, which suggests discretionary macro managers underperform systematic macro**

13 https://deepmind.com/about/, https://ai.google/research/teams/brain.
14 'Man vs. Machine: Comparing Discretionary and Systematic Hedge Fund Performance', Harvey, C.R., Rattray, S., Sinclair, A. and O. Van Hemert, *The Journal of Portfolio Management*, 2017, 43 (4), pp. 55–69.

managers, even after adjusting for volatility and factor exposures over the measured time period. How do you think this debate will shift with the advent of machine learning?

From my experience, machine learning strategies have the most to offer towards the faster end of the spectrum of strategies deployed by most systematic macro managers. Furthermore, not all systematic macro managers will make use of such strategies.

So the impact on performance at the group-wide level of systematic macro managers is likely to be modest, at most.

Do you have any thoughts on the increased competition among quantitative managers?

Increased competition is likely to mean that only managers offering genuinely differentiated alpha (arising from machine learning or other novel sources) will be able to resist fee erosion. This is clearly a much wider issue than just relating to machine learning.

What in your opinion distinguishes a good from a mediocre quant manager?

I have quite a few criteria!

- an independent risk management team that monitors for the build up of inadvertent portfolio exposures
- a wide range of diversifying strategies so that undue reliance is not placed on any one strategy or concentrated group of strategies
- a joined-up understanding of strategy design, portfolio construction, trade execution and risk
- a long track record of trading through a wide range of market environments
- a stable, international, multi-disciplined and diverse team with low turnover that contains both new recruits and old-timers (like me!)
- state-of-the art computing hardware and software
- active engagement with the outside world; for example, through academic collaborations and publications
- contributing to rather than just taking from the open-source community
- an open culture where staff collaborate rather than operate in silos

- a test-trading program where the latest research ideas can be verified in live trading without risking client capital

- an honest research culture where nobody seeks to hide research that does not work, or to pretend it does!

How do you decide when a model no longer works?

It's rare in our style of trading for a model to suddenly stop working, and many models are kept fresh through periodic refits. Sometimes the components of a model are superseded by new models, and in that case they get turned off.

More generally the amount of trading capital a model obtains in the portfolio will be driven by its long-term risk-adjusted return and correlation with other models. This means that a model which consistently underperforms or fails to diversify will naturally receive a diminishing allocation as time progresses, although obviously this de-allocation occurs with some lag.

If the structural assumptions underpinning a model fundamentally change (for example, a currency peg is implemented or relaxed) then turning off the model in that market is warranted.

What do you think is the best investment time horizon to apply machine learning? How important is real-time data?

Within our suite of trading models, machine learning has the highest representation at the faster end, with holding periods extending from intra-day out to multiple days. Faster signals than that certainly exhibit greater non-linear structure, however such effects are hard to capture as alpha in the client-scale funds typical of large systematic managers like us. In a nutshell, they are just too fast. However, when applied in trade execution, such effects may offer an advantage in reducing transaction costs, for example, enabling orders to be front- or back-loaded depending on the short-term predictability of the limit-order book. Real-time data is essential for that.

Are there any other important developments in the quantitative space worth noting?

There is a good deal of research effort being deployed on modelling text and other alternative data sources, and the range of instruments being traded continues to extend. These are just the latest pieces in the industry's ongoing hunt for diversification through new models, new markets and new trading horizons. Machine learning and Big Data fit somewhere as pieces in that hunt.

Can you comment on some of the other interesting areas apart from machine learning that the Man-Oxford Institute is currently working on?[15]

Within the University of Oxford, the Engineering Science Department's hub for machine learning houses both the Oxford-Man Institute (OMI) and the broader Machine Learning Research Group (MLRG). Research activities span a diverse range of topics with applications ranging from astronomy to zoology, with examples including detecting disease-bearing mosquitoes, identifying exoplanets from data gathered using NASA's Kepler space telescope, systems for remote fault detection and monitoring, and making energy networks and storage more efficient.

Research in the MLRG also addresses the broader societal consequences of machine learning and robotics, for example, their impact on employment. Alongside the OMI's strong research focus on machine learning and data-centric methods for finance, its members, associate members and graduate students undertake a broad range of interdisciplinary and collaborative projects, for example, assessing the impact of regulation – and breaches of regulation – on markets, and investigating the relationship between future earnings and the language used in corporate announcements.

On a side note, do you think there is a premium for illiquidity?

My experience would suggest there is, however it is hard to disentangle this from the inverse premium associated with a market's ease of access. In particular, I have seen the same algorithms trade in easily accessed liquid markets and hard-to-access illiquid markets and do much better in the latter. But I should add that this has been against a backdrop of non-standard central bank, regulator and government measures[16] which typically have more impacted the liquid easily accessed markets. Will that continue? Who knows. Also, if you look across the industry, the half-life of trading strategies tends to be monotonic with their time

---

15 http://www.oxford-man.ox.ac.uk/Areas-of-research.
16 In response to the Global Financial Crisis.

horizons. Slower strategies typically last longer, but with lower Sharpe ratios, than higher frequency strategies.

As a scientist, do you have any thoughts on the premium for sustainability?

My colleagues in Man Numeric have spent almost two years unpacking environmental, social and governance (ESG) data, conditioning for statistical biases and removing exposures to other factors, and thereby have obtained something meaningful and orthogonal. This is the closest thing I have seen to an ESG or sustainability factor. Of course, it is quite possible that as more people focus on ESG and sustainability that a premium may emerge – it is a changing environment where ESG and non-ESG activities could become advantaged or disadvantaged by policy.

How do you see the investment industry evolving over the coming decade?

At the industry level, I expect to see more consolidation as both fee erosion and the costs of doing innovative state-of-the-art research take effect.

Closer to home, some currently 'cutting-edge' alphas (including some machine learning models) will transition into alternative betas, while a new cohort of data science researchers will seek out new alphas to replace them. Discretionary managers will make extensive use of data dashboards that deliver assimilated Big Data views.

Run-of-the-mill computer hardware (and whatever the smartphone has become in a decade's time) will make today's state-of-the-art systems look just as ridiculous as those from 2009 do today.

Who will have the edge in leading the AI research of the future? Apart from yourself, are there certain leading academics, corporations or even countries that you could identify?

Internationally, North America and China have been the leading investors in AI and machine learning research for some time, with Europe, Australasia and the rest of the world now trying to compete, if somewhat belatedly.

I'd expect how this funding landscape evolves to be the deciding factor in the shape of AI developments over the next decade. That said, the traditional model of methodological AI research being undertaken in universities has changed significantly over the last 10 years, with a lot more now originating in blue-sky company laboratories *and* being openly published, with a corresponding drift of staff from universities to these laboratories.

Without a strong source of people to replace these university researchers, the research landscape could become fundamentally changed. To mitigate this, joint industry–university collaborations such as the Oxford-Man Institute may become more common, enabling academics to operate effectively in both camps, rather than exclusively in one or the other.

What keeps you busy outside of office hours?

Family, enjoying the wonderful countryside around Oxfordshire, various sporting events where my son competes, and a fascination with restoring bygone mechanical and scientific instruments.

Could you elaborate?

Inventions from before the microchip. For example, a Wimshurst machine, an old Victorian instrument that generates enormous electrostatic charges. It's not as big as the one in the Oxford Museum, but mine works. And the artificial horizon from a World War Two Spitfire.

A very peculiar hobby indeed! You really are an eccentric scientist. What would you be doing if you weren't in this field?

It's a bit random that I am in finance at all. The probability and statistics I researched when working as an academic was in extreme value theory, with applications in hydrology such as how high to build flood defences. I started looking at financial data only because it fitted well with a computational statistics module I was teaching. Eventually, I was hooked, and thought I would try the industry for a few years. Well … it's now been 18 years! I still do some academic research, and if I wasn't at Man AHL it would probably still be my day job. Being sat in Oxford, in an academic building, I get the best of both worlds.

Having close proximity to internationally leading research groups in the multiple disciplines we've found useful is why I am based in Oxford. Most PhDs we hire are from scientific backgrounds like physics, engineering, maths, statistics, econometrics or computer science, with very few having academic finance or business school backgrounds. We have found that we can teach trained research scientists the finance they need to know to thrive as a quant researcher, but it's more difficult to equip a finance person with sufficiently advanced skills in the relevant scientific techniques. I'd say that the ability to extract information from noisy data – which is something that is practised in the experimental sciences – and having an open, inquisitive mind are the most important things.

My final question: investing: art, science or skill?

All three. But it's rare to find all these in the same person at the same time, which is why we believe in teams.

Thank you for your time.

Conclusions

This chapter was dedicated to help the reader understand the resurging interest in artificial intelligence and Big Data in the Digital Age as well as their impact on investment decisions. While artificial intelligence has been around since the 1950s, deep learning has become extremely popular since 2012, when a deep learning system for image recognition beat competing systems based on other technologies by a significant margin. Unlike much of the media hype, Anthony remains however, quite sanguine about the possibility of algorithms becoming aware and 'taking over' as evil robot overlords. He definitely rates this in the domain of 'science fiction rather than science fact'.

More practically, he suggests investment fields that could benefit from AI, Big Data analysis and deep learning could be more prevalent at the daily, intra-day and faster speeds, where there is a relative abundance of data. Developing trade execution and smart order-routing algorithms is another ideal domain for the use of machine learning. Another area where machine learning is having significant impact is in exploiting text-based data. In terms of the 'future centres of research excellence' for artificial intelligence in the investment field, he remains somewhat surprised that large corporations like Alphabet have not become involved already. A partial explanation might be the large proportion of machine learning researchers who want to work on applications involving computer vision, self-driving cars, consumer apps and seemingly anything other than finance.

At the investment industry level, he expects to see more consolidation as both fee erosion and the costs of doing innovative state-of-the-art research take effect. Some currently 'cutting-edge' alphas (including some machine learning models) will transition into alternative betas, while a new cohort of data science researchers will seek out new alphas to replace them.

Internationally, North America and China have been the leading investors in AI and machine learning research for some time. The traditional model of methodological AI research being undertaken in universities has changed significantly over the last 10 years, with a lot more now originating in blue-sky company laboratories and being openly published, with a corresponding drift of staff from universities to these laboratories.

Without a strong source of people to replace these university researchers, the research landscape could become fundamentally changed. To mitigate this, joint industry-university collaborations such as the Oxford-Man Institute may become more common. In an increasingly complicated world with abundant availability of Big Data, investors considering allocating resources to AI and analysing Big Data would do well to heed Anthony's advice:

'The lesson is always to fit a simple model first, and then only adopt a more complicated machine learning model if the extra predictive accuracy (value) it provides is worth it. Give me the simplest model that does the job every time.'

— CHAPTER 4 —

RETHINKING THE ALPHA BET

An interview with Stan Beckers
on alpha, beta and costs

'You have to learn the rules of the game.
And then you have to play better than anyone else.'
Albert Einstein (1879–1955)

Like the elusive Holy Grail, alpha is something everybody seeks, many claim to have, and few are willing to share. Eugene Fama once famously said 'an investor doesn't have a prayer of picking a manager that can deliver true alpha'.

In addition, we mentioned in earlier chapters, in increasingly rational markets dominated by institutional flows, capital provision may drive excess return down together with cost, until a Berk and Green Equilibrium is reached in major asset classes.[1] How then will the total amount of alpha change with the rise of the Digital Age? How much alpha will remain out there for the masses of long only and hedge funds?

---

1   Berk, J.B., and R.C. Green, 'Mutual Fund Flows and Performance in Rational Markets,' *Journal of Political Economy*, 2004, Volume 112 (6), pp. 1269–1295.

Any discussion of alpha hinges on the exact definition of alpha. Disentangling the returns to certain risk factors from those representing pure alpha is no easy task. Like the Grail, everyone assumes alpha exists, but no-one seems sure of how to identify it. Alpha will be equal to that part of excess returns not explained by beta factors (market risk exposures) or any random errors.

Alpha is a zero-sum game (negative after fees), expensive, requires active management, is uncorrelated with beta, and may be generated using asset allocation, security selection or market timing; beta has a positive expected return from exposure to systematic risk factors, comes at cheaper fees, tends to be associated with passive management, and is potentially correlated with other betas. Examples of traditional betas are equity, term, credit, size and value. Examples of non-traditional betas are carry, momentum, volatility, insurance and regulatory risk.

When alpha transforms into beta in the Digital Age

Skill can also be thought of as 'divine inspiration'. It's a finite commodity and, as in any skill-based game, the more highly skilled players gain at the expense of the lesser-skilled ones. Therefore, alpha is something you take away from the competition and nets out to zero. After fees it's a negative-sum game.

The most straightforward and intuitive explanation of alpha is skill-based returns that cannot be replicated by following a formula or some recipe or procedure. From that perspective, the idea that an algorithm could possibly create 'alpha' would remain a paradox, until the algorithm becomes sentient or self-learning. Yet, it remains difficult to disentangle alpha and beta, as we have not uncovered all the betas as yet. Arbitrage pricing theory extended the capital asset pricing mode and leads to the discovery of additional beta factors. As the world evolves, we become more knowledgeable. Fundamental or 'skill-based' managers will say their edge lies in experience, wisdom and their insights as to the specifics of individual countries, sectors or securities. 'Systematic managers' allegedly exploit persistent market inefficiencies and do not even attempt to develop in-depth knowledge of the securities they invest in. The latter group has gained a substantial market share as investors demand structured investment processes and are ironically most at risk from the Digital Age as their formulas become more widely adopted.

Following developments in financial engineering, an explosion in beta building blocks has become available through passive funds and ETFs. But is all alpha and beta created equal? In this interview we discuss the re-engineering of alpha and beta in detail.

Introducing Stan Beckers

Stan Beckers is Executive Fellow and Chair of the AQR Asset Management Institute at London Business School and Non-Executive Director and Chair of the Risk Committee at Rothesay Life in London. He was a member of the Management Board of NN Group and CEO of NN Investment Partners (previously known as ING Investment Management) until 2017. He has more than 30 years of professional and leadership experience in finance and asset management with organisations such as BlackRock, Barclays Global Investors, Kedge Capital and WestAM. Stan was also one of the early partners at BARRA (now MSCI BARRA) where he started and ran the non-US operations for 20 years. Over the years, Stan Beckers has served as a member of the investment committee of pension funds and on the supervisory boards of KAS Bank and Robeco in the Netherlands. He has taught at Universities such as UC Berkeley, the Free University (VU) of Amsterdam, Cass Business School, London School of Economics and Catholic University (KU) Leuven. Stan has published over 50 papers in various academic and practitioner journals such as the *Journal of Finance*, the *Journal of Financial and Quantitative Analysis*, the *Financial Analysts Journal* and the *Journal of Portfolio Management*. He received a PhD in Finance from the University of California at Berkeley.

Stan, thanks again for your time. Can you explain to our readers some of the work you currently do at the London Business School and your areas of research interest?[2]

I am chairing the AQR Asset Management Institute, which was established through a generous grant by AQR to further strengthen the

---

2   https://www.london.edu/faculty-and-research/research-centres/aqr-institute-of-asset-management.

position of LBS as a leading centre of learning and research in asset management. The Institute organises seminars and conferences, it invites guest lecturers and sponsors research.

In terms of areas of research, I have three projects going.

First, I am interested in mutual fund performance persistence, which is the Holy Grail of investment. I look at equity and fixed-income managers using the Morningstar database and see whether you can identify performance persistence criteria. It is well known that fees tend to be a negative indicator, in the sense that that leaves less for alpha. However, I also find some evidence of momentum in the sense that funds that have done well recently continue to do well for a little while – possibly driven by fund flows – before they reverse. I am also looking at factors such as tracking error, the liquidity of the underlying instruments, the type of share class, and others.

Second is the performance of fallen angels – stocks that fall out the index. People always look at additions and whether that adds extra returns. My hypothesis is that those stocks that exit the index will go on a secular decline. However, the preliminary evidence seems to contradict this!

Third is the question whether index funds 'outperform' the corresponding ETFs. Contrary to my initial thoughts, the preliminary evidence is that ETFs have on average lower tracking error, lower fees and higher alpha. Possibly the broader use of stock lending is an explanation I am looking into.

Which areas of academic research would you expect to be most impacted by new technology developments?

I think, in general, the flood of 'new' data that comes at us from social media, the way of treating that data through natural language processing, machine learning and artificial intelligence with a commensurate rise of the data scientists is certainly something to consider.

Do you think it will impact short-term investors (such as high-frequency traders) more than long-term investors?

That's probably true. Although some of the new data, like satellite imaging and information from the Internet of Things, is also potentially worthwhile for long-term investors.

Can you comment in general on the trends in alpha, beta and costs?

True alpha is a zero-sum game, so on average your alpha is what you take away from the competition. An ever-increasing component of what traditionally was considered as 'alpha' has now been identified as a risk premium (or beta). Finally, there is an irreversible secular downward trend in management fees and costs in general.

How do you think the amount of alpha will change in the Digital Age?

My thought is that deep down the only source alpha is investor irrationality. If all investors were rational there would be no alpha and we would have efficient markets.

So the real question is: will the Digital Age increase rationality? I don't think so. For example, take populism, which is certainly not rational from an economic perspective, but nevertheless is on the rise. Look also at the amount of noise in social media. So I believe the amount of alpha will not change as investors continue to behave irrationally.

Do you think however that the signal-to-noise ratio will then decline because there is so much noise?

That's a hypothesis that's hard to substantiate, but I could sympathise with the statement that the amount of noise has increased. So it may be less easy to detect signals.

The number of alternative beta and ETF providers has exploded, offering low-cost exposure to a wide range of markets and market segments. What kind of new, exotic beta strategies and ETFs will we see, and how will this impact market efficiency?

We haven't seen the end of the growth of factor-based ETFs which are now spilling into fixed income, commodities and currency. So the deconstruction of alpha is continuing at pace. However, I am not sure whether the promised liquidity of the ETFs always matches that of the underlying instruments. This could be a disaster waiting to happen, as all crashes are in essence liquidity crashes.

Some people argue price discovery may have moved away from stocks into ETFs as they become more easily traded.[3]

I'm not sure ETFs improve price discovery, given that they just repackage underlying assets. There's no straight answer here, but there's certainly a dark side to the growth in ETFs.

What are examples of recent financial innovation that you've come across?[4]

There are a few:

- *Data sources.* Getting your hands on information nobody yet has, by legal means, rather than insider info. We are now at the stage where hedge funds are launching their own satellites.

- *Processing speed.* Processing data more quickly than the competition. This is probably more in the realm of the high frequency traders though, locating as close to the exchange as possible to reduce information latency.

- *Insight.* The true source of differentiation is processing information in a more insightful manner. Transforming data into information and then into insight is what sets genius apart. It is neither the tools nor the infrastructure that is the true differentiator: it is the way in which it is applied.

There are applications like Natural Language Processing (NLP) of course, but everybody is using the same NLP on the same CEO/CIO statements and financial reports (except for those who forget to eliminate the legal disclaimers from the analysis). So we are now progressing into body language algorithms on films. But in the end technology is a means to an end. The intelligent/creative application is the differentiator.

---

3   Over US$5 trillion was invested in ETFs as of 2018. Research indicates stocks with higher ETF ownership display significantly higher volatility. The increase in volatility appears to introduce undiversifiable risk in prices, as stocks with high ETF ownership earn a significant risk premium of up to 56 basis points monthly. Itzhak, B., Francesco, A.F., and R. Moussawi, 'Do ETFs Increase Volatility?', *Journal of Finance*, 2017, 73(6), pp. 2471–2535.

4   We distinguish between financial innovation and financial engineering. Financial innovation is something truly new (like exposure to a new risk premium, or say finding some new behavioural patterns in high frequency trading based on Big Data or AI text recognition or other). Financial engineering is repacking existing betas (like say some hedge funds, ETFs do) or altering payoff patterns (like tail risk hedging products).

Speaking about innovation, while the majority of ETFs offer plain vanilla passive equity index exposure, the existence of leveraged and inverse ETFs in essence gives retail folks the power of a hedge fund strategy in a single click, potentially also with some counterparty risk. What do you think about that?

They are a danger absolutely and have no role to play in standard retail investor portfolios. They are not investment but gambling tools. Possibly, you could see them as short-term hedging tools, but I'm not a fan.

What are your thoughts on the wide range of outcomes investors derive from some of the alternative beta providers?[5]

Luckily there is no unique definition of value or momentum or quality. If we think about value being things that are fundamentally cheap, one can define (relative) cheapness based on yield, book value, enterprise value, cashflow and so forth. As the market switches attention and emphasis from one characteristic to another, different 'versions' of value will tend to outperform. It's the same thing with momentum. Do you use 3-, 6- or 9-month momentum? Occasionally 6-month will outperform 9-month and vice versa. So I don't have a problem with different outcomes for the same characteristic as long as they cover a similar risk premium. Market attention shifts all the time.

What do you think of the recent trends (decline in returns) in alternative risk premia strategies? Cyclical or structural?[6]

If we think about the most basic premium, the market risk premium, we know the long-term premium is around 5% to 6%. However, we have gone over long periods where the market didn't deliver 6% on average. We also know that market volatility is around 20%. So I think the under-performance we're observing is cyclical as long as we're talking about true 'established' risk premia. However, a non-negligible number of 'risk premia' are the result of data mining and academics trying to get their papers published. These premia tend to magically disappear as soon as they have been discovered. I've long been an advocate of an academic

---

5 For example, investing in a 'carry' or 'momentum' strategy can lead to vastly different outcomes depending on the manager, trading strategy and implementation efficiency employed – which makes the claim to beta an oxymoron, as it becomes dependent on manager skill. A recent study suggested an average correlation of only 0.35 between managers and noted differences in design and implementation in well-known risk premia. 'Understanding Multi Alternative Risk Premia Strategies', J. Skeggs, L. Liu, Societe Generale, January 2019.

6 'Alternative Risk premia: Crisis or Opportunity?', M. Aked, B. Kunz, Research Affiliates, December 2018.

Journal of Insignificant Results to be able to judge what is a true find and what is data mining!

One of the industry's most decorated 'alpha sources', Warren Buffett's performance was recently 'disentangled' and found to be lacking alpha, after controlling for exposure to the factors such as leverage and quality. What are your thoughts on this? Reality or academic oversimplification?[7]

Buffett's track record has been studied and deconstructed into a number of risk premia. There's nothing wrong with that. In a similar vein a four-star chef's signature dish can be deconstructed and ex-post written up in a cookbook: that doesn't make him/her less of a four-star chef.

What Warren Buffett has achieved is still remarkable, even more so because he has not been doing anything magical, but he did so by combining well-established risk premia.

Again, a four-star chef uses ingredients you and I can buy in the supermarket but combines them in a consistent/genius fashion that nobody else thought of.

If somebody says 'it was only combining ingredients', that doesn't make the person a four-star chef!

In your opinion, is there alpha to be made in 'factor timing'? I note one of your recent articles discusses that topic.[8]

It's the same as with market timing. For those that can do it, obviously it's a source of value add. However, it is virtually impossible to demonstrate or prove this skill as it is a binary decision at any point in time, and the number of times that people make market timing decisions is not large enough to gather enough data points. So in theory it's possible to be a successful market or factor-timer; in practice it's hard to demonstrate. Often the skill is more in the storytelling rather than in the results!

---

7   Frazzini, A. and D. Kabiller, Pedersen L.H., 'Buffett's Alpha', *Financial Analysts Journal*, 2018, 74(4), pp. 35–55.

8   'What is Value in an Equity Market?', *Journal of Investment Management*, 2017, 15(3). Michael Suen, Hany Guirguis, Stan Beckers and Ted Theodore. Investors can gauge whether the equity market is cheap or expensive by referring to a historical time series of the value index. The authors also develop a tactical asset allocation strategy based on the trend of the value index.

The number of US-listed companies has fallen to almost half what it was at its peak in 1996.[9] Paradoxically, the number of US equity funds has surged ahead during this time, nearly matching the number of listed stocks in the country, and the number of ETFs has now overtaken the number of stocks. What do you think the implications are for alpha and active management?[10]

True alpha-hunting active managers will not use ETFs (except possibly for hedging purposes). Stock pickers should be/are looking for individual stock mispricings – not for risk premia as offered by some ETFs. As long as the growth of ETFs does not impact liquidity in the underlying shares, these stock pickers can continue to build positions as before. So from this perspective the growth of ETFs does not impinge on a stock picker's ability to generate alpha.

Actively managed ETFs may emerge at some point. So far, ETFs are largely intelligent market/factor based harvesting of risk premia, but they are not delivering alpha.

On the topic of alpha in hedge funds, from our previous interview in *2020 Vision*:

'My basic premise is that people invest in hedge funds looking for alpha. Unfortunately, it turns out there are lots of betas embedded in the fund of fund returns. So the hedge fund industry is far removed from being institutional quality, because people are not getting what it says on the label. Most hedge funds are not focused on delivering a pure alpha product, or any type of product that can justify their fees (on average).'

Do you still hold that opinion?

Yes. There is – on average – still a huge disconnect between fees and what is delivered. To the extent that hedge funds deliver risk premia then the 2+20 or 1.5+15 fee is not justified.

Fees are exorbitant, and although fees have come down, the world hasn't changed.

---

9 https://qz.com/1272280/there-are-now-almost-as-many-equity-funds-as-there-are-stocks-for-them-to-invest-in/.

10 Grinhold, RC, and Kahn, RN, 1999, *Active Portfolio Management*, McGraw-Hill. Two of Stan Becker's former colleagues at BlackRock demonstrated that Information ratio = Information coefficient (ability to forecast) × √ (Breadth of opportunities).

So, what do you think are justified fees?

My rule of thumb has always been that a manager can claim one-third of the alpha they are delivering. So to claim 2 and 20 you have to get double-digit returns before fees.

Hedge funds have not delivered an excess return over cash anything close to that. So hedge funds still overcharge.

Over half of hedge funds are currently 'adopting' artificial intelligence (AI) or machine learning technology to inform investment decisions and generate trading ideas.[11] This includes hedge fund managers like Brevan Howard and Winton using machine learning for macro insights.[12] How do you think this will impact the amount of alpha available to the hedge fund industry?

I'm not sure they will change the amount of alpha. In fact, the mis-application of new technology may benefit others. I came across a hedge fund recently with the following investment criteria: average holding period maximum 10 days, using new data without any economic or financial rationale and delivering a Sharpe ratio of minimum 5! That seems to me an extreme form of data mining that will lead to a fair bit of noise trading! I was at a New York conference recently where there was this oversupply of data scientists who knew everything about data science but nothing about economics or finance. That's a recipe for disaster! (Or opportunity for others, perhaps.)

New data, the Internet of Things and all that information will become more widely available. That will help. But in general it is hard to be truly innovative. If I think back to the days of the legendary Peter Lynch at Fidelity, who staked out supermarkets to observe the buying behaviour of customers, or the CIO of Robeco having a direct line to the harbour master in Rotterdam to get the low down on shipments, there is nothing new under the sun. Satellite imaging can now achieve the same thing more systematically. But the idea is relying on the same information as 20 years ago.

Some of the larger pension funds also invest significant time and resources into the potential benefits of AI, possibly because they

---

11 https://www.barclayhedge.com/majority-of-hedge-fund-pros-use-ai-machine-learning-in-investment-strategies/.

12 https://www.fnlondon.com/articles/alan-howard-backs-artificial-intelligence-data-venture-20180705?mod=article_inline and https://www.fnlondon.com/articles/winton-names-execs-to-lead-spun-out-data-unit-20180619?mod=article_inline.

can fund it with their large asset base, but not necessarily because they have an expertise or edge in machine learning. What do you consider some of the potential benefits for pension funds?[13]

The main focus of a pension fund is long-term asset allocation and risk management like ALM, LDI. Coming back to the earlier point you mentioned: most of these new techniques have a shorter term horizon, so are less relevant. The biggest impact I would expect to be on risk mitigating, stress testing and scenario analysis. Climate change analysis probably falls under one of those long horizon things as well. We suspect it may have an impact over 20 to 30 years, so how is a pension fund preparing for those eventualities?

You've worked for large Anglo Saxon and Dutch firms. What are the various views and convictions on ESG issues and climate change? For example, a number of Dutch pension funds have incorporated the UN's Sustainable Development Goals (SDGs) into their investment policies.

It's a dominant theme in Europe (Dutch, Scandinavians funds) although it's slowly catching on in the US. Asia is still further behind (apart from Japan). So, I think sustainability is a theme that will not go away. Some regions are probably slower and a bit more resistant to recognising the facts. But regulators are increasingly asking questions on ESG and climate change. So it's inevitable and irreversible.

What is in your opinion the academic/practitioner consensus (if any) on the benefits of sustainability exposure/climate change hedging (reducing carbon footprint) from an investment (rather than moral) perspective?

From an investment perspective: the jury is still out on the return impact of an ESG focus. My summary is that it's not statistically proven so, therefore, it's a free option. If it hasn't been proven to add value but also doesn't detract, then why not add it if it doesn't cost you anything in the return space and possibly helps you in the risk space? There are still theories of course that neglected (excluded) stocks could outperform, although the data so far doesn't seem to bear this out.

---

13 For example, some mentioned manager selection, scenario analysis, dynamic factor analysis and risk management. Refer for example to https://www.gpif.go.jp/en/investment/research_2017_1_en.pdf. The Government Pension Investment Fund of Japan tested AI to assess managers. APG teamed up with TNO and Maastricht University.

In one of your recent articles[14], you suggest: 'Lagged social media and news can help forecast next month's global stock market return. However, adding social media information to news-based sources does on average not improve the results of a market timing investment strategy. Overall, the news-based equity fundamentals sentiment is the more consistent and reliable source for monthly timing of the MSCI World Index.' Can you explain for our readers the practical implications of your research? Also, how do you deal with 'fake/outdated news'?

I was intrigued by the question whether social media contains anything not already in established news sources. By putting the two next to each other (news and social media) I came to the conclusion that social media in aggregate is so polluted, it doesn't add anything to what's already in the news. So, whereas news can help in timing the market, social media as a whole doesn't add anything. Maybe there is a source somewhere that does, but in aggregate all together social media is one bunch of noise!

In terms of strategic research, which areas do you think institutional investors should focus on? For example, strategic asset allocation, security selection, new asset classes, market timing, portfolio construction, risk management, and principal–agency issues.

Beyond any doubt it is strategic asset allocation, especially now in a low-return environment. There is increasing importance of the less liquid assets such as commercial real estate infrastructure debt, real estate debt and mortgages. Pension funds have less of that potential mismatch between illiquid assets and long time horizon.

Do you believe in an illiquidity premium after fees?

Definitely! Certainly in the fixed-income space. For private equity I suspect that's harder to substantiate because the fees are so high.

Can you comment on the trend towards 'dynamic asset allocation' and 'real return' strategies and the academic evidence that short-term market timing from tactical tilting adds value?

It all comes back to a previous question. Can you add value by doing DAA or marketing timing? I'm sceptical. It's hard to identify who's really

---

14 Beckers, S.,'Do Social Media Trump News? The relative importance of social media and news based sentiment for market timing', *Journal of Portfolio Management*, Multi-Asset Special Issue 2019, vol. 45 (2) pp. 58–67.

good at it. It's even harder to identify a good dynamic asset allocator than it is to find a good stock selector or bond manager.

I'd be very reluctant to give money to somebody who claims to be good at it.

What keeps you busy in retirement?

Apart from my activities at the London Business School and various non-executive positions? Daily running and cycling. I have five grand-children and a sixth one on the way. I also like to travel. I have a son in Melbourne, Australia, so we try to make it over to Australia at least once a year. I do travel a bit. On average, every week I spend two or three days in London, a day in Luxembourg and am in Belgium for the weekends.

Before I forget, what do you think about the diversity movement?

I am absolutely convinced that more diversity improves investment performance. Of all the limited academic evidence I've seen so far and incidental evidence, I would say that women are better investment managers than men.

Why do you think that?

Well, I think that is intuitive: men have too high testosterone levels, which leads to overconfidence. They then trade too often and too aggressively. Women have less ego, so their views are less clouded. So the industry will benefit hugely from more women. Unfortunately, the industry is still dominated by big-ego males, which makes it hard for women to get into the industry.

So it's a good thing you retired then to make way for more women!

Exactly! [Laughs.]

How do you see the investment industry in 10 years' time?

The words that come to mind are:

- leaner
- less profitable. We've only seen the start in the reduction of fees. We now see zero-fee ETFs emerging. I have also seen traditional

active managers splitting alpha 50/50 after no (or even negative) management fee

- fewer players

- more regulated

- more passive.

So, I see significant change. It will remain as one of the most profitable industries, but the cost-to-income ratio of 65% will not be sustainable. Consolidation and size will become determining factors.

I feel I retired at a crossroads for the industry.

Finally – investment: art, science or skill?

Passive management is a science.

Active management is an art.

You need a minimum amount of skill for passive management.

For active management the skill hurdle is high.

Skilful artists are rare. Much rarer than the abundance of supply that's currently out there for active management!

Thank you for your time.

Conclusions

'Choose work that you love and you won't have to work another day.'
Confucius (551–479 BC)

Stan mentioned he feels like he retired at a crossroads for the industry. But even after officially retiring, Stan keeps an active mind by testing various hypotheses, such as performance persistence, fallen angels and fund versus ETF performance.

He agrees short-term investors such as high-frequency traders will be impacted more than long-term investors by new AI technology and Big Data. He considers that deep down the only source of alpha is investor irrationality. In his view the real question is: 'Will the Digital Age increase rationality?' He does not think so, citing populism as an irrational example from an economic perspective. The amount of noise and irrationality in social media all point towards continued support for alpha. He also observes that social media is so polluted, it doesn't add anything that's not already in the news for investment signals.

While more and more alpha is repackaged, he considers the under-performance we're observing in various risk premia to be cyclical, but he also notes there has been a proliferation of risk premia. Not all the new products represent 'true established risk premia'. The rest is a result of marketing and academics trying to get their papers published.

He is somewhat concerned about the growth of ETFs, which are now spilling into fixed income, commodities and currency. This may be a problem in the making during the next crash.

In terms of the impact of technology, he notes a few developments:

- *Data sources (by legal means, rather than insider info):* As an active manager there are only so many ways to beat the competition. We are now at the stage where hedge funds are launching their own satellites.

- *Processing speed:* Data gets processed more quickly, so high-frequency traders are locating as close to exchanges as possible.

- *Insight:* The true source of differentiation is processing in a more insightful manner. That will be the true source of alpha generation. Not sharing the secret sauce is the way to stay ahead. He cites Renaissance as an example.

In general though, Stan suggests there is not much new under the sun in terms of the data we are looking at, or the algorithms we are using. In the end, the technology is a means to an end. The intelligent application is the differentiator. As Stan mentions:

> *'A four-star chef uses ingredients you can buy in the supermarket. He can combine them in a consistent fashion that nobody else thought of. If some-body says "it was only combining ingredients", that doesn't make the person a four-star chef!'*

CHAPTER 5

INVESTMENT FIRMS IN THE DIGITAL AGE

An interview with Julia Hobart on investment firms, technology and diversity

'The stock market is a device for transferring money from the impatient to the patient.'

Warren Buffett

The CFA Institute identifies challenges for investment firms in the coming decade, including fee pressure, lower market returns, increased service and compliance costs, and reduced net inflows as more people reach retirement age while facing a low-return environment.[1] New technologies promote new business models, and investment firms are faced with consolidation. Although it's uncertain what the catalyst would be, the industry may become dominated by a few very large investment managers that have leveraged technology to enhance efficiency. In addition, any of the FAANG tech titans has the potential to be among these dominant investment industry players in the future.

---

1 'Investment Firm of the Future: Alternative business models and strategies for a more forward-thinking industry', CFA Institute, 2018.

The fund management industry needs to find radical reductions in the existing cost base to allow investment for growth. A recent Morgan Stanley/Oliver Wyman report[2] suggests revenue growth for the industry over the next five years will remain flat.

Fund management industry growth

Global revenue composition – base case, 2018–2023(f), USD BN

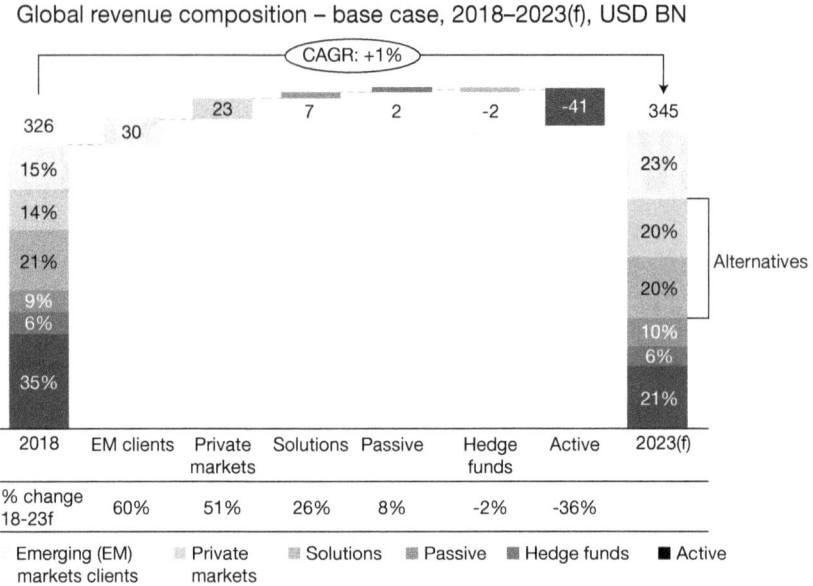

% change 18-23f	60%	51%	26%	8%	-2%	-36%

Source: Oliver Wyman

As with other industries that have undergone dramatic pricing pressure, asset managers need to decide whether to stay and fight in traditional active territory or move to areas of growth in, for example, emerging markets, private markets, or helping segments other than the dwindling DB plans, such as DC plans, high-net-worth individuals, or sub-advisory. Technology, efficiency and the right business focus will become increasingly important.[3]

Getting the client proposition right is also increasingly important. Given the emphasis that investors place on aligning interests, it is

---

2   'Asset Managers & Wholesale Banks: Searching for growth in an age of disruption', Morgan Stanley and Oliver Wyman. https://www.oliverwyman.com/our-expertise/insights/2019/mar/wholesale-banks-asset-management-analysis-2019.html.
3   https://www.oliverwyman.com/our-expertise/insights/2019/jan/asset-management-trends-2019.html.

concerning that only approximately one-third of retail investors and a quarter of institutional investors think their investment advisor or firm consistently puts their interests first.[4]

At the same time institutional asset owners are significantly more aware and better resourced than ever before. Asset owners have become more conscious of the investment management value chain. Many asset owners recognise that in order to reduce inefficiencies along their investment management value chain, they must not only push cost down for their external fund managers, but also improve their own internal processes and capacity for innovation. They also face tremendous challenges. The rise in world debt reflects stimulus programs and the failure to turn budget deficits into budget surpluses. Implicit and explicit retirement needs are ballooning, with an ageing population in many developed markets.[5]

Introducing Julia Hobart

Julia is a partner in the Wealth and Asset Management practice at Oliver Wyman in London.

Her key areas of expertise include advice on business strategy to clients operating in the investment arena. This includes organisational and operational effectiveness, product design and investment processes, and relevant responses to the changing industry environment.

Julia has co-authored a series of reports published by the World Economic Forum, including 'The Future of the Global Financial System'[6] and 'The Future of Long-Term Investing'[7]. She is also one of the authors of Oliver Wyman's bi-annual 'Women in Financial Services' report, which seeks to provide insight and solutions on gender challenges and differences across the financial services subsectors.

She joined Oliver Wyman in 2004 from Mercer, following its acquisition by MMC, and has worked for over 25 years in the investment field, as a portfolio manager and investment consultant before her current role as a strategy consultant. She has worked with a wide range of

---

4 'The Next Generation of Trust: A global survey on the state of investor trust', CFA Institute, 2018.
5 The world's six largest pension systems face a joint shortfall of $400 trillion by 2050. Source: 'We'll Live to 100 – How Can We Afford It?', World Economic Forum, 2017 and 'Investing in (and for) Our Future', World Economic Forum, 2019.
6 www3.weforum.org/.../WEF_GCP_Future_of_the_Global_Financial_System_pager.pdf.
7 www3.weforum.org/docs/WEF_Future_of_Long_term_Investing.pdf.

clients, including asset managers, insurance companies, SWFs, pension funds and banks.

At Mercer, Julia headed its Investment Consulting business in Continental Europe. She then led its Manager Advisory practice, providing strategic advice to asset management clients, before transitioning the business to Oliver Wyman. Julia holds an MA in Mathematics and Computer Science from Cambridge University. She is a member of the Advisory Council for AIMSE Europe (the Association of Investment Management Sales Executives).

We discussed how megatrends are impacting investment firms for the future, in terms of technology, diversity and regulation, and also Julia's work on long-term investing.

Julia, many thanks for participating. Can you introduce our readers to what you consider to be the most interesting topics of discussion for investment firms today?

There are four topics on my mind.

The first one is the perennial question of: how do you differentiate yourself as an investor and how do you add value?

The second is how to be cost effective? And how to use technology to achieve it. I like to be a bit radical here. Rather than cutting costs *by* 10%, how about cutting cost *to* 10% of what they currently are? We need to challenge ourselves more and move away from the incremental approach, which is unlikely to move the dial sufficiently.

The third is around distribution, and impacts commercial asset managers. There is a revolution happening in distribution whereby distribution is increasingly being captured by a shrinking number of vertically integrated organisations. This is where FAANG could disrupt, given their extensive customer access. What is the most effective way of accessing and servicing clients? Although technology is an enabler here, it highlights the fact that technology should be viewed in conjunction with other attributes.

The fourth is a way that I find useful to shift one's thinking: if you were to disrupt your organisation, what would you do? This is helpful to get one thinking about different business models, what clients want, what is redundant, different client access and service, different propositions and different investment tools. It also helps us to focus on where the weaknesses are.

What are the main differences in your views with regard to how these topics influence institutional asset management firms versus asset owners?

The nuance is quite subtle. If you are an asset owner you have a choice as to whether you do things yourself or get somebody to do it for you. Asset managers don't have that choice – although they can decide what products and services they will and won't provide. Cost is universal though. Everybody needs to be alert to being more efficient, and that feeds into whether to insource or outsource.

For everyone, it is really hard to be honest about what you are good at and where you add value. As an asset owner you become attached to what already exists. It is therefore hard to be agile, as it feels much more personal. Still, they should be asking: what are our competitive advantages? Is it a longer time horizon? Or do we have a structural advantage to deal access? Or can we use our size and provenance; for example, investment clubs of likeminded asset owners, who can take advantage of investing collectively at a much lower cost.

If you are a commercial asset manager, to some extent you are both anticipating and responding to your clients' demands. What do clients want, and how can you deliver it? And increasingly, is it adding value? Look at the current vogue in private assets, the rationale being to pick up the illiquidity premium, to provide diversification and sometimes a liability match. However, often the cost of managing the investments is high and the fees correspondingly high. So there is a question as to whether, after fees, the net returns to investors are worth it. The asset manager can control only part of this equation, but it is important to keep the value-for-money point front of mind.

As part of the changes in the distribution landscape, we are seeing a shift from 'pure' distributors to vertically integrated players who have extended their activities down the activity chain. The latter has been fuelled by the growth in outcome-oriented products such as multi-asset and lifecycle options. So as an asset manager, you need to decide whether you are just a manufacturer selling products through a distributor or you are doing both distribution and manufacturing. From the client's perspective, the challenge then is how to evaluate what you have bought both at a product level and the integrated level.

In its 'Investment Firm of the Future' report, the CFA Institute suggest 72% of respondents expect the pace of industry consolidation to speed up, and 55% believe the biggest challenge will be fee or cost pressures. What's your take on this?

Everybody has been predicting consolidation for over a decade! And if you wind forward I think we will have far fewer players and in fact less capacity in the industry, driven by cost pressure. But I take a slightly nuanced view. There seems to be a perception that scale is the answer to profitability. I don't think it's that simple. I think if you're delivering a more commoditised product, then yes scale is critical. But there is still room for value-adding strategies – these may be smaller-scale products but they can still be attractive for boutique businesses. I do still believe there will be a place for specialists who are expert in their areas.

Digital disruption is hitting investment firms, with some firms adapting existing processes and others doing a complete workplace overhaul.[8] What's your view on this? Is it better to *adapt* existing processes or *disrupt* and start from completely new business models and employee requirements?

I suspect we are all hidebound by incremental thinking, and so I believe that if you want to dig a hole, the best way is to dig in a different place. I think it is better to start anew. But that is quite scary, so there is an argument for starting small and building up from there. Whether its small or a big bang, you do need a vision of what you want to do, and for that you need to challenge yourself.

Big Data and artificial intelligence – how do investment firms best apply this?

It is hard to do it incrementally. But a big bang approach is really hard and risky. People don't like change, and worry about their jobs. So there are lots of forces pushing against it.

Big Data lends itself to certain parts of the value chain, such as business development and sales analytics. We have heard a few managers describe their early use of AI and machine learning within the investment engine. But it's early stage and many managers are looking at how

---

8   Major banks such as JPMorgan Chase, Goldman Sachs, and Citigroup are teaching investment bankers to code, as artificial intelligence and online lending platforms shape the future of the industry. https://www.techrepublic.com/article/why-big-banks-are-requiring-workers-to-learn-coding/.

to leverage the time of analysts and portfolio managers but are certainly not replacing them, at least as yet.

This already necessitates a change of skills required of the front office. But in time these roles could be automated to some extent. The question is whether you adapt current investment approaches using AI, or you start anew with a completely new business model?

I can't see humans being completely replaced by machines. We can still think more tangentially and relate things in a non-linear way. In a future world, there will most probably be some purely AI-driven managers, but I would like to think there will also be some 'bionic' managers where humans work with the machines, each doing what they do best. That would entail a step change from what the industry does today.

In the institutional world, there is currently a lot of focus on ESG. How do investment firms relate to those topics? Is the absence of a consensus on whether it impacts investment returns a constraint on these matters? For example, many investment firms have ESG as part of their investment beliefs, but don't adjust their actual investment process much.

In some jurisdictions investment firms are now required to embed ESG thinking into their investment process. But the problem is that it has also resulted in some greenwashing. That said, there has been a step change; the industry has gone well beyond negative screening and into more proactive/thematic sustainability, most recently climate-related debates and corporate engagement.

This is all great, and some organisations are making real positive changes. However, while there is little doubt that responsible investing is the right thing to do, there are now so many different ESG products and practices that buyers need to be very clear about what they want and what they are getting.

In the CFA 'Investment Firm of the Future' report, 53% of respondents say the business case for improved diversity in the industry is strong, yet only 14% say the speed of uptake of diversity and inclusion practices will be fast. Could you expand for our readers on how you see the uptake and influence of diversity for investment firms?[9]

My frustration is that progress is very slow! And although the headline board numbers are improving, there are too few women CEOs

---

9   https://info.cfainstitute.org/DI_Report.html.

or women controlling P&Ls. Some say it's a pipeline problem – which is true. But there is an issue of the 'missing middle' – we haven't yet fixed how to make mid-career better for women: to foster, support and ultimately retain more women at that level. It is a big issue, and we need to turn our attention to it.

Are you aware of any recent literature that proves a diversity premium (excess returns, not priced in)?

We did a report with the IFC earlier this year which looked at venture capital and private equity in emerging markets. For this we did extensive performance analysis and concluded that gender-balanced teams (defined as 30% to 70% men or women) outperformed and achieved higher realised returns.[10]

Do you have any views on the outlook for growth and profitability for investment firms in China or emerging markets?

Well, I'm not sure how many Western asset managers have made money in China so far. Foreign managers are trying to build credibility and volume, but progress has been slow, and as a foreign manager you have to play a long game. However, the potential size of the asset pool is incredibly enticing and, with an acceleration in the pace of liberalisation, foreign asset managers will now be able to own a majority of a local fund management company from next year. So the opportunity has become very real.

The early stages of foreigners entering a market are often difficult. Even US managers, when they started selling in the UK 30 years ago, their pitches went down awkwardly with UK clients. The apparent similarities of the two countries turned out to be importantly different. The successful companies rapidly became more local, sometimes buying local firms. There are lessons to draw for China, where being local and having a distributor relationship will be key.

What's your view on the alpha versus beta debate?

Alpha is typically smaller scale and beta typically needs to be done at large scale. I do believe there are people and organisations who can deliver alpha (defined as value added over a replicable benchmark).

---

10 https://www.oliverwyman.com/our-expertise/insights/2019/mar/moving-toward-gender-balance-in-private-equity-and-venture-capi.html.

However, I think alpha skill is much rarer than the capacity for it in the industry, and often it resides in smaller organisations. To deliver alpha, the most important thing is to do things differently. But that is difficult in an industry where the penalty of getting it wrong is increasingly high.

Any other thoughts on alpha?

Measuring alpha or persistent skill is full of traps. You'll often find strongly performing products or strategies, and discover that style has played an important part – was that luck or skill? You try to normalise for the style factors, but if you normalise too much you end up with no information at all. The other confounding factor is people moving jobs. And how much of the performance is down to the individual or the team or the wider firm? So, following an individual's real record is quite hard. But there are certainly some organisations that have strong team stability and organisational consistency over multiple decades. Often they are partnerships, although that is not a prerequisite.

What is your view on public versus private markets?

Investment in private assets is very much in fashion, and fashion always worries me. However, I think there is justification for private assets. I am linking private assets with illiquid assets (although an important distinction: all private assets are typically illiquid but not all illiquid assets are private). I won't attempt to give a full rationale for why private assets, but one fact that has stunned me is the narrowing of public markets. Over the last 20 years, the US and UK markets have halved in terms of number of stocks and therefore breadth of the market, so it's much less representative of exposure to the overall economy than in the past.

Private markets, and particularly venture capital, contain a disproportionate exposure to technology across multiple sectors, which is underrepresented in public indices. But don't invest just because it's private – as ever, caveat emptor.

Could you comment on some of the World Economic Forum reports you worked on? 'The Future of the Global Financial System' and the 'Future of Long-Term Investing'? How can the global financial system contribute to sustained economic growth and social development? How do they best manage various stakeholders?

There are a few learnings from the Future of Long-Term Investing report that I particularly like.

First, it's really hard to maintain a long-term view. Even archetypal long-term investors such as sovereign wealth funds struggle with this because they are being so scrutinised. While the objective is long term, there is greater short-term pressure. Another segment, mutual insurance companies, has competitive pressures, regulation and policyholder owners, all of which shorten the time horizon. And, secondly, regulation is also a confounding factor. So, having a truly long-term view is really hard, no matter how desirable. There are a few prerequisites: trust is critical (between owner and manager, principal and agent), having short chains of command, and having a set of balanced metrics that focus on the long term as well as short term.

Of the 50-plus organisations we interviewed for the report, we noticed that everybody wanted to have the long-term view, but surprisingly almost none used any metrics that would help to reinforce the long-term view and navigate progress. In fact, there was only one organisation that seemed to have mastered the art – they had lower frequency metrics as well as the more standard quarterly and annual risk/return data. They also had an outstanding record of outperformance.

I'm a strong believer in taking the long-term view for two reasons. First, I don't think many people are very good at timing markets. But I believe you can be more confident about long-run trends. The second reason is that most organisations are taking a much shorter view due to external pressures, so if you think on a different timescale you are more likely to be able to see value.

What new research projects are you working on at the moment?

Well, we have been doing a study for the UK Treasury looking at the feasibility of DC schemes investing in venture capital and growth (later stage) equity. The short story is that there is a very strong case for longer term exposure to VC and GE as part of a diversified DC pension pot. Over the longer term, VC and GE deliver a premium return over public markets.

You have been an asset manager, asset consultant and strategy consultant. Which of these careers have you found most rewarding and why?

I'm glad I have done all three. Each has complemented the next career. But temperamentally, I am a consultant. The reason is that I like to evaluate a situation, diagnose the issues, and then come up with solutions. That for me is the exciting bit. In a broad sense that describes strategy consulting.

What keeps you busy outside of office hours?

That would be family and friends. I also run. I've run several half marathons, but am taking a break from them for a bit, and I enjoy skiing and cooking. I never have quite the time to do all the things I'd like to do! Oh yes, I listen to podcasts while I run. I like to learn about new things.

How do you see the investment industry in 10 years' time?

I see a world that has been through disruption. Conceivably it may originate from a FAANG, but it will be a different business model. And it will require a step change, whereas at the moment we're changing incrementally.

There will be considerably less institutional money, which is the historic provenance of most large asset managers. With DC, decisions are much more around individuals, whose needs are ever increasing given longevity, less state assistance, potentially lower market returns, and other issues. This will in turn challenge what is offered, what it costs and how asset managers will deliver it.

This is ripe for challenge, with someone coming in with a different model and different value proposition. It could be from within the industry, but equally it could be an outsider. The question for me is whether this model will squeeze out the more specialist (and hopefully higher performing) asset classes. I think there will always be a place for strong-performing asset classes and managers, but it will be important to have an objective way to measure them.

Finally – investment: art, science or skill?

It's all three. But my view is that you can't succeed for very long without skill of some sort. So if I have to choose one, it is skill.

Thank you for your time.

Conclusions

With uncertain economic conditions ahead, the fund management industry needs to find radical reductions in the existing cost base to allow investment for growth. At the same time, institutional asset owners are significantly more aware and better resourced than ever before. Asset owners have become more conscious of the investment management value chain.

This then touches on the perennial question of: how do you differentiate yourself as an investor and how do you add value? As an asset owner you have a choice as to whether you do things yourself or get somebody to do it for you. As an asset manager, you don't.

She suggests there will be a change of skills required in a more technological industry. For the longest time you had analysts who do the research, and the portfolio manager with hypotheses. The portfolio manager skill is in portfolio construction. As Julia points out, that could all be automated to some extent, apart from the hypothesis.

While parts of the process will become increasingly automated, there is little danger of portfolio managers being replaced by machines as long as they can demonstrate skill.

Regardless of the rise of AI and Big Data, you can't succeed for very long at anything without skill of some sort. As Julia concludes:

'We can still think more tangentially and relate things in a non-linear way. In a future world, there will most probably be some purely AI-driven managers, but I would like to think there will also be some "bionic" managers where humans work with the machines, each doing what they do best. That would entail a step change from what the industry does today.'

PART III

EAST VERSUS WEST

CHAPTER 6

THE ROAD LESS TRAVELLED

An interview with Dr Mark Mobius on emerging markets

'I've toured rubber plantations in Thailand and road-tested bikes over the pothole-ridden roads of rural China. I've choked on roasted camel's meat, sheep's eyeball, guinea pig and dined (surprisingly well) on scorpions on toast, all to find undervalued companies before other investors do. I think you could safely say that I'm driven.'

Mark Mobius, in *Passport to Profits*

Emerging markets continue to fascinate investors, and whatever they do, they always promise an exciting ride.[1] In this chapter we discuss some of the fundamental changes in emerging markets. At a broad level, the pros and cons of investing in emerging markets have long been widely

---

1   Several definitions of 'emerging market' exist; for example, from the IMF or United Nations. Emerging market index providers generally start from the World Bank's Gross National Income (GNI) per capita measure to classify a country as emerging market or developed market. For MSCI, a developed market must have a GNI per capita 25% above the World Bank high-income threshold – $12,056 in 2017 – for three consecutive years. However, the MSCI Emerging Markets Index contains some very developed high-income countries such as Taiwan and Korea, where access by foreigners remains limited. Indeed, over 75% of the MSCI Emerging Markets Index is related to more 'developed' East Asian economies.

acknowledged. The arguments *in favour* of exposure to these markets include:

- These markets reside in economies which are seen as dynamic, have achieved stronger economic growth than more developed economies, and look set to continue to do so. This could potentially lead to appreciating currencies.

- By 2030, emerging market economies are expected to account for 50% of global GDP, and 75% of global growth.[2] In short, emerging markets are the *future giants*. By 2030, China is expected to become the largest economy in the world, overtaking the US, whereas India will become the third largest.

- In many of these countries, the emergence of a professional and consumption-orientated middle class is driving a strong pick up in domestic demand. At the same time, an enormous pool of cheap labour combined with often artificially controlled, undervalued currencies means that these countries are super-competitive against developed economies in manufacturing and, increasingly, in services.

- These markets normally trade at a discount to developed markets, suggesting that investors are not required to pay up for the greater growth potential. Naturally, the discount reflects the higher risk of the sector, especially in terms of corporate governance.

- Scope for added value from active management is greater due to the lower proportion of institutional ownership and less efficient dissemination of information.

The major *negatives* include:

- Volatility is high for a range of reasons, including the narrow economic bases of the underlying economies plus the various crises, including political and currency crises, which have afflicted the sector on a reasonably regular basis. Volatility is increased by the tendency for contagion across markets; that is, when a crisis develops in a particular emerging or Asian market, it frequently spreads to other emerging markets, including those where there is no logical link with the original crisis.

---

2 HSBC Global Research estimates (2019).

- Transaction costs are higher and liquidity lower than in developed markets. The lower liquidity itself leads to volatility as the markets have difficulty absorbing the positive or negative cashflows which occur when they move into and out of favour with institutional investors.

- Standards of investor protection trail those of the more developed markets. Issues under this general heading encompass broad legal systems, corporations law, stock exchange regulation – including information disclosure and corporate governance – as well as repatriation laws.

Introducing Dr Mark Mobius

Mark has spent more than 40 years working in Asia and other parts of the emerging markets world. Mark joined the Templeton organisation in 1987 as President of the Templeton Emerging Markets Fund in Hong Kong. He has also served as Joint Chairman of the World Bank and on the Organization for Economic Cooperation and Development (OECD) Global Corporate Governance Forum's Investor Responsibility Taskforce, among other high-profile posts. He is a member of the economic advisory board of the International Finance Corporation. In 2018, Mark retired from Franklin Templeton after 30 years to announce the launch of Mobius Capital Partners, a fund management firm focused on investing in emerging and frontier markets as he moved back to London.

Mark has received numerous industry awards, including being named as one of the 'Ten Top Money Managers of the 20th Century' in a 1999 Carson Group survey and 'Emerging Markets Equity Manager of the Year 2001' by *International Money Marketing*. He was rated among the 'Top 100 Most Powerful and Influential People' by *Asiamoney* magazine in 2006. He was named as one of *Bloomberg Markets* magazine's '50 Most Influential People' in 2011 and awarded the Lifetime Achievement in Asset Management by Global Investor London in 2017. Mark holds a bachelor and master's degrees from Boston University, and also earned a PhD in economics and political science from MIT. Mark has studied at the University of Wisconsin, University of New Mexico and Kyoto University in Japan.

Mark is the author of several books, including *The Investor's Guide to Emerging Markets* (1994), *Mobius on Emerging Markets* (1996), *Passport to Profits* (1999), *Mutual Funds* (2007) and *The Little Book of Emerging Markets* (2012). Given his extensive travel experience as he spends most of his time jetting around the globe looking for the gems in exotic countries, some investors have nicknamed him the 'Indiana Jones of investing' and the 'Dean of emerging markets'.

Mark, thanks for your time. After 30 years as an emerging market strategist with Franklin Templeton, you decided to start a new firm in 2018. What prompted this?

The challenge of doing something new at age 82 is so enticing! Here was a chance to do something different and make a difference. So in 2018 Mobius Capital Partners was launched by myself, together with Carlos Hardenberg and Greg Konieczny from Franklin Templeton.

Your new firm has the intention of bringing environmental, social and governance improvements to companies in the developing world. Why this angle, and why now?

The interest of investors in ESG is growing as it is becoming mainstream and a critical issue. So I decided to look at this more carefully. Really, sustainability is related to ESG. 'E' is about making the environment more renewable and sustainable. 'S' is about creating societies with social stability. 'G' is about being a good, sustainable operator of companies with good shareholder rights. So sustainability crosses all three.

As a firm, we are focusing on the 'G' as most important because that in my opinion drives the 'E' and the 'S'. We do that by working on the governance aspect with companies.

The best approach for ESG in emerging markets is, in my opinion, not negative screening but engagement. So, you should have a willingness to actually work with management. Not in an aggressive style, but in a cooperative way. Not all companies are willing to do that, however. If they are approachable, they are willing to make changes. A number of organisations like MSCI or Sustainalytics rank sustainable companies. The performance of the higher rated sustainable companies over the last five years tends to be better. So the track record is there, albeit a bit short.[3]

3　Refer for example to https://www.msci.com/www/blog-posts/has-esg-affected-stock/0794561659 and https://www.msci.com/www/blog-posts/can-esg-add-alpha-/0182820893 from MSCI.

Would your style of investing in smaller companies also work better from a governance improvement perspective as you can gain a bigger stake?

Not really. We've found the size of the holdings is not the key. It is about how you communicate and receptiveness of management. Unless you want to become aggressive and take over the company, of course.

How easy is it to judge emerging market companies on an ESG basis given the lower transparency and quality of the data?

Actually, the transparency of data is a problem for both developed markets and emerging markets. A number of accounting scandals of major corporations occurred in developed markets, so it is a global issue. With regards to the economic data, a lot of it is not publicly available so it's important to be on the ground, which is why we travel a lot. For example, I still travel at least 200 days a year.

What would be the catalyst for the P/E discount to developed markets to disappear?

I think the P/E discount represents two different issues: emerging companies are growing faster, so the 'E' depresses the P/E, and second and more important, the big money does come from developed markets. Those investors tend to have a home bias and see emerging markets as a very risky area of the world. So I would say there is a general reluctance to invest, which leads to a discount.

Some people suggest for those folks with a home bias, US multinational companies (such as Apple, Starbucks, McDonald's and Nike) are still a good way to access emerging markets. What do you think of that?

Yes, of course that is a good option for people who do not like to venture far from home. We must also remember that for those folks there are emerging market companies listed in developed markets – like Alibaba on the NYSE – which are easy to access. At the core though, my main interest is onshore investing, especially with China opening up.

Talking about China, despite the increased weight in the MSCI emerging market index, some investors remain concerned about the corporate governance in China. What's your view on this?

Well, personally, I think corporate governance in China is improving. The Chinese government is behind better governance, especially for state-owned enterprises. Once they say 'this is what we need', the companies will follow through. We're looking at improvements in disclosure and the treatment of minority shareholders. So I think China will be doing very well.

Institutional investors are increasingly wondering whether they should invest across the full range of emerging markets or China specifically, given that China is now such a dominant part of the MSCI Emerging Market Index. Do you have any views on that?

Yes, China's weight in the various indices – including the MSCI EM Index – is growing, and it's important to pay attention to that since it indicates where the huge amount of money in index funds and ETFs will be going. But for active investors, it is important to *not* try to construct portfolios in line with the index but to do something different from the index. More and more investors have made big investments in index-related funds such as ETFs, and now want something that will not be correlated with the index in order to be diversified and not be exposed to index risk.

What is your view on the 'one belt, one road' policy?

I think it is a good initiative. I've seen the results on the ground in various countries and they're doing a terrific job building up the infrastructure. These countries need the infrastructure badly. But as the Americans who ventured overseas have learned, such an effort may not always be appreciated by the locals. There are some issues about the Chinese bringing in their own staff rather than employing locals to do the job, and concerns about Chinese domination.

Despite the high GDP growth, equity investors have not made any real returns in China over the past 20 years, mainly because of high dilution.[4] What do you think will change that going forward?

That depends on the companies you invest in, of course. I think it is hard to make a generalisation. Some companies will do very well, some won't. In theory one would expect higher GDP growth to lead to higher earnings per share growth all else being equal, but in the end it is all about bottom-up stock picking. As I said, it's better to be benchmark agnostic.

To what extent should investors factor in currency as a source of returns when buying emerging markets (from a USD perspective)? Does Balassa-Samuelson apply in practice?[5]

I think it is very important. In the long term, currencies in fast-growing companies should appreciate against the USD because of the higher GDP growth and stronger foreign exchange positions, as well as lower inflation. However, from a portfolio perspective, we look more at individual companies and whether they are net exporting or importing. Then we assess the impact of the currency behaviour on the company's profitability.

Speaking about bottom up, from your 40 years of experience, what style factors work best in emerging markets equities, if any?

It would be nice to say value is key in emerging markets, but in reality it's all about forecasting growth. Emerging markets move on what people perceive to be the growth of the company or economy. At the end of the day though, capital growth comes as a result of value, be it value in earnings, on the balance sheet or value in management – then there is a good opportunity for growth. You have to be flexible and open minded. In some instances, observing momentum/technical analysis and examining price movements can be important, as at the end of the day the market is a forward-looking instrument. We do invest with a small/midcap bias.

---

4   From 1997–2017, the US experienced 1% to 2% real GDP growth on average, but investors earned 5% real from domestic equities. In contrast, China experienced 9% to 10% real GDP growth, but close to 0% real return from domestic equities. L'Her, J.F., Masmoudi, T. and R.K. Krishnamoorthy, 'Net Buybacks and the Seven Dwarfs', *Financial Analysts Journal*, 2018, v74(4), pp. 57–85.

5   The Balassa-Samuelson effect (1963) suggests countries with high productivity growth (such as emerging markets) should also experience higher real exchange rates in theory. In practice, emerging countries such as China may follow a weak currency policy to retain export competitiveness.

Do you have any views on commodity prices?

A lot of people think commodity prices are a key driver for emerging markets success, as we have large exporters like in Latin America or South Africa. But China is a net importer, so it is not the be-all and end-all of emerging markets forecasting. One thing is very clear, however: I'm quite bullish on commodities as demand for coal, iron ore and others will continue to be strong as these emerging economies continue to grow at a rapid pace.

You recently commented you quite liked India, despite the usual political upheaval. Can you comment on the reasons for that?[6]

The growth is faster than China, and the country is in transformation because of Modi's reforms. For example, the Goods and Services Tax (GST) introduction eliminated tax differentials between different states. The GST, which aims to bring India's 1.3 billion-strong population under a single market for the first time since the country's independence from British rule in 1947, came into force in July 2017, after a lengthy parliamentary process.

What is your view on Latin America? You once said: 'One of the problems in Latin America is that the growth rate in the economies has not been as fast as in Asia. The reason for that is government policies.'

A number of things are happening here. In Mexico, you have a leftist president who will not want to privatise state-owned enterprises, so that will hold back the economy. Nevertheless, they are heavily tied to the US so they should do fine with the US growing. Brazil is going through momentous changes and reforms which will drive the economy and result in higher growth.

Argentina will have to follow Brazil going forward, depending on whether Macri is able to maintain the government and make the reforms required. Colombia and Chile are doing well. So, I believe Latin America should be doing well overall, with Brazil leading the reform path.

Having said all that, at this stage Asia has more faster growing countries, so Asia is a larger focus at present, also in terms of sheer size.

---

6   https://economictimes.indiatimes.com/markets/expert-view/4-things-mark-mobius-is-looking-for-as-he-plans-to-invest-in-india/articleshow/66329851.cms.

What interesting countries do you think will enter the MSCI Emerging Markets Index in the coming years?

There are so many frontier markets like Bangladesh and Vietnam that are interesting candidates.

How do you think advances in technology will influence emerging market investing?

Well, I think technology has a massive impact on emerging markets and economic growth. It enables them to leapfrog over technology; for example, from no telephony systems to 4G smartphones.

For us as fund managers, we look at how individual emerging market companies are using technology and bringing innovation into our portfolio. And also, we use it to lower the cost of research and transactions. In the regionally expansive and diverse emerging markets, the ability to directly WhatsApp or Zoom with management teams is fantastic.

What do you think makes a good fund manager? In my previous book you mentioned 'discipline, humility, love of study and the willingness to work hard'. With your new firm's governance angle, I understand you are now 'interviewing millennials who are more interested if their coffee is made from sustainable farming!'[7] How important are ESG and fintech skills?

I think curiosity and the ability to learn and to keep an open mind are key. Technology has had a big impact. The discipline now requires you to have technological skills as well to look at the wider list of opportunities to do your research. In terms of ESG, we have one member with that specific background.

What interests do you have outside of work?

None! I work 24/7 researching companies, looking for opportunities and talking to clients.

More seriously though, I do love to take time out to sightsee some of the cities I visit. I do cycling and fitness. It's not that I particularly like to exercise, but I need to do this to keep healthy to keep doing the work I am doing.

---

7   https://citywire.co.uk/funds-insider/news/why-mark-mobius-didn-t-retire-and-what-comes-next/
    a1116237.

I also read books on the plane. I just finished *The Curve* by Nicholas Lovell, about how the internet is being used to get things for free but focuses on people with special offerings to turn freeloaders into super fans. The book encourages you to embrace giving some things away for free. By stimulating interest and cultivating communities, you'll build relationships with your audience and your fans, who'll want more of what they love. I also like history and technology, and also fiction like John Grisham.

At what age will you finally retire?

No age in mind – I have a passion for what I do!

Final question – investing in emerging markets in the future: art, science or skill?

I would say it will remain an art. It requires solid judgement to talk about the future of businesses and companies. We are in the future business, predicting the future. You have to combine all your knowledge, but in the end, that synthesis is still an art. It's a subjective decision-making process. I don't think this will change much because of technology. Like artists using various techniques and tools, you use technology, but as an investment professional your view is the key. It is the subjective judgement you have to make. It is up to the individual to make the decision.

Thank you for your time.

Conclusions

Emerging markets may rise and fall, but Mark Mobius just keeps on going with no plans for retirement, even starting a new firm at age 82. He notes one of the reasons for starting the firm as being the interest of investors in ESG, which is becoming mainstream and a critical issue. The best approach for ESG in emerging markets is, in his opinion, not negative screening but engagement. He focuses on the G, and suggests there are signs of improvement in governance in emerging markets, especially in China where there is a government-led initiative.

In terms of investment style, he suggests investing in emerging markets is all about forecasting (perceived) growth, and to remain flexible and open minded. He also suggests emerging market investors shouldn't really pay attention to indices, and that it is better to invest benchmark agnostic and bottom up to access the best companies. Mark considers the P/E discount a function of emerging companies growing faster, and secondly, a home bias by developed-market investors who see emerging markets as risky.

In terms of technology, he considers this to have a massive impact on emerging economies as it enables them to leapfrog over technology stages; for example, from no telephony systems to 4G smartphones. For investment research, he uses the latest networks to lower the cost of research and transactions in the regionally expansive and diverse emerging markets. He acknowledges technology has had a major impact on his dealings, and that the investment discipline now requires you to have technological skills to look at the wider list of opportunities.

However, for all the developments in technology, Mark remains convinced that the investment decision-making process at its core will remain an art. It requires solid judgement to project the future of businesses and companies, and at the end of the day, Mark still considers that synthesis an art or a subjective decision-making process. Technology, to him, remains a tool, rather than potentially replacing the decision maker. We must remember Mark has a long history in investing, and learned the investment basics from the legendary John Templeton.[8] As Mark notes: 'Sir John Templeton was quite a personality. The thing that impressed me the most about him was he was very frugal. He was very patient, very even-tempered.' The words of Sir John Templeton probably describe best why Mark thinks humans will never be replaced by machines:

> *'Even if we can identify an unchanging handful of success principles, we cannot apply these rules to an unchanging universe of investments – or an unchanging economic and political environment. Everything is in a constant state of change. The wise investor recognises that success is a process of continually seeking answers to new questions.'*

---

8   Sir John Marks Templeton (29 November 1912 – 8 July 2008) was an American-born British investor, banker, fund manager and philanthropist. In 1954, he entered the mutual fund market and created the Templeton Growth Fund. In 1999, *Money* magazine named him 'arguably the greatest global stock picker of the century'.

CHAPTER 7

CROSSROADS

An interview with Ray Dalio
on identifying conflict

*'The ideas of economists and political philosophers, both when
they are right and when they are wrong, are more powerful than is
commonly understood. Indeed, the world is ruled by little else.'*
John Maynard Keynes (1883–1946)

Economics is concerned with the production, consumption and transfer of wealth, and from a broader perspective, forms an integral part of how we live and react to one another. The inherent difficulty in studying economics as a subject is multiplied a thousandfold by a factor insignificant in physics or mathematics: forecasting the adaptive and collective behaviour of individuals and crowds governed by self-interest. Any attempt to isolate economics from other disciplines like politics, history, philosophy and ethics therefore reduces its power to explain what is happening in the world. While the pursuit of happiness gives meaning and purpose to our lives, focusing on GDP alone does not give a good measure of economic performance, and even less of wellbeing. The philosophies of materialism and capitalism are being challenged within many countries by events political, economic and environmental in nature.

In addition, the intersection of politics, economics and philosophy[1] has often led to a bloody crossroads; for example, capitalism versus communism. The philosophy of nationalism can lead to embargoes, trade wars and foreign exchange controls. Some even consider the philosophy of protectionism equivalent to the philosophy of war.[2] Yet, great civilisations are often not conquered from without by war, but destroyed from within, combining a decline in morale, a class struggle, and despotism with failing trade and consuming wars.[3]

We are now at a crossroads where the US and China are locked in trade tensions. At the root of most conflicts lies the quest for resources. It may be disguised as ideology, nationalism or even religion, but without an economic motive there is no lasting impetus for a (trade) war.

The US has truly awakened the sleeping dragon. Already ranked second in the world by GDP size, by 2030 China will overtake the US as the world's largest economy.

Introducing Ray Dalio

'I believe that all good things taken to an extreme can be self-destructive and that everything must evolve or die. This is now true for capitalism. I believe that capitalism is now not working for the majority of Americans.'

Ray Dalio, founder of Bridgewater Associates

In an era where Julian Robertson and George Soros have left the scene, Ray's firm is one of the few original global macro money managers still actively managing money. A baby boomer himself, Ray has been trading since the age of 12, buying and selling stocks while caddying at the local golf course. After graduating from Harvard Business School with an MBA in finance and with two years of work experience, Ray founded Bridgewater in the 1970s at the age of 25 in a spare bedroom

---

1 Some might also include religion. Philosophy is the rational investigation of truth, whereas religion makes the same kind of truth claims based on faith. Both religion and philosophy ask questions like: what is good? What does it mean to live a good life? What is the nature of reality? Why are we here, and what should we be doing? How should we treat each other? What is really most important in life?
2 'The Conflicts of Our Age', chapter 24. *On Human Action*, Ludwig von Mises (1949).
3 https://www.linkedin.com/pulse/why-how-capitalism-needs-reformed-parts-1-2-ray-dalio/ describes the widening income/wealth/opportunity gap, existential threats and the rise of populism.

in his apartment on East 64th Street in New York, specialising in managing credit and currency exposure. Bridgewater has since evolved into the largest hedge fund worldwide. Ray officially relinquished his Chief Executive Officer title in 2011 to take on the title of 'Mentor'. He remains one of its three co-Chief Investment Officers.

Ray has appeared in the *Times* list of 100 most influential people in the world, and also on the Bloomberg Markets list as one of the 50 most influential people. Ray has a number of essays and publications to his name, including *How the Economic Machine Works: A template for understanding what is happening now* (2008), *Principles: Life and work* (2017)[4], *Principles to Understanding Big Debt Crises* (2018)[5], *Why and How Capitalism Needs to Be Reformed* (2019) and *Economic and Investment Principles* (forthcoming). Investors and policymakers around the world subscribe to Bridgewater's newsletter *Daily Observations*, and Ray's insights into the working of the world's economy have led to appearances in financial publications and media outlets, including CNBC, Bloomberg and *The Wall Street Journal*. In 2011 Ray and his wife joined Bill Gates and Warren Buffett's 'Giving Pledge', vowing to donate more than half their fortune to charitable causes within their lifetime. Ray has created the Ray Dalio Foundation to channel his philanthropic contributions.

When we first interviewed Ray 12 years ago in 2007 for *2020 Vision: Investment Wisdom for Tomorrow*, we focused on Ray's work as a hedge fund manager. We discussed the potential paradigm shift involving the separation of alpha and beta, a future of investing consisting of efficient beta creators (such as indexers and ETFs), and post-modern portfolio theory and risk parity, a concept he first considered in 1989.

Twelve years on, Ray has taken on a mentoring approach, and in this conversation we ask him for an update on the economic environment, sources of conflict within and across countries, and where he would put the marginal $1 to invest.

Ray, thank you for participating again. Twelve years after our first interview, and you're still in the competition for alpha at an age when most macro managers from your era have retired. Clearly you're still busy investing and writing books. I understand you are working on

---

4 *Principles: Life and work* was a New York Times #1 bestseller and Amazon's #1 business book of 2017. Refer also https://www.amazon.com/Principles-Life-Work-Ray-Dalio/dp/1501124021.
5 https://www.principles.com/big-debt-crises.

a new book: *Economic and Investment Principles*. What can readers look forward to?

I'm in a transition phase of my life in which my goal now is to pass along the principles that helped me to be successful.

Does that mean you are actually giving away part of the secret sauce?

While I won't give away confidential decision rules, I will pass along principles that I believe will help people see economics and markets in a way that is different from how most people do, and that has been invaluable to me and Bridgewater.

It will be something like my book *Principles for Navigating Big Debt Crises*, which is available free online at principles.com/big-debt-crises or in print form on Amazon, though it will be focused on economics and investments.

Let's talk about the current investment environment. You mentioned some time ago that 1937 was perhaps the most analogous period in history in terms of the rise of populism, money printing and wealth disparity. Do you still hold this view?

Yes, I still hold that view. As was true in the late 1930s, central banks today can't lower interest rates and can't put enough money and credit in the hands of those who will spend it, so they don't have much power to reverse the next downturn.

Can you comment on the rise of populist left and right?

There is a lot of conflict between populists of the left and populists of the right because of the large wealth and opportunity gap, and there is a rising world power challenging the existing world power – both of which were also true in the 1930s.

The interactions of those forces, plus the tech revolution, are likely to be the major drivers of the economy and markets over the next few years.

Some groups argue that the money created through QE to date has not gone to the consuming public but has gone to the banks, which have funnelled it into the financial markets and remain conservative in lending. In their view, QE in essence was deployed to reverse

the debts of banks and prop up the stock market. In other words, it bailed out the rich, but failed the poor. What's your view on that?

It's true that the central banks' printing of money and purchases of financial assets drove up financial asset prices, which helped those who had financial assets more than those who didn't.

It is true that this has widened the wealth gap, but it's not true that it was a ploy to help bankers.

It was a necessary move that didn't do much to help those who were poor because the money and credit did not trickle down to them much, because lending to them was imprudent because they weren't creditworthy.

So what was the impact on the overall market?

The QE you asked about equalled about US$15 trillion, which is why there is so much money in the hands of investors and why all asset prices are so high that real and nominal yields are low and the future returns of assets will be low.

That happening at the same time as new technologies are replacing people in middle-class jobs and leading to the widening wealth gap.

Do you have any thoughts about gold, given the increase in money supply after QE, and given the low/negative nominal and real yields in many countries?

I believe that most investors are underweight in gold, which will likely perform well. In addition, it can serve as an effective diversifier, so I'd buy enough to get my allocation up to at least 5% of my portfolio.

A key to keeping low interest rates is inflation staying low. What's your view on why global inflation remains so low despite tight labour markets? Is it due to the low velocity of money (banks being reluctant to lend) or something else?

Technological advances have kept all prices low and have widened corporate profit margins. Globalisation had the same effect. That has led to chronic goods deflation and slow labour cost increases.

What's your view on the de-globalisation that we're currently seeing? (For example, the rise of nationalism, populism, protectionism, trade wars.)

I think that populism, nationalism and protectionism are the natural consequences of the forces mentioned earlier.

How long will the current environment last? What are its causes, and what are the potential catalysts for change?

De-globalisation will be with us for a long time as the US and China will seek to disentangle themselves in order to reduce their vulnerabilities to being cut off by the other in the event of conflict.

You've always had a positive view on China, arguing for a soft landing due to tax cuts and fiscal stimulus, but also due to technological advances and strong leadership. Is that fair to say?

I'd say, generally speaking, that the Chinese system is being run better than the Western system. Its track record over the last 40 years speaks for itself.

Does the technological big brother aspect in China concern you at all?

Each system has its pros and cons. There is an orderliness and efficiency that is gained by top-down systems when they are run well. On the other hand, bottom-up systems are more conducive to creativity when they are run well.

So, if you had the marginal $1 to invest, would you invest it in China or the US?

It depends how much of my portfolio is already in each. Diversification is very important to me. Since most investors are way underinvested in China relative to the US at the same time as 1) China's marginal growth rates are going to be much faster, and 2) given the relative pricing of these two countries' assets, I would put that marginal dollar into China.

Do you have any strong views on the impact of AI on investment management? How effectively can it be applied, and what are the dangers with the abundance and noise of Big Data?

I think most investors who try to use AI will fail because a strategy based on using AI to find the key relationships to bet on won't be able

110

to compete with deep understanding. It's more likely to produce data mining that will be costly.

However, using Big Data and algorithms that reflect a deep understanding will remain a big advantage.

So, does man still beat machine?

Brains are still better for imagining and thinking logically, and computers are still better for processing lots of information. If you use each for what it does best, that will produce the best results.

What would you do differently if you had to start all over again?

I wouldn't change anything. Life is a journey, so the goal is to enjoy the twists and turns, not to go directly to the destination. I can't imagine changing anything, including the mistakes that have helped me learn.

What do you think makes a good investment manager?

The ability to be comfortable holding an independent point of view.
Constantly questioning whether that view is wrong.
Common sense.
A passion for the game.

What would you have done if you had not entered this business?

I couldn't say, other than it would have led me to travel to faraway places and meet people with radically different points of view, it would have been entrepreneurial, and it would have been playing a game that provides relatively quick feedback.

How do you see the investment industry in 10 years' time?

The investment business will consist of alpha generators and beta replicators, and the alpha generators will have very smart people who understand financial engineering and are equipped with fabulous information technology. The amount of money firms will expend in the competition to produce alpha, and the levels of sophistication that this will produce, will be commensurate with the fees that they earn, which will increasingly differentiate between the various gradations of quality. In others words, the quality of play will increase dramatically.

Finally – investment: art, science or skill?

There are all sorts of ways to make money in the markets. However, I believe that the best way, and the way that increased competition will drive investing forward, is art and skill systemised into science.

Thank you for your time.

Conclusions

Like many of our interviewees, Ray represents the wisdom of a great generation in finance.

Ray founded Bridgewater in the 1970s at the age of 25 in a spare bedroom in his New York apartment. At age 69, he is in a transition phase in his life in which his goal is to pass along the principles that helped him become successful. As he notes: 'Life is a journey, so the goal is to enjoy the twists and turns, not to go directly to the destination. I can't imagine changing anything, including the mistakes that have helped me learn.'

Ray acknowledges that QE lifting asset prices at the same time as new technologies are replacing people in middle-class jobs is leading to the widening wealth gap. Though investors have had investing tailwinds over the past decade, Ray notes de-globalisation will be with us for a long time as the US and China will seek to disentangle themselves in order to reduce their vulnerabilities to being cut off by the other in the event of conflict. Markets that still comprise the bulk of most portfolios, such as developed equity and bond markets, have become more efficient and more richly valued at present. But as Ray notes:

> 'Diversification is very important to me. Since most investors are way underinvested in China relative to the US at the same time as 1) China's marginal growth rates are going to be much faster and 2) given the relative pricing of these two countries' assets, I would put that marginal dollar into China.'

On the impact of AI on investment management, Ray notes 'most investors who try to use AI will fail because a strategy based on using AI to find the key relationships to bet on won't be able to compete with deep understanding. It's more likely to produce data mining that will be costly.'

The investment business will consist of alpha generators and beta replicators, and the alpha generators will have very smart people who understand financial engineering and are equipped with fabulous information technology. The amount of money firms will expend in the competition to produce alpha, and the levels of sophistication that this will produce, will be commensurate with the fees that they earn, which will increasingly differentiate between the various gradations of quality. In others words, the quality of play will increase dramatically. Using Big Data and algorithms that reflect a deep understanding will become a big advantage. As Ray notes:

> *'Brains are still better for imagining and thinking logically, and comput-ers are still better for processing lots of information. If you use each for what it does best, that will produce the best results.'*

PART IV

ALTERNATIVE INVESTMENTS

CHAPTER 8

ALTERNATIVE INVESTMENTS OF THE FUTURE

An interview with Dr Keith Black on alternative investments

'Alternative investments are often defined not by what they are, but by what they are not. That is, an alternative investment is a position in something other than a long position in either equity or debt. Generally speaking, the alternative investment markets encompass hedge funds, venture capital and private equity, real estate, and managed futures.'
Mark Anson, *The Handbook of Alternative Assets* (2002)

While Anson was among the first attempting to define the wide variety of alternative assets back in 2002, institutional asset allocation remains firmly focused on hedge funds and private equity. According to a Preqin survey[1], as of December 2017, private equity and hedge fund assets under management represented a combined 75% of the US$8.8 trillion alternative assets industry. As the industry is predicted to reach

---

[1] https://www.preqin.com/insights/blogs/the-future-of-alternatives-the-classes-of-2023/24217.

US$14 trillion in funds under management by 2023, participants are expecting this share to reduce to 69%, as other alternative asset classes such as infrastructure, natural resources, private debt and real estate gain in prominence. Examples of various alternative assets and their uses are shown in the diagram below.

Alternative assets

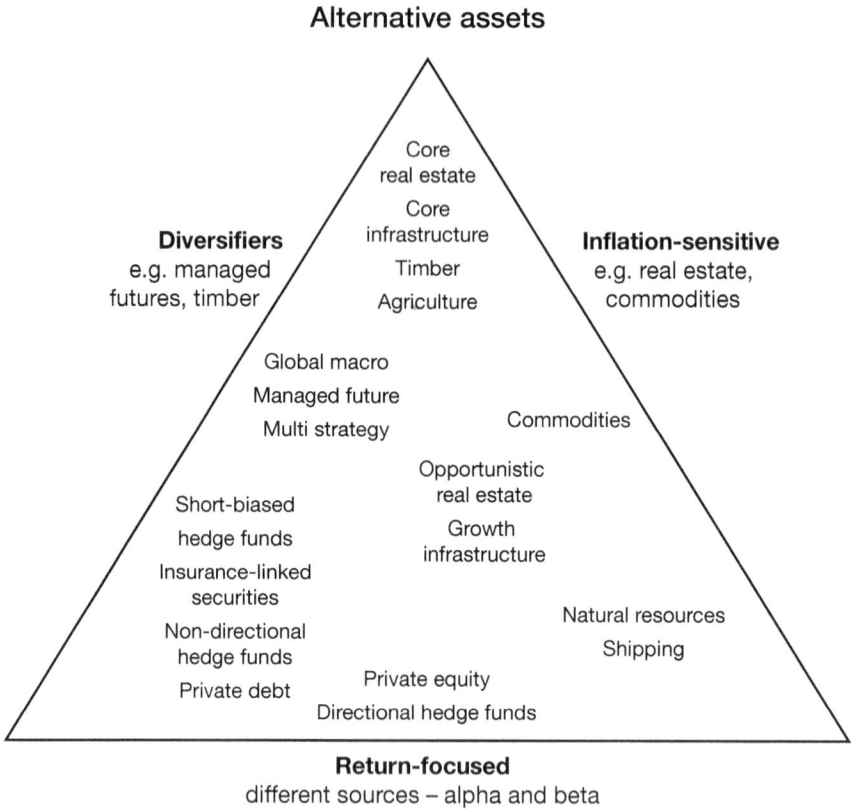

Diversifiers
e.g. managed
futures, timber

Core
real estate
Core
infrastructure
Timber
Agriculture

Inflation-sensitive
e.g. real estate,
commodities

Global macro
Managed future
Multi strategy

Commodities

Opportunistic
real estate
Growth
infrastructure

Short-biased
hedge funds
Insurance-linked
securities
Non-directional
hedge funds
Private debt

Natural resources
Shipping

Private equity
Directional hedge funds

Return-focused
different sources – alpha and beta

Source: Mercer

In this chapter we will focus on the new types of alternative assets that will gain prominence in investor portfolios, the impact that AI and machine learning will have on the various segments, and also how they might impact the knowledge base required to enter the industry.

Who better to ask about the latest academic and practitioner knowledge base and discussions in alternative investments than the Managing Director of Curriculum and Exams for the Chartered Alternative Investment Analyst (CAIA) Association?

Introducing Dr Keith Black

Keith Black has over 25 years of financial market experience, serving approximately half of that time as an academic and half as a trader and consultant to institutional investors. He currently serves as Managing Director of Curriculum and Exams for the CAIA Association. During his most recent role at Ennis Knupp + Associates, Keith advised foundations, endowments and pension funds on their asset allocation and manager selection strategies in hedge funds, commodities and managed futures. Prior experience includes commodities derivatives trading, stock options research and CBOE floor trading, and building quantitative stock selection models for mutual funds and hedge funds. Keith previously served as an assistant professor and senior lecturer at the Illinois Institute of Technology.

He contributes regularly to the *CFA Digest*, and has published in *The Journal of Wealth Management*, *The Journal of Trading*, *The Journal of Investing* and *The Journal of Alternatives Investments*, among others. He is author of the book *Managing a Hedge Fund*, as well as co-author of the 2012 and 2015–16 second and third editions (respectively) of the CAIA Level I and Level II textbooks. Keith was named to the *Institutional Investor* magazine's list of 'Rising Stars of Hedge Funds' in 2010. Keith earned a BA from Whittier College, an MBA from Carnegie Mellon University, and a PhD from the Illinois Institute of Technology. He has earned the Chartered Financial Analyst (CFA) designation, and was a member of the inaugural class of the Chartered Alternative Investment Analyst (CAIA) candidates.

Keith, many thanks for participating. Some of the key themes for institutional investors in relation to alternative assets are the increased allocation to more exotic assets, globalisation of portfolios, focus on ESG, changes driven by new technology, and low-cost risk premia substitutes. Are there any other themes you have identified?

As I travel around the world, it seems everybody is thinking different but the same.[2] Every person I speak to is basically doing the same things: investing more globally, moving away from liquid fixed income and more into alternatives. Those trends are literally every investor in every

---

2   The global footprint of CAIA is now 11,000 members in 90 countries so Keith travels a lot.

country, regardless of the size of the funds. Part of that is driven by the search for yield, which makes products like real estate, infrastructure and private debt more attractive. A less obvious but equally important trend is the increased fee sensitivity. Investors are reducing hedge fund allocations and moving more into liquid beta products or direct investments.

How are these themes being picked up by the CAIA curriculum? I note the current and integrated topics at Level II, but are there any other mechanisms?

The CAIA Association just finished a process called 'global practice analysis', which is a term used in professional education whether you're training doctors, dentists, teachers or alternative investment analysts. You're trying to align your curriculum with what's going on in the market, and the training practitioners need to succeed in their work. We surveyed our members and had global panels and focus groups, asking them a long series of questions to see what's important to them. The result of that was our members told us we were generally teaching what they needed to learn, which is a good result.

We followed up with an asset allocator advisory panel, planning semi-annual meetings with CIOs of SWFs, pension funds and E&Fs. As we started in 2002, we now have an increasing number of CAIA members moving into CIO roles. While we rewrite our textbooks every three or four years, the current and integrated topics you mention are updated every year. The reason we do that is because some things can move quickly. For example, we have an article on UN PRI for a real asset portfolio, and blockchain in clearing and settlement. While both the global practice analysis and asset allocator panels tell us that CAIA is educating investors in productive and comprehensive ways, there were several trends that we picked up from these discussions that will make their way into the curriculum of the future.

What do you see as key factor for success in the industry?

You need to learn as much as you can! Continuing education is so important. Some folks ask me, 'should I take CAIA or CFA?' I say you should probably do both. CFA charter holders can now start CAIA at level 2. It's not just the learning, but also the networking. CAIA provides many opportunities for continuing education, as we offer over 150 live events at our 30 member chapters each year, and we also publish the

Journal of Alternative Investments and the *Alternative Investment Analyst Review*.

In alternative investments, the willingness to learn new things is a key factor for success. I myself have a computer science degree from 1988. I can tell you, there's not much demand for PASCAL and Fortran programmers today! So, I recently took a class in Python and am studying for the new credential from the FDP Institute.

FDP Institute?

That's a new designation – we're starting to cater for the rise in what we call 'Financial Data Professionals'. First, you learn Python and Statistics – a series of courses that take about 30 hours of study at a coding boot camp – as part of your entry into the FDP program.[3] We're looking for people with CFA, CAIA and FRM backgrounds who understand finance but want to learn more about our profession's digital future. We train the FDP candidates to understand artificial intelligence, Big Data and machine learning applications for financial markets. Topics include textual analysis, data ethics, robo advisors, GDPR and European data security, and so on. Big Data is so important as earnings surprises aren't necessarily surprises anymore.

What do you mean by that?

Well, investors today collect electronic footprints by examining your email, credit card receipts, cell phone location or social media posts. A good example would be Tesla. Is it really worth US$30 billion, or will it become insolvent or sold cheaply within a year or two? Investors can try to estimate Tesla revenues by buying a list of automobile registrations from the insurance companies every week to find out how many Teslas are actually getting sold and registered. By searching out information in real time, investors may be less surprised by quarterly earnings reports

What do you think about ESG integration for alternative assets?

At CAIA we try to be education focused and focus on the facts. We never say everyone should invest in alternatives. We say they are complex; if you invest in them consider each of these variables. Similarly,

---

3   https://fdpinstitute.org. Companies like DataCamp, Dataquest and METIS offer a series of short courses based in Python, ahead of enrolling in the FDP program.

we're spending a lot of time right now on ESG. Some people see ESG everywhere, and some don't believe any of it!

We try to take that middle ground. We see some obvious applications of ESG and some where it doesn't make sense. On the 'E' or environmental side, the cleanest application is in your real asset portfolio – if you're investing in mining and energy or are building infrastructure or real estate assets, sensitivity to environmental issues is an imperative.

On the 'G' or governance side, you have activist hedge funds who deal with proxy voting, executive compensation and board structure. Investors have long been concerned about these issues, so this concern is nothing new.

It gets really interesting when you come to the 'S' or social issues. Someone with progressive politics may not agree with someone with a religious point of view. There is a huge diversity of social goals across investors. At universities everywhere, the students are pressuring the investment committee on divestments without the students actually understanding what's inside the investment portfolio. I personally question the social impact that divestment of public companies has from an investor's portfolio. As the universities sell, some other investors will buy those shares, so capital availability to the corporations is not directly reduced. Divestment doesn't punish the company. It can be more effective to engage with company management and state your case about how their operations could improve from an 'E', 'S' or 'G' standpoint. Rather than punishing the bad actors, I think the social side is probably better served by impact investing in private equity and private fixed income. When you make an impact investment with a measurable social goal and new focused capital, that works. It gives more accountability from a philanthropy and social angle.

Traditionally, the 'ethical' discussions around hedge funds focus on 'are hedge funds allowed to short in the interests of the greater society and financial stability, especially during times of crisis?'

I don't think that any rich person is inherently good or bad or hedge funds are inherently good or bad. We need to look at the specifics of each actor in the market. What's wrong with being short? Shorting reduces market volatility, as short sellers sell stock at high prices and hopefully buy stocks at lower prices. Short sellers can keep companies honest, reveal fraud and make the market safer.

Nowadays people are discussing, 'is the idea of an ESG hedge fund even possible, as hedge funds' focus should be on maximising absolute returns?' What is your view on this? Does it make sense to go long 'virtue' and short 'sin'.[4]

Would there be a reward for being long virtue? There's an article in the *FAJ* that basically says that ESG is a risk management exercise.[5] Let's say you have two publicly traded utility companies, one with dirtier coal versus another focused on cleaner energy such as gas or solar. If investors aren't concerned about the environmental outlook of these companies, the two utilities may trade at similar valuations as measured by yields or P/E ratios. The article says these stranded assets are potential liabilities, which might cause millions of dollars in clean-up costs for the coal utility if and when environmental regulations are tightened. If the clean and dirty companies are trading at the same valuations, risk management is about being long the cleaner company – that is, if and when the Americans catch up to the Europeans with tighter regulations! So, rather than an ethical or religious or scientific point of view, I would look at this as a risk management exercise, as companies with more risky operations may eventually face lower profits when regulations change or their reputation is tainted through a somewhat predictable scandal.

I haven't seen any studies that show cleaner assets actually have better returns than dirtier assets, but that doesn't mean such studies don't exist. I see this more as an 'unconstrained (market based)' versus 'constrained (mission based)' return objective. One of the things that has been difficult is the US pension regulations have historically stated that trustees should invest solely in the best interest of the beneficiary. That makes it difficult for public pensions to put a significant tilt to ESG if they can't prove that this tilt enhances return or reduces risk. There is recent change in law that allows pensions to consider factors other than returns, so we will see how this develops. For universities and endowments, their mission may be more important than maximising returns.

---

4 https://www.aima.org/educate/aima-research/from-niche-to-mainstream-esg.html found that 40% of hedge fund managers surveyed were practising responsible investment, while half reported increased investor interest in ESG. There are almost as many descriptions for hedge funds as there are descriptions of ESG investing.

5 Andersson, M., Bolton, P. and F. Samama, 'Hedging Climate Risk', *Financial Analyst Journal*, 2018, v72(3), pp.13–32.

Regulation is increasing in the alternative asset management industry on both sides of the Atlantic.[6] How do you see this impacting the alternative investment industry, in terms of cost, transparency, but also idea generation and the ability to generate excess returns?

I am going to answer that slightly differently. In 2008, the US and Europeans had to bail out the banks. Because of the focus on risk-based capital, capital adequacy ratios and stress tests, banks can't lend to the middle market speculative companies. So, increased regulation that caused the withdrawal of banks from proprietary trading and more risky types of lending has created an opportunity for private capital.

What do you think of regulation for the hedge fund industry?

Well, there is a huge consolidation in the hedge fund space, with the top quartile of hedge fund firms controlling 90% of the assets. With the increased importance of investment and operational due diligence, investors are regulating even where governments aren't. The size of compliance and due diligence and regulatory issues means that hedge funds have to spend a lot of money to meet investor requirements. Do they have external administration, a reputable auditor, top 10 software systems, and so on. Scale is beneficial, as the largest firms can make the investments required to pass the due diligence screens. The bottom 40% of hedge funds control less than 2% of assets, and will continue to struggle to gather assets if they can't meet the requirements of large investors.

As mentioned in the introduction of this chapter, Preqin suggests infrastructure, natural resources, private debt and real estate will gain in prominence as alternative assets. What additional risk factors do you think investors get access to that they can't access through public markets?

The main issue here is factor diversification. What most people don't realise is that both stocks and bonds have negative exposure to rising rates and rising inflation. A traditional 60/40 portfolio will be pretty challenging return wise when rates and inflation rise. Each of these real asset areas has a neutral or positive exposure to rising inflation. Some investors allocate 30% of their portfolio to real assets to offset the negative exposure to rates found in a long-only stock and bond portfolio.

---

6   For example, Dodd-Frank/the Volcker Rule, Basel III, MIFID, TCFD, but also the Alternative Investment Fund Managers Directive (AIFMD).

People are underestimating inflation risk. If the world moves towards tariffs, there will be increasing demand for domestic resources which is going to drive up prices (in addition to a higher cost for imported goods).

Real assets are now the largest part of the CAIA curriculum! Even larger than hedge funds and private equity, as real assets are diverse and complex investments.

But, I am concerned about the real asset space. In that same Preqin survey you mentioned, it says 40% of investors want a larger allocation to private equity, private debt and real assets. A couple of pages later we find US$2.1 trillion in dry powder, half for private equity, half for real assets. It seems that there are some crowded trades. While investors want ever-increasing allocations, the General Partners (GPs) can't put the money to work. I would say there is also a 'negative' overcrowding risk factor.

There is a school of thought that, in the long run, listed and unlisted commercial real estate and listed and unlisted infrastructure in essence lead to the same returns. Therefore, the appraisal-based nature of unlisted assets mainly leads to (perceived) diversification benefits from a portfolio context, rather than additional returns. What's your view on that?

I have had this discussion with a number of large pension plans. If private real estate has 6% measured volatility and REITs 16% volatility, some investors think the public market is at least twice as risky! Actually, REITs are less risky than they appear, as they are picking up volatility from public stocks, while private real estate is more risky than measured due to the infrequent valuation. The appraisal-based nature of private markets uses quarterly or annual marks. At the end of the day, the main drivers of the asset class are pretty similar.

If we remove one quarter of autocorrelation from private real estate, the volatility and correlation to equity probably doubles. The real volatility of both public and private real estate is probably somewhere between 6% and 16%. There is, however, higher leverage on the private side.

But there is a way for private market investors to differentiate themselves. Private market managers with preferential deal flow can add value. In public markets, everybody can see things, so it's hard to get a deal, especially in real estate. In private markets, you might get better access to tenants, and so on. The ability to add value on the private side is much higher.

Also, you never should be using mean variance optimisation (MVO) with private assets because many of these alternative assets have non-normal returns and smoothed returns to appraisal-based assets! An unconstrained MVO will want to have high allocations to private real estate, private equity and infrastructure. And then comes the nasty surprise when liquidity dries up and markets turn over and investors didn't properly value the illiquid nature of these assets.

When we last met, you were discussing the merits of private debt at a Sydney seminar. Can you for our readers briefly reiterate why you think private debt will play an increasing role in institutional portfolios?[7]

The middle market companies that banks no longer lend to employ one-third of the people who work in the US and European economies! This system has clearly broken down as banks have pulled out after 2008, so borrowers need to find new lenders to meet their needs for capital. Private debt investors have always had opportunities in distressed and mezzanine debt. Mezzanine debt feeds the Leveraged Buyout (LBO) markets. Recent growth has been very strong in the direct lending markets. As banks turn down middle market borrowers, lenders are now hedge funds, private equity funds and private debt managers. These lenders may charge borrowers coupons that are 200 bp higher than those companies could previously access from bank lenders. Investors like this higher coupon as they are searching for yield, but the borrowers end up with a higher interest burden.

On the positive side, most of private debt is in floating-rate notes. As yields rise, floating-rate loans have less interest rate risk, with semi-annual resets based on LIBOR or whatever benchmark rate comes after LIBOR. The problem though is that we have borrowers that might be rated B by the rating agencies now servicing an extra 200 bp of interest costs, which could impair debt servicing ability. I am concerned about the covenants and underwriting discipline. More disciplined lenders would

---

7   The non-bank private debt market continues to increase. In the US this figure has grown from 60% in 2002 to 90% by 2018, and Europe from 20% in 2002 to 70% by 2018, based on estimates from S&P Capital IQ. There are two key distinctions between high-yield bank loans and high-yield bonds. The former are floating-rate instruments and, in the event if a default, they are senior to bonds.

prefer senior secured debt, carefully evaluate the collateral, and look for negative terms like trapdoors and black holes in the loan agreements. A lot of private debt is covenant lite.

In terms of commodities, how do you see the future research into commodities evolving?

Commodity indices are weighted by global production or global demand. If we do land in a post-carbon future, the weight to fossil fuel energy in commodity indices is likely to decline. Wind, solar and/or battery power may be added to commodity indices as markets evolve. Because the weights on commodity indices are reviewed annually, indices will look different in 20 years.

Having said that, there may not be enough lithium or cobalt in the world to build enough batteries the way electric car makers want to do it! We're really going to strain natural resources! If Elon Musk hits his production goals, he's going to use more cobalt or lithium than all the phones, computers and cars in the world combined. Vehicle wise, there may be constraints to quickly reach a post-carbon future without significant technical breakthroughs.

The main drawback for solar and wind is that they don't generate much power at night or when it's not windy, so they provide less stable sources of energy than nuclear, coal or gas. If we can somehow store wind- and solar-generated power in an economically efficient battery system, that would speed the adoption of these technologies.

Can you comment on the institutional demand for commodities?

Institutional demand is a lot smaller than it used to be! Commodity indices are coming out of an 80% drawdown. Stock indices are now four to five times above their 2009 lows, but some commodities are still at half the price they were 10 years ago. If commodities drive inflation and inflation is returning, most people are very underweight commodities at this point in the cycle. The institutions that were in commodities 10 years ago may not be invested there today. There has been concern on contango in the commodity markets, but there has been a lot of work on commodity investing regarding roll yields. By moving back and forth across contract maturities, investors can diversify or get out of the way of contango markets. Gorton and Rouwenhorst demonstrate that by buying commodities with the tightest inventories you have the least problem with contango and also the most upside from a supply shock.

What do we really know about alternative assets? For example, for traditional assets, we have 100-plus years of global data, based on actual daily observations. However, for alternative assets, we mostly have data from the early 1990s, and then mostly self-volunteered and appraisal-based in nature.

What has happened in financial markets since 1990? There's been a banking crisis in 1990, the 1998–2000 tech bubble, the 2000–08 real estate bubble. We've had some of the biggest cycles of the last 100 years in the last 20 years! The last 20 years are pretty representative for huge cycles in credit and equity. Apart from inflation spikes, I wouldn't know what 100 years would buy us in terms of additional insights. People are being smarter on how to work with these databases. In the CAIA curriculum, we talk about backfill bias, survivor bias and selection bias. Maybe the best way to evaluate these investments is through funds of funds, where these biases are substantially reduced.

One thing that did strike me is that the 1990s history of hedge funds looks so different from the recent history. So, if you segment hedge fund returns into the first 15 years and the last 15 years, the results are very different! Perhaps the database is maturing, or so much money has come into the space that alpha is being forced lower as markets are becoming more efficient.

Do you have any strong views on the alternative risk premia versus hedge fund debate?

Hedge funds used to outperform liquid alternative risk premia, and maybe that's due to the database issues we were previously discussing. Under UCITS and '40 Act legislation there are limits on leverage, shorting, concentration and liquidity. In liquid alternative funds, the managers don't have the full set of tools available to private hedge fund managers. Even though hedge funds charge 1.5+15 and liquid alts have a fee advantage at 1.5%, hedge fund managers still outperformed.

That's not necessarily going to invalidate the case for liquid alts. Hedge funds appeal to a different audience. For example, a high-net-worth investor who has just $500,000 to allocate to alternatives will likely go to liquid alts or funds of funds rather than invest in a single hedge fund or private equity fund.

Strategy by strategy, the returns to liquid alts are highly correlated to hedge funds. The return differences are small, especially in the liquid strategies (say equity long/short), with liquid alts returns 50 to 150 bp behind hedge funds. If you're a retail investor and you want $50k in managed futures, it's immaterial whether you make 15% or 19% during the next drawdown. You're there for the diversification, and liquid alts give you similar return/risk characteristics to hedge funds that are hard to replicate in traditional financial instruments.

The *Journal of Alternative Investments* is certainly throwing up new and exotic alternative assets of the future. For example, initial coin offerings (ICOs), longevity risk, protection strategies, private credit, volatility, collectibles and alternative assets in emerging markets. Are there any that you consider would be of particular interest to large institutional investors?

Large investors are not yet into crypto. The volatility is too high and the valuation models too uncertain. Something I learned in a crypto course is that the custody issues are frightening! It's a non-starter. People are really afraid of the next 'hack of the week'. We need that bulletproof custody, like large prime brokers offer, before institutions can move in to cryptocurrencies.

Insurance strategies, longevity risk and private credit really stand out to me. At our recent Alts Chicago conference, people were talking about life insurance strategies and catastrophe bonds. These are certainly interesting. For secondary buyers of life insurance, it's like investment-grade fixed income with unknown duration, and some credit risk with the counterparty, usually a huge global insurance company. The main risk is duration extension or a long life doubling-up on pension funds.

Collectables are iffy. Individual investors go big into them, like classic cars. Sure, some pension funds have been investing in coins and stamps, but there are cases where these investments have physically disappeared! There are also issues with scale and custody costs, as pension funds often need to invest at least $100m to make a difference in their portfolio.

Do you have any strong views on green/natural resources as an alternative private market allocation? I was reading a recent *Journal of Alternative Investments* article suggesting 'a distinct lack of consensus in our brief review of the green investment literature when assessing the benefits of investing in green assets for financial

portfolios. The inconclusive evidence on the relationship between green investments and financial performance has often discouraged investors from taking green approaches to investing'.[8]

Yes, as I mentioned earlier, we should distinguish between 'mission-based' and 'market-based' returns. For example, there's a consulting firm that only deals with impact and ESG investments. They will say the market-based return is 8%. Given the investment risk, investors deserve to earn 8%, but a specific investment may yield just 4%. The risk is quantified and the return is easy to see. Then investors need to make the choice whether the ESG characteristics of that investment are worth 400 bp as a contribution to the investor's mission. We need to calibrate those two. What's really holding ESG back is the perception that constrained investors have lower returns than unconstrained investors. Do you want to make money or do you want to do good? More money for being nice would open the floodgates of allocation to ESG strategies.

The pace of new IPOs has decreased to its lowest proportion of the total number of listed companies since 1980. At the same time, the median age of firms seeking an IPO has risen. This suggests that it is harder for public equity investors to access early-stage growth companies.[9] What implications do you think this will have for private versus public equity performance?

Private equity and venture capital investing will continue to be strong if the managers have a sourcing advantage. As companies stay private longer and go public at higher market caps, the public markets are deprived of the majority of the capital appreciation offered by these firms.

What does the CAIA material suggest on the existence of the illiquidity premium (net of fees) for private market investors?[10]

There's a big dispersion across managers, so we do believe in an illiquidity/ complexity premium. Before accessing these managers, allocators need to invest in operational and investment due diligence, as well as manager access and education. Or you can hire a manager research consultant.

8 Martinez-Oviedo, R., and F. Medda, 'Real Natural Assets: The real green investment alternative', *The Journal of Alternative Investments*, 2019, 21(3), pp. 53–69.

9 Refer for example: 'What is the point of the stock market (in a capital-light world)?', Fund Management Strategy, AllianceBernstein, 2019.

10 There have been a lot of discussions about the illiquidity premium, and whether such a premium actually exists for the average investor after taking out the impact of private equity leverage and fees and biases in the data. So far, the consensus seems to be that a positive net return after fees depends mainly on access to top-quartile GPs and also vintage year.

At present, investors generally allocate capital to alternative investments through funds of funds, managed accounts, indexed products or direct investments. Institutional investors with the requisite resources and a focus on fees are now moving to a hybrid allocation model whereby they move more activity in-house. Has any study been done on the impact of increased institutional fund flows on the returns to alternative assets, which are generally more capacity constrained?

There are different takes on this. If you look at what Norway is doing, they are very large, very in-house, and operate with very low expenses. With 95% in public liquid assets, they are mostly indexed. As Norway is moving toward a 5% allocation to real estate, they are finding a market impact from that size of investment. Some investors may simply be too large to allocate effectively to the full range of alternative investments.

In the US, CalPERS started moving out of hedge funds, as it was hard to invest to scale in the hedge fund market. Hedge funds were a small part of the portfolio, but a big part of the pension fund's due diligence budget! They just thought they couldn't afford the due diligence work on the hundreds of hedge funds they would have needed to invest in to reach the desired allocation size in their portfolio.

The Canadian model, demonstrated by investors such as CPPIB and Ontario Teachers, are doing exactly the opposite. They are trying to be as private and illiquid and direct as they can. They are buying huge portfolios of companies and owning them for decades. While Norway and CalPERS are staying cheap and in-house, CPPIB and Ontario are doing the opposite. CPPIB is now one of the biggest investors in private credit. CPPIB and Ontario Teachers employ very talented investors who are well rewarded when the funds have strong performance.

With the ongoing insourcing trend among large institutional investors, are you aware of any studies discussing the relative merits of in-house versus outsourced teams?

OCIOs (outsourced chief investment officers) can benefit smaller investors who used to have to invest in funds of funds with extra fee burden or avoid investing in alternatives altogether. The OCIO is like a commingled multi-manager setup, so something like a fund of funds without the fund of funds fees. In practice, you see a declining dispersion between small and large endowments, as the difference in returns to large versus small endowments in the NACUBO survey has declined substantially over the last 10 years.

For example, firms such as Commonfund group investors together to create scale benefits. Smaller endowments don't employ investment staff, but may have the University Treasurer spending just 20% of her time in the CIO role. It's hard for one person to run the whole portfolio, so the default then becomes index funds or funds of funds. Once the endowment starts working with an OCIO, they have greater resources and access to more cost-effective alternative funds.

In terms of alternative asset research, which areas do you think institutional investors should focus on?

Inflation risk is underrated, so investors might be well served to increase their real assets allocation. All-weather portfolios are important. Investors need defensive strategies in their portfolio to hedge against the next market drawdown, whether volatility strategies, macro/managed futures or sovereign debt. Tail risk hedging has benefits, but investors need to be aware of the high cost of purchasing direct hedges. Investors shouldn't allocate their entire portfolio to 'risk on' assets, but take the time to understand how 'risk off' assets can benefit the portfolio during times of market crises. Many investors are depending on central banks to protect them and bail them out, but that's not going to be as easy or as feasible in an increasingly populist world!

What future topics or updates to the CAIA curriculum are you considering at the moment?

More ESG, more private credit, and a greater focus on asset allocation strategies. We spend a lot of time talking with CIOs and are adding their insights into our curriculum.

In the Digital Future, which alternative asset classes are expected to be most impacted by AI and machine learning, and in what manner?

It's more about roles than asset classes. I was reading an article today about how a single investment advisor from one of the large banks will find it harder to do business on their own. Big firms are transitioning from persons to teams with books. It's becoming harder to be a standalone investment advisor, as technology like robo-advice or Python-based applications are becoming more pervasive. We talked earlier about asset prices becoming more efficient. There is so much data out there you can use to predict trends and earnings. Earnings aren't a surprise as much, as technology-enabled funds can read your cell phone, credit card and emails as inputs into their trading strategies. Markets are moving faster and faster.

How do you see the alternative asset industry in 10 years' time?

I see more investors with larger assets. There will be higher barriers to entry. It's going to be harder and harder to be a startup manager. Alternatives are going to be more mainstream. There's going to be an alternatives alpha and beta business. The managers with real alpha will sustain very high fees. But managers who are not creating positive alpha will be crowded out by liquid alternative beta and factor-based ETFs. Managers will increasingly have to prove outperformance to sustain high fees and levels of asset growth.

What keeps you busy outside of office hours?

I sit on a number of not-for-profit boards. As a consultant, I write papers on option and volatility investing, as well as working in litigation support as an expert witness. There are constant disputes in hedge funds and private equity regarding fees, risk and due diligence between professional investors. I assist the attorneys by explaining how alternative investments work.

For hobbies, I'm on a rowing team, where I spend early mornings on the Connecticut River with eight of my teammates. My son is in college for music and theatre, so I enjoy attending his shows. We live halfway between New York and Boston, so we take our son to many of the Broadway shows. We are also active in our church.

Finally – alternative investment: art, science or skill?

I'd say skill. But a huge part of this is access. Access to the right managers, access to the right education, access to the right risk models, and access to the right investment opportunities. If you don't have access then you should be in the lowest fee products.

Thank you for your time.

Conclusions

As Keith travels around the world he is struck by how everybody seems to be thinking different but the same about alternative assets. Every person he speaks to is basically doing the same things: investing more globally, moving away from liquid fixed income, and more into alternatives. An equally important trend is the increased fee sensitivity, with investors reducing hedge funds and going into liquid beta products or direct investments.

Similarly, Keith is spending a lot of time on ESG. He acknowledges 'some people see ESG everywhere, and some don't believe any of it!' On the 'E' or environmental side, the cleanest application is in a real asset portfolio. On the 'G' or governance side, activist hedge funds deal with proxy voting, executive compensation and board structure. When you come to the 'S', Keith considers the social side better served by impact investing rather than divestment.

In terms of the impact of regulation, the withdrawal of banks has created an opportunity for private capital. He also notes the huge consolidation in the hedge fund space, with the top quartile controlling 90% of the assets.

From a portfolio context, he considers alternative assets useful for factor diversification. Both stocks and bonds have negative exposure to rising rates and rising inflation. To offset a 60/40 negative exposure to rates, Keith suggests you need at least a 30% allocation to real assets. Real assets are now the largest part of the CAIA curriculum. As investors continue the debate about public versus private markets, Keith concludes:

> 'At the end of the day, the main drivers of the asset classes are pretty similar ... But there is a way for private market investors to differentiate themselves. Private market managers with preferential deal flow will have a much higher ability to add value.'

— CHAPTER 9 —
PRIVATE INVESTIGATIONS

An interview with Professor Ludovic Phalippou on myths surrounding private equity

'The world is full of obvious things which nobody by any chance ever observes.'
Arthur Conan Doyle (1859–1930)

Institutional investing in private equity has been popular ever since US endowments pioneered increasing allocations to alternative assets in the 1980s.[1] Since then, private equity investors have been through the 1990s tech bubble, the 2000s buyout boom, and are now in an era where there are increasingly fewer public companies remaining. Banks are reluctant to lend, with increased regulations and capital constraints such as Basel III.[2] Public markets – especially in the US – are trading at rich valuations following one of the longest economic booms in history. Private markets have become the intermediary of choice for the financing needs of many, and more money has been raised, invested and distributed back to investors than in any other period in history.

---

1 Yale for example increased its allocation to private equity (venture capital and buyouts) from less than 1% of assets in 1985 to 31% today. Refer also *Pioneering Portfolio Management: An unconventional approach to institutional investment* (The Free Press, New York and London), 2000, and http://investments.yale.edu/reports.
2 As an example, in 2002 non-bank lenders comprised 60% of the loan market in the US, and 20% in Europe. By 2018 it was closer to 90% for the US and 70% for Europe. Source: S&P Capital IQ.

At the same time, returns have slowly declined. The pace of technological change is increasing in almost every industry segment, making it harder to forecast future winners and losers. Competition has driven deal multiples to historic highs, driven by a dearth of attractive targets and stiff competition.

Valuations in private equity

Average EBITDA purchase price multiple for US LBO transactions

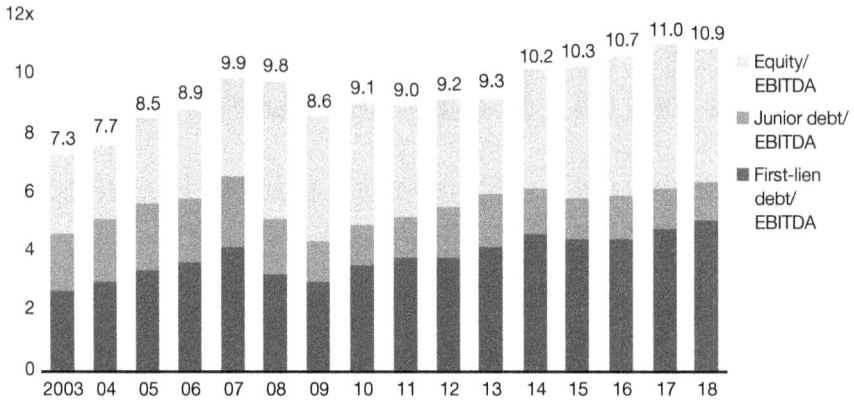

Source: LPE

Dry powder, or uncalled capital, has been on the rise, and hit a record high of US$2 trillion in December 2018 across all fund types.[3]

Introducing Professor Ludovic Phalippou

Dr Ludovic Phalippou is Professor of Financial Economics at Saïd Business School and the Queen's College, at the University of Oxford. He teaches asset management and private equity, and has received several best teacher awards. He specialises in private market investments, with a focus on fee tracking, interest alignment and return benchmarking. He has worked with large institutional investors on their private equity investment decisions and benchmark systems, and acted as Head of Private Markets Research for the BlackRock Investment Institute.

He has been named as one of the '40 most outstanding Business School Professors under 40 in the world' and listed in 2016 as one of the

---

3 https://www.bain.com/insights/year-in-review-global-private-equity-report-2019/.

20 most influential individuals in private equity in Europe by *realdeals* magazine. Ludovic has strong links with senior practitioners in the industry, and routinely appears at conferences and in the media, including the *Economist, Financial Times* and *New York Times*. His research has been published in the *Journal of Financial Economics*, the *Journal of Finance*, the *Journal of Financial and Quantitative Analysis* and the *Review of Financial Studies*, among others. His paper 'How Alternative are Private Markets?' was one of three 2018 recipients of the Jack Treynor Prize. He is also author of the book *Private Equity Laid Bare*.

He has presented at seminars around the world at all major academic conferences. His work has been downloaded over 50,000 times on SSRN.com and is ranked among the top 100 business authors worldwide. He has been cited over 2,000 times according to Google Scholar.

Ludovic achieved a degree in Economics from Toulouse School of Economics; a Master in Economics and a Master in Mathematical Finance both from the University of Southern California; and a PhD in Finance from INSEAD.

Ludovic, many thanks for participating. In your book *Private Equity Laid Bare*, you state: 'Over the past fifteen years, I have been actively researching the private equity industry. Data point after data point, article after article, I found that virtually everything sold as a fact was not quite so.' Can you expand on that for our readers?

There are two perspectives on private equity: the *corporate finance* perspective and the investor's *(investment management)* perspective.

On the corporate finance perspective, there have been a lot of myths of private equity financiers being short-term focused, causing major bankruptcies, and sucking dry companies on the way there.[4] The data points show this is not true. Private equity financing is shown to be about increasing company resources, rather than bankruptcies.

From the *investment management* perspective, there is a lot of hype about the Yale Endowment PE program or top-quartile PE firms such as KKR delivering 25% to 35% per annum over the past three decades or more, and you as an investor being able to get it too. None of this is true. Technically this reported number may be compliant, but people think this means you earn these rates of return on your capital over this time

---

4   This may have had its roots in popular literature like *Barbarians at the Gate: The Fall of RJR Nabisco*, written by investigative journalists Bryan Burrough and John Helyar in 1989.

period, just like you would if you had invested in the S&P 500 index, but it is not true. The number used in the PE industry is an IRR, not a rate of return; no-one earned 25% to 35% return on their capital in PE. In fact, it has little to do with how much investors actually earned.[5] On average, people have received $1.50 for every $1 invested, and an average holding period of 4.5 years.

I think a third myth is the fees. On the surface they seem very standard at 2 and 20, but this leads to a high annualised fee. When I published the first paper estimating an annualised fee for LBO funds and reported 7% a year, I was accused of all sorts of things. Today this result has been replicated in many ways, and this figure is routinely cited.[6] After these fees, the average LBO fund returns about the same as the average US stock.[7] The magnitude of the rent raises the question of why does the marginal investor buy buyout funds? In early work, I explored one potential – and probably the most controversial – answer: some investors are fooled. I show that the fee contracts are opaque and difficult to quantify, and performance difficult to benchmark. It's also important to know that not all contracts are the same in the details. Different definitions lead to very different fee levels. It is a myth to think that all funds charge the same fees.

In terms of private markets research, which areas do you think institutional investors should focus on?

Performance and expectations are the most important ones. Benchmarks should be realistic. People observe the past and say, 'the past has been good, hence the future will be as good'. Warren Buffett for example

---

5 'The fact that IRR math is easily gamed is well known and can make mediocre investments look brilliant. Two investments with the same IRR can produce completely different profits.' (https://www.oaktreecapital.com/docs/default-source/memos/2006-07-12-you-cant-eat-irr.pdf.) The so-called public-market equivalent, or PME, is a better way to track performance. By that method, buyout firms are trailing stock markets. Refer also https://blogs.cfainstitute.org/investor/2017/10/30/private-equity-presentations-are-they-tall-tales/ and https://www.bloomberg.com/news/articles/2018-07-02/buyout-firms-profit-goosing-scheme-spurs-backlash-from-clients.

6 Phalippou, L., 'Beware of Venturing into Private Equity', *The Journal of Economic Perspectives*, 23(1), pp. 147–166. https://papers.ssrn.com/sol3/papers.cfm?abstract_id=999910

7 The historical excess performance of private equity funds remains a topic of discussion. For example, in 'Private Equity Performance: What do we know?', Harris, S., Jenkinson, T., and S.N. Kaplan in *The Journal of Finance* 69(5), 2013, find evidence of outperformance for buyouts using data to 2008, but not for venture capital. Ludovic notes the period from 1999 to 2008 as a rare decade in the history of the US stock market where large stocks underperformed smaller companies. Compared to the S&P 500 benchmark over the period, private equity did better. But he also notes that private equity did as well as the average stock in the US in that time period. He mentions that since 2009, the S&P 500 has performed in line with other stock size categories and in line with private equity.

has had an amazing 19% p.a. in his first three decades. I believe that he is below the S&P 500 over the last decade. People like superheroes and keep on chasing past returns. It is more important to be forward looking by focusing on the fees and getting the contract details right. In a low-interest environment, what do you think of the hurdle rate? The catch-up? These little details are very important to align interests and to make sure you will pay fees only for genuine outperformance.

There have been a lot of discussions about the illiquidity premium, and whether such a premium actually exists for the average investor, after taking out the impact of private equity leverage and fees and biases in the data. So far, the consensus seems to be that a positive net return after fees depends mainly on access to top quartile GPs and also vintage year. Do you agree? What would be the other key success factors?

People think an illiquidity premium is normal. This makes no sense to me. For example, I could take your money and for 20 years lock it away for you and invest in the S&P 500. But you wouldn't earn anything extra. I don't see a natural mechanism for a premium just because something is illiquid. Similarly, if nobody cares about being locked up and money is pouring into private equity, how can there be an illiquidity premium? I find it a weird and flawed idea.

Sometimes people say, 'ahhhh … but private equity outperformed public equity, so there must be an illiquidity premium'. I can see some smart beta having a premium over many stock indices, but that does not mean they earned an illiquidity premium.

What should investors who can't access top-quartile GPs do?

With funds from the KKR, Bain, Blackstone and others available to investors, I actually don't think that there is so much of an access issue, at least not for buyouts. Yes, for some parts of venture capital.

PE firms have many ways they can use to present themselves as top quartile to prospective investors. And then they say that there is performance persistence, hence the future will be good too.

But is it really true? What are we seeing? The reality is that the literature has found no persistence in top-quartile buyout fund performance – see for example literature by Tim Jenkinson.[8] There is

---

8   Braun, R., Jenkinson, T. and I. Stoff, 'How Persistent is Private Equity Performance? Evidence from Deal-Level Data', 2015. https://papers.ssrn.com/sol3/papers.cfm?abstract_id=2314400.

some small persistence in venture capital. The problem though is that people don't really understand how these numbers work. For example, funds 2 and 3 may have eight overlapping years of returns. So, if I do a persistence check, then of course I will see a correlated return between these two funds. The question is: could you predict the performance of fund 3 when it was raised from the performance back then of fund 1 and/or 2, and the answer is no (even in venture capital).

Everybody can create things to become top quartile – 99% of firms are 'top quartile', which is not supported by data. Part of the trick toolbox is choice of vintage year (was that the year you started fund raising, the year of your first investment, first close, last close?), choice of universe (benchmark shopping), and sometimes indirectly selecting investments.[9] There's bound to be some combination that shows you to be top quartile. In the old days, many general partners used venture economics universe as their returns were so much lower than everybody else.

In the institutional world, there is currently a lot of focus on ESG, diversity and climate change. How does the academic/practitioner research on private equity react to those topics?

I think private equity is well suited for that. If you want to change the world, you have to be able to control the company.

In private markets, the lack (and quality) of data has always been an issue for serious research.[10] Is there any prospect that the increased use of machine learning and artificial intelligence will impact private markets research and inefficiencies?

We do a lot of work on that. Machine learning is helpful when there is a lot of data to analyse. In private equity, this is the opposite on most issues. An exception is legal documents, and this is something I am currently working on.

---

9 You can also redefine your objective to say you're always correct. For example, if your large buyout funds bomb, but your late-stage VC funds do well, you might just simply market your late-stage VC. Or say you focus on – for example – the $100 to $250 million segment. Remember, it is all voluntary reporting. There are no rules or regulations.

10 For example, Phalippou shows that in commonly used samples, accounting values reported by mature funds for non-exited investments are substantial and provides evidence that these mostly represent living dead investments. After correcting for sample bias and overstated accounting values, average fund performance changes from a slight outperformance to a substantial underperformance of 3% per year with respect to the S&P 500. Phalippou, L. and O. Gottschalg, Performance of Private Equity Funds. EFA 2005 Moscow Meetings. Available at SSRN: https://ssrn.com/abstract=473221.

In 15 years of private markets research, what do you feel has been your most important 'a-ha' moment?

I quite like my Yale endowment paper.[11] I collected all their data; it started as a bit of a joke, but I think it debunks the 'Yale is a model' myth. The reality is we cannot really tell if Yale did well. The article shows a random investor with a long and 'average' track record in venture capital computing its return following the GIPS recommendations would display a 30% return over a long horizon, and that this number would hardly change from one year to the next, which is similar to what is shown in the annual reports of Yale Endowment.

What do you see as the hallmark of a successful long-term private equity investor?

I think that would be the ability to distinguish between marketing hype and facts, and the ability to have a balanced conversation with a general partner. Not being lured just by the promise of high returns. Use size to get concessions. So, somebody who is successful should not be afraid to stir things up from time to time, as it will pay off in the end.

US foundations used to attract a lot of press coverage for their superior investment performance, much of which can be traced back to their early asset allocation decision to move into private equity. Would you consider them among the most successful private equity investors? How transferable are their advantages for other investors? (For example, long time horizon, ability to absorb fees and illiquidity, and alumni networks.)

As I said, I think this is a myth. There was a good paper on this by David Yermack at NYU.[12]

Based on a comprehensive sample of more than 28,000 organisations drawn from Internal Revenue Service filings for 2009–16, they find endowments badly underperform market benchmarks, with median annual returns 5.53 percentage points below a 60/40 mix of US equity and Treasury bond indices, and statistically significant alphas of −1.01%

---

11 Phalippou, L., 'Yale's Endowment Returns: Case Study in GIPS Interpretation Difficulties', Spring 2013, *Journal of Alternative Investments* 15(4), pp. 97–103.

12 Dahiya, S. and D. Yermack, 'Investment Returns and Distribution Policies of Non-Profit Endowment Funds' (27 December 2018). European Corporate Governance Institute (ECGI) – Finance Working Paper No. 582/2018; Georgetown McDonough School of Business Research Paper No. 3291117. Available at SSRN: https://ssrn.com/abstract=3291117 or http://dx.doi.org/10.2139/ssrn.3291117.

per year. Smaller endowments have less negative alphas than larger endowments, but all size classes significantly underperform. Higher education endowments, the majority of the US$0.7 trillion asset class, do significantly worse than funds in other sectors.

Here's another updated table that proves this point. As you can see, over 10 years there has not been a meaningful performance difference between the large and small endowments, and most have under-performed the 60/40 Vanguard passive fund.

Performance of endowments versus passive funds

Size of endowment	3 years	5 years	10 years
Over $1 billion	6.8%	8.2%	6.0%
$501 million to $1 billion	6.2%	7.4%	5.6%
$251 million to $500 million	6.1%	7.3%	5.7%
$101 million to 250 million	6.0%	7.1%	5.6%
$51 million to $100 million	6.0%	7.0%	5.7%
$25 million to $50 million	6.0%	7.0%	6.1%
Under $25 million	6.2%	7.5%	5.8%
60/40 Vanguard	**6.1%**	**7.2%**	**6.2%**
70/30 Vanguard	**7.1%**	**8.0%**	**6.6%**
90/10 Vanguard	**9.2%**	**9.7%**	**7.1%**

Source: NACUBO, Portfolio Visualiser

What are some of the more recent articles that you have (co-authored) yourself? What new academic research projects are you working on at the moment?

I am working on a project which looks at private market factors – that is, factors not available in public markets – in asset classes such as real estate, infrastructure and natural resources. Is infrastructure an asset class? Are natural resources an asset class? There is also a paper coming out on secondary markets, and competition. These will be posted on SSRN.com and LinkedIn in due course.

Do you think private equity returns will converge to public equity returns?

I would say this is already the case.[13] I don't think they have ever diverged, especially when compared to small/mid-cap stock indices (and even excluding adjustments for leverage and such). All the vintage years from 2006 to today, taken together, have a return close to the S&P 500. So now you see managers benchmarking themselves to the MSCI World. Because of the emerging market low performance in US dollars, private equity is still shown to outperform public equity. But what does a US buyout performance have to do with emerging markets?

In the Digital Future, where technology and knowledge will become increasingly important, will book smarts win over street smarts in private equity?

You definitely need both to succeed. You also need to be as transparent as possible and minimise potential conflict of interest, and be as well informed as possible.

How do you see the private equity industry in 10 years' time?

I have a paper called 'The Future of Private Markets'.[14] Asset owners derive little benefit from the continuous trading of capital claims offered by public markets, and the number of listed companies is decreasing. However, private markets are not as efficient, and delegating investment management in private markets is challenging due to inherently strong agency conflicts, and minimal regulatory protection. Insourcing private market investment capacities is a solution (a.k.a. the Canadian model), but it presents some often-overlooked challenges. Alternative solutions include private market platforms controlled by multiple asset owners.

I think we will see highly specialised funds with better alignment. Markets will shift towards the large asset owners. LPs will become GPs. They will be empowered.

---

13 https://www.nakedcapitalism.com/2018/08/oxford-professor-phalippou-since-2006-private-equity-produced-sp-500-returns-reaping-400-billion-fees.html. A common rule of thumb is that private equity should outperform the relevant public equity benchmark by 300 basis points (3%). Funds launched have, on average, performed in line with the S&P 500, which delivered annualised returns, including dividends, of 8.6% between January 2006 and the end of March 2018. Being 'fair' means using PME, 'public market equivalent', which is widely acknowledged to be the more accurate way to compare private equity returns to public market returns, rather than IRRs.

14 Ludovic, P., 'The Future of Private Markets', 30 June 2018. https://papers.ssrn.com/sol3/papers.cfm?abstract_id=3170928.

If not for excess returns or an illiquidity premium or top quartile performance, why would institutional investors invest in private markets?

Well, there is the diversification argument. For example, as I said there may be private factors. Or it may be a way to get exposure – for example, to China – as China has a small public market, so we can use private equity instead. Or you may want to engage in impact investing as I earlier mentioned and need the element of control. Or somebody thinks they can really select the right manager and have a right mechanism in place. And then there are people who are really so big and need to deploy large amounts of capital quickly through co-investments. As a small investor, if you know your private equity managers around you pretty well that is also okay.

What are you teaching your students as key factors for success in the industry?

I use my book *Private Equity Laid Bare* as a textbook. But I bring a lot of practitioners into my lectures with different perspectives as well. The main thing is not to be naïve, and be exposed to all sides of any argument. This is what education is about. There is a lot of marketing going around. Critical thinking is important. There are masses of people going into the sector. I tell them: 'do it for the right reasons, and if something sounds fuzzy it probably is because it is not real (like the IRR issue).'

What keeps you busy outside of office hours?

I cycle a lot. I engage in cycling competitions. I taste a lot of wine as well (although not at the same time!).

Finally – investment: art, science or skill?

All of them together, but I'm biased to think that science plays a bigger role than art!

Thank you for your time.

Conclusions

With the amount of money flowing into private equity on the promise of high returns, attention to the contract details is becoming even more important, as is attention to reported performance. Ludovic notes there are two popular perspectives on private equity, the *corporate finance* perspective and the investor's *(investment management)* perspective, both of which he considers in need of adjustment.

On the corporate finance perspective, there have been a lot of myths of private equity financiers being short-term focused, causing major bankruptcies, and sucking dry companies on the way there. The data points show this is not true. Private equity financing is shown to be about increasing company resources, rather than bankruptcies.

From the *investment management* perspective there is a lot of hype about the Yale Endowment. He suggests his 'a-ha' moment was proving that the Yale Endowment may be a myth. Ludovic suggests the reality is we cannot really tell if Yale did well.

He considers private equity, especially impact investing, well suited for changing the world from a sustainability perspective, as you have to be able to control the company.

Machine learning he considers helpful when there is a lot of data to analyse. In private equity, this is the opposite, due to the opaque nature of the industry. So, in terms of actual applications, he investigates its use for limited partnership agreements, which are often 200-plus pages.

As to 'the future of private markets', he thinks we will see highly specialised funds with better alignment. Markets will shift towards the large asset owners. LPs will become GPs. As Ludovic notes as the hallmark of a successful private equity investor:

'I think that would be the ability to distinguish between marketing hype and facts, and the ability to have a balanced conversation with a general partner. Not being lured just by the promise of high returns. Use size to get concessions. So, somebody who is successful should not be afraid to stir things up from time to time, as it will pay off in the end.'

PART V

A BETTER TOMORROW

— CHAPTER 10 —

BUILDING A SUSTAINABLE WORLD: OPPORTUNITIES IN REAL ESTATE AND INFRASTRUCTURE

An interview with Professor James McKellar and Assistant Professor Sherena Hussain

'Real estate cannot be lost or stolen, nor can it be carried away. Purchased with common sense, paid for in full, and managed with reasonable care, it is about the safest investment in the world.'
Franklin D. Roosevelt (1882–1945)

Real estate has been among the first investments of man, long before stock markets existed. One of the earliest known pieces of investment advice and diversification was described in the Talmud: 'a person should invest 1/3 of his wealth in real estate, 1/3 in business and hold 1/3 on hand.'[1] For centuries, commercial real estate, notably in cities, has been at the heart of the arts and culture, thriving businesses and innovative ideas. The sheer number of people who live in cities now and who are expected to move into them in the coming years is startling. Around two-thirds of the world's population is predicted to live in an urban area by 2050, which means there are major financial implications and potential disruption to businesses and governments, as well as a need to create sustainable cities.[2]

Private sector infrastructure investing, on the other hand, is a more recent phenomenon, as traditionally these assets were held in public hands. While infrastructure has been seen as a suitable institutional investment in Australia, Canada and the UK since the 1990s, it only recently increased in popularity in the US.[3] For long-term investors, the long duration, inflation hedging and steady cashflows hold considerable appeal.

Infrastructure and real estate are closely linked. Infrastructure initiatives are catalysts in the economic development process, often with major external benefits that are reflected in the productivity and returns to both physical and human capital and accelerating growth. Infrastructure can fundamentally alter the economics of real estate investments, on the one hand, while real estate development creates the need for and value of infrastructure.

Introducing Professor James McKellar

James McKellar, FRAIC, FRICS, is Professor and Director of the Brookfield Centre in Real Estate and Infrastructure Schulich School of Business, York University, Toronto, Canada. Prior to joining York University, he was a faculty member at the Massachusetts Institute of Technology (MIT) and served as the first Director of the Center for Real Estate at MIT. In addition to MIT, he has held faculty appointments at

---

1   The Talmud is the compendium of Jewish law compiled between the 3rd and 5th century. It explains the financial logic of the '1/3 strategy' by claiming it provides an optimal mix of returns as real estate is 'safe' and thus offers a core sustainable return; while business offers a higher return due to its higher risk; and cash on hand provides liquidity for unexpected expenses. This rather naïve investment strategy is commonly referred to as the '1/N rule', which in practice has outperformed many other types of diversification strategies.
2   Over 90% of urban areas are coastal, which means that most cities on the planet are vulnerable to the effects of sea levels rise and extreme weather effects.
3   Traditionally, projects were financed through municipal bonds with tax concessions.

the University of Pennsylvania and the University of Calgary. He was also Adjunct Professor at Johns Hopkins University in Washington, DC. He has lectured at universities in North America, Asia and Europe, and addressed various industry and government groups across the world.

Professor McKellar has both a Master in Architecture and Master in City Planning from the University of Pennsylvania, and a Bachelor of Architecture from the University of Toronto. Professor McKellar has a life-long involvement in the real estate industry, and has consulted to businesses and governments in many parts of the world on real estate matters covering housing, development, finance and investment, asset management, and market performance. In the past several years, his teaching and research has focused on the emerging field of infrastructure and the business models driving large-scale public infrastructure projects, as well as the topic of sustainable cities as it pertains to the challenges of urbanisation across the globe. He is a Fellow of the Royal Architectural Institute of Canada (FRAIC) and the Royal Institute of Chartered Surveyors (FRICS).

Introducing Assistant Professor Sherena Hussain

Sherena Hussain is an Assistant Professor in the Program in Real Estate and Infrastructure at the Schulich School of Business, York University. Her professional work and research involves the structuring of transaction models and frameworks in infrastructure and commercial real estate in a manner that attracts new business models and investment mandates. Her papers have been published in *Public Management Review* ('Rethinking the Role of Private Capital in PPPs: The Experience of Ontario, Canada'), *World Economic Forum* ('Developing Master Planning for Resilient Infrastructure Within Existing Urban Centres'), and the *Journal of Economic Policy Reform* ('Peeking into the Black Box of Infrastructure Investment', forthcoming). Professor Hussain is also a legal professional, having practised tax and infrastructure law at McCarthy Tetrault's Toronto office for several years and Infrastructure Ontario, the Province's Public–Private Partnership agency.

Professor Hussain holds a combined Juris Doctor-Master of Business Administration degree, Graduate Master Diploma in Real Estate and

Infrastructure, and Bachelor of Business Administration. She is the recipient of numerous accolades, including the Hennick Medal for academic excellence and multiple prizes in the areas of tax, contract, commercial/corporate, real estate, trust and estate law. Professor Hussain is also the Academic Director for the Sustainable Infrastructure Fellowship Program, a G7 initiative that – alongside 12 large institutional investors of infrastructure – trains senior government officials from emerging markets on how to develop and finance long-term sustainable infrastructure projects.

James and Sherena, thanks for your time. Globalisation, urbanisation, ageing populations, technology and sustainability issues have become central concerns for real estate and infrastructure developers and investors. Could you comment on those and other trends that you see influencing real estate and infrastructure projects?

James: These are trends that will have significant effects in both developed and emerging economies. North Americans represent around 5% of the world's population but consume approximately 30% of the world's resources to sustain their lifestyle. The world's richest 10% account for approximately 60% of all private consumption.[4] These are not sustainable ratios, particularly when the rest of the world aspires to what the developed world currently enjoys. China and India alone will add 915 million more urban dwellers between 2010 and 2050, a 92% increase.[5]

India is the big loser. Not only does it have the fast-growing economy that will be slowed, but it's already a hot country that will suffer greatly from getting even hotter. India bears a huge share of the global social cost of carbon – more than 20%.[6] It also stands out for how little it actually contributes to the world's carbon emissions. It is a serious equity issue. India would need to add about 500 gigawatts of renewable capacity by 2030, nearly seven times the current total, just to meet the growth in demand without building a new coal plant. The IEA expects carbon emissions from India's power sector will increase by 80% through 2040, even with renewable generating plants currently planned.[7]

---

4   World Bank Development Indicators.
5   *AIQ*, issue 008.
6   *MIT Technology Review*. May/June 2019.
7   *MIT Technology Review*. May/June 2019.

Sherena: Urbanisation and ageing populations are affecting different regions differently. The opportunities and challenges are quite distinctive. Ageing population is more what the mature markets are facing, and they are forced to rethink the type of infrastructure they are building. Payment streams are changing as obligations for funding are falling on an increasing smaller base of working people.[8]

For emerging economies, you see a variety of younger demographics with different propensities to pay. This gives rise to new business models, particularly because the same infrastructure that was built 60 years ago in mature markets will not resonate well in emerging markets. When paired with changes in technologies, societal structures and cultural dynamics, there is a global rethinking of how to approach infrastructure in a more productive and impactful way.

James: As an example, we use century-old systems to pump purified water to each house that leaks or gets stolen along the route. Why not pump unfiltered water and have it filtered at the point of consumption, or capture and reuse 'grey' water on-site? This is where technology may help. Emerging markets are where the investment opportunities in infrastructure of the future will likely be found, given these global trends. Challenges in the developed countries will be to reduce demand and address the negative impact of a highly consumptive society. The challenges for emerging markets will be to increase the supply of everything including food production, fresh water, sanitation, communications and mobility with business models that can attract private investment.

Sherena: New business models reflecting new technologies raise the possibility of stranded assets based on functionally obsolete infrastructure systems. Stranded assets are an increasing risk for long-term investors and institutional funds that are increasingly relying on research units to deal with this topic, particularly as it applies to the consequences of climate change. Yet stranded assets can arise from more factors, more than climate change in the traditional sense. The materiality of social and governance considerations, such as community development and transparency, are also factors that can affect the long-term risk/return profile of infrastructure investments. Creativity, relationship building and common interests are critical to the viability of infrastructure business models globally.

---

8 *AIQ*, issue 008.

James: The increasing use of hybrid public/private delivery models is also important. Unfortunately, many governments, including many in developed nations, don't like to mix public and private initiatives. 'Public' typically infers a free good whereas 'private' infers user charges in addition to taxes. In emerging markets, this legacy may not exist to the same extent. In many developed economies, 'privatisation' carries a stigma; somehow private capital is 'bad money'. Private capital often struggles to achieve a social licence to legitimise its presence in infrastructure deals.

That's somehow similar to the general discussion from shareholder to stakeholder?

James: Yes, and the discussion on ESG which is gaining increasing prominence among large institutional investors.

Sherena: And ESG is not merely a mandate or a set of compliance checks. Large direct institutional investors are increasingly embedding this perspective across their investment and asset management processes within all asset classes, including infrastructure and real estate.

Institutional investors continue to increase allocations to real estate and infrastructure in the search for steady 'real' returns. How do you think this increased institutional interest is impacting deal flow and pricing?

James: Increasingly large pools of private equity capital are chasing a diminishing pool of investment-grade opportunities across the globe. Competition for assets is driving down returns and directing investors into more Core + and Core ++ opportunities to meet their return objectives. Prices are going up, returns are going down, and this is a long-term trend. Investors will increasingly turn to 'greenfield' projects in both emerging and mature markets, despite their previous aversion to the risks these entail.

The 'infrastructure gap' may be a false claim though depending how you define the gap.

What do you mean by that?

James: Often-quoted reports are arriving in very large numbers to emphasise the extent of the infrastructure gap. McKinsey's report of

June 2016 is one example.[9] McKinsey estimates that to keep up with projected growth, the world needs to invest US$3.3 trillion annually in economic infrastructure through 2030. This amounts to US$49.1 trillion in the period 2016 to 2030, or 3.8% annual spending of GDP. On the other hand, levels of 'dry powder', sums that have yet to be invested, reached records in 2018.[10] Investors allocated a fresh US$85bn for infrastructure funds last year, up US$10bn on 2017, according to Preqin.

In defining the magnitude of need, it's not clear what is being measured. For example, the US Southwest has 13 deep water ports, but may only need two. Do you need to fix all 13 for political reasons? So the measurements can be flawed. The underlying issue is: what does this gap reflect? There are substantial amounts of private money looking for infrastructure opportunities, and yet there are many governments bemoaning the lack of funds to close their gap.

Sherena: Governments and investors often use similar terms but mean different things. Governments speak of the need for financing infrastructure and investors speak of investing in infrastructure. Are they referring to the same thing? PPPs (public–private partnerships) hold some appeal to bridge the gap, but PPPs mean different things to investors versus governments. Governments may constrain themselves to classical risk transfer PPP models based on high leverage, whereas investors are seeking value-added opportunities based on equity returns. I have written a paper on this which has found that such models have been crowding out private capital, with much fanfare among governments with fiscal capacity to substitute public money for private dollars.[11] Governments seek 'greenfield' projects, whereas institutional investors are attracted to 'brownfield' projects with a track record of performance. So there's quite a difference in perspective on PPPs as investors come on board in later rounds and with different investment parameters. Seldom do the two sides speak to each other at the formulation stages of a project.

James: Most infrastructure projects are launched by governments, and the dilemma is they are launched with business models that are not attractive to investors. They decide on a solution to get from point A to point B, implement the solution through a highly structured proposal

---

9   Bridging the Infrastructure Gap. McKinsey Global Institute. June 2016.
10 'Infrastructure Fund Set for Boom Year After 2018 Record'. *Financial Times*. 19 January 2019.
11 Hussain, S. and Siematycki, M. 'Rethinking the Role of Private Capital in Infrastructure PPPs: A Case Study of Ontario, Canada', *Public Management Review*, 2018.

call, and then may discuss it with potential investors. Governments do not understand that investors are not bankers or lenders. Institutional investors currently prefer equity over debt, want to invest large sums, seek value-added opportunities, and buy operating businesses, not assets. Investors need to be brought in early in the process, be involved in identifying possibilities, and prefer to see a pipeline or portfolio of projects to gain their attention.

Sherena: We are currently witnessing the rise of infrastructure debt as a way for institutional investors to gain exposure to infrastructure. The return upside from debt is limited, thereby limiting the pool of investible projects to those where de-risking has occurred, whether through government assumption of risk or from a strong counterparty. Again, the disparity between mature and emerging markets manifests. Mature markets may have governments with a strong enough fiscal position to de-risk projects from a debt perspective, whereas emerging markets largely do not. The outcome is a shallow debt market in emerging markets or ones that rely heavily on external parties to assume currency, political or revenue risk.

Infrastructure has some characteristics akin to real estate: a long life cycle, heterogeneity, illiquidity and inflation hedging ability. However, a defining feature of infrastructure is the prevalence of 'natural monopolies or oligopolies' in the provision of essential services and of economies of scale created by large distribution networks. For our readers, can you explain what you consider the major differences in return drivers between the two asset classes?

James: Infrastructure is subject to two major risks that set it apart from real estate, namely sovereign risk and regulatory risk. Also, it is more prone to political or ideological barriers; for example, aversion to 'privatisation' of public services. Infrastructure models also fall into two camps with very different risk/return profiles: those based on availability payments that underwrite significant risk in return for lower cost of money, as payments are looked upon by institutional investors as akin to government bonds; and, revenue-based infrastructure that carries with it significant revenue risk for the investors, but more upside in terms of value creation.

Sherena: There are some other characteristics that set it apart; for example, infrastructure projects have complexity and capital intensity.

Infrastructure as an asset class is still not as well defined, in terms of behaviour and benchmarks. Also, unlike real estate in today's market, infrastructure is heterogeneous and is not a commodity – investors view infrastructure less as an asset transaction and more as an investment in an operating business. This is most clear when we recognise that institutional investment in infrastructure can occur through an investment into an asset itself, or into a platform company that invests in infrastructure projects. As exposure to infrastructure grows within a portfolio, the heterogeneous nature of infrastructure assets can begin to dim and the financial characteristics of infrastructure investments begin to behave similarly.

James: Real estate is a private business and very reliant on personal relationships. You build, you rent, or you sell, usually in a specified sector such as office, industrial or retail, or housing. Infrastructure is a very public business, reliant on transparency and high levels of public acceptance and accountability.

So, infrastructure is more heterogeneous, real estate more homogeneous?

James: I think that's a fair point. Infrastructure requires a much higher skill level given the complexity of transactions, the longevity of the assets, the direct connection between capital and operating costs, and the public services provided.

Sherena: The public dimension of infrastructure adds to the complexity. Take PPPs for example; they usually depend on the transfer of a public monopoly, the division of risks, the involvement of regulatory bodies, and detailed and complex legal agreements among many stakeholders. The question of land ownership and the structure of a concession agreement adds to this complexity.

So, is it fair to say that because of all the additional risks (complexity, project, regulatory risks) you would expect on average higher returns from infrastructure than real estate?

James: That's a difficult one to answer. It really depends on your infrastructure portfolio and your investment horizon. LPs and GPs may build in capital appreciation given a defined time horizon. Institutional investors usually don't have a time horizon and rely on yield. They have to price long-term risks such as functional obsolescence, the impact of new technologies, potential effects of climate change, or the vagaries of political leaders. They have to contend with sovereign risks. When investing in real estate, the value proposition is very different and value can be more readily monetised and benchmarked against some index. Real estate values are driven by rents paid by users or tenants. So, the whole model is different. For infrastructure, governments want to drive down the cost of capital, whereas investors want to drive up the return on equity. They are not aligned in their use of capital.

Sherena: For many projects, greenfield in particular, there's very limited upside available. Whereas in the context of real estate, which has a more private dimension, when an asset manager deals with a tenant, there is an opportunity to create value for both parties in the transaction. It's only when infrastructure assets are conceived more broadly that the upside potential of a particular project can be identified, and focused asset management activities can be deployed to derive greater value.

James: Infrastructure also takes a longer time frame to implement (leaving aside, for example, renewable energy) compared to real estate.

What do you see as the difference between listed and unlisted markets for real estate and infrastructure investing? Do they represent different drivers (and thereby different returns) or is it mainly a question of appraisal-based values? For example, they are both exposed to economic growth, interest rates, regulatory risk, and more. Do you think there is an illiquidity risk premium (after fees)?

Sherena: I think there's a dimension related to transaction cost that comes with being able to deal with a private investment as opposed to a listed fund. There's also the challenge of liquidity. For infrastructure funds with longer investment horizons, you will find they have very little intention to ever sell, unless there is a seismic shift in the regulatory environment or relationships change. For listed infrastructure there are additional factors that come into play. In many ways, there are still those that think listed infrastructure is a cross between equity and bonds in the way the public market behaves. We're still waiting for the data to give us an answer on listed versus unlisted. The jury is still out on this debate.

For institutional investors there have always been benchmarking issues regarding unlisted real estate and infrastructure.[12] Most benchmarks do not relate to their actual strategy and risk exposures. Can you comment on this?

James: You can benchmark some real estate, like pension funds do through their sharing of data and given the homogeneity of many asset classes in their portfolios. For infrastructure, it's really hard to aggregate data, as you're dealing with an operating business, a very different set of risks, and different regulatory regimes. With real estate – there's a lot more of it, and you have large institutional portfolios with data sets tracked over long periods of time. Benchmarks in real estate are tied to performance measures for managers – so-called 'attribution analysis'. Investors want to know if their managers are meeting or exceeding a particular benchmark. In real estate, benchmarks serve to figure out whether you're getting value for your fees. For large institutions (especially in 'the Canadian model') they are for a large part managed in-house, not through external managers, and so benchmarking is a comparative exercise against other funds.

Sherena: Reports to the plan holders in Canada are very personalised and distinctive. So it's really hard to generalise to see how one large investor does compared to another. It really depends on their portfolios. As well, if assets are held privately, valuation methodologies can smooth out performance quite a bit, leading to the perception that infrastructure is less volatile than other asset classes. Benchmarks are only as good as the methodology they subscribe to.

James: At a recent Berlin infrastructure investment conference an academic got up to present the results of a benchmark exercise. It was received with a great deal of scepticism. The challenge of collecting and comparing data across heterogeneous infrastructure assets was something that investment managers took issue with. Those in the room were quite vocal about the quality and consistency of the data underlying the analysis.

---

12 More popular unlisted benchmarks include NCREIF or EDHEC, IRR (which is sensitive to the timing of the cashflows), industry peers, or listed equivalents such as the FTSE EPRA NAREIT for real estate or the FTSE Global Infrastructure indices.

For infrastructure as an asset class, natural monopolies and industries enjoying economies of scale are often regulated by government restrictions on prices, returns, output levels or barriers to entry. Consequently infrastructure investments may require compensation for regulatory risk. Has there been any study done to estimate the size of this 'regulatory' risk premium compared to standard equity?

James: I don't know of any. Big investors tend to mitigate some of this risk by having people in the right countries, collecting local knowledge, and engaging local partners who have their ear close to the ground.

Sherena: I know there have been attempts to do so. But it really depends on how regulatory risk is defined. It is very challenging. Investors may look at this differently. Again, we need to find the data to support this.

As in other alternative asset classes, asset owners and fund managers have long been at odds when it comes to demonstrating value and performance with illiquid asset classes like real estate and infrastructure. Managers (GPs) say they have better deal making skills, while asset owners (LPs) point to their high fees. Are you aware of any studies (Canadian or other) that examine the relative performance of in-house versus externally managed portfolios?

James: This is a very interesting issue. The 'Canadian pension fund model' is in-house management. What these pension funds tell us is that they are looking at the people running the businesses they acquire. When they fly off to look at an airport, they look at it from a business perspective and will acquire in-house technical skills to do just that. Funds no longer hire just financial analysts; they now look to acquire in-house technical specialists that may run from farming to telecommunications, or at least be able to communicate with their local partner.

Comparable to say how Warren Buffett invests?

James: Yes, one only need look at the performance of Canada's large pension funds to see returns over many years similar to those achieved by Warren Buffett. They manage mostly in-house, and have the advantage of size to acquire the technical specialities required. They also make it clear that they buy businesses, not assets, and managing these businesses effectively is what sets these institutional investors apart.

Sherena: I would agree that I'm not aware of any studies. Their investment philosophies are quite different. It's going to be challenging to get an apples-to-apples comparison because of the lack of data.

How do investors best create 'excess returns' in real estate and infrastructure? Would that be from asset selection, manager selection or asset management (operational value creation), or something else?

James: Primarily through value creation and driving up revenues on the asset management side; for example, increasing retail sales in an airport purchase. Airports have a huge revenue stream from retail. Our big pension funds have big retail and real estate exposure, and it is this nexus between infrastructure and real estate that provides a competitive advantage in some sectors. For the institutional owners, driving up value does not mean selling the assets, it is about increasing returns. For an external manager like Brookfield, a value increase may be sufficient motivation to sell as they will play arbitrage in the market.

Sherena: There's also the opportunity to drive down costs and create networks. Companies such as Brookfield look at not just the infrastructure asset but the whole value chain, where the infrastructure asset sits, and whether they can influence inputs or outputs with various stakeholders to create a pipeline of value and a future source of transactions. For Brookfield, it is excellence in asset management. Pension funds may look at the ability to scale up with local partners as a way to create value. One asset alone may not be able to achieve this. But when looked upon as a network or a platform for investment in subsequent assets, excess return potential becomes more apparent.

So, for institutions it is more buy and hold?

James: For sure, as they will have to replace the hole in the portfolio once they sell. Pension funds are governed by their fiduciary responsibility to their pensioners. They need a steady cashflow to fund their obligations, and pension contributions alone will not be enough. This situation grows more acute as the workforce ages and pensioners begin to outnumber those still working.

Sherena: There may be reasons for selling of course, like regulatory risks or misalignment with partners. As well, portfolios are always subject to rebalancing depending on changing perspectives on risk, return and mandate alignment.

The ESG debate is intensifying. Investors are trying to arriving at a consensus of what makes good ESG, and agree it has become much more sophisticated. What do you think makes for good ESG in real estate and infrastructure?[13]

James: ESG is something that most investors agree with but admit that definitions are fuzzy and concepts are not well understood. Despite the best of intentions to deal with ESG, it is fair to say there are still no generally accepted standards as to what ESG entails, or means. One good example is GRESB that has developed an ESG benchmark for real assets that's being embraced by investors. Unfortunately, there is no discourse on the impact of ESG on returns. CDPQ in Canada has made a significant commitment to build in ESG targets for their investment opportunities.[14]

Sherena: Some of the Canadian direct investors have been practising it for a long time, long before it became a 'buzzword'. It just never had that practice being simplified as ESG! It's hard to define social and governance requirements (more so than environmental requirements). We are also beginning to see how ESG is incorporated into the investment and asset management decision process.

Which one is the most important: 'E', 'S' or 'G'?[15] What is the literature evidence that an ESG focus creates superior returns in real estate and infrastructure?

James: The 'E' tends to gain the most attention (especially climate change, because of the potential to create stranded assets), but more recently the 'G' is getting a lot of attention. There is very little literature on the investment impacts of ESG on infrastructure. Professor Avis Devine in the Brookfield Centre is doing groundbreaking research on

---

13 James and Sherena are interacting closely with 12 large Canadian institutional investors in the delivery of the Sustainable Infrastructure Fellowship Program, in collaboration with the Government of Canada and in partnership with the Sustainable Infrastructure Foundation and the Schulich School of Business.
14 https://www.cdpq.com/en/news/pressreleases/from-commitment-to-action-la-caisse-publishes-its-second-stewardship-investing.
15 The renewable energy industry has benefitted from environmental, social and governance interest, and in particular from concern for environmental and climate-related risk.

the impact of 'green buildings' on portfolio value.[16] Are certified green buildings adding value? Professor Devine is working with data from a large Canadian real estate firm to address this question.

Sherena: This is where things can get a little fuzzy. If a government official in an emerging market builds a toll road, they would say that's a sustainable investment. That's counterintuitive as this implies more cars and thus more carbon dioxide. The government would claim they are introducing mobility, an important social objective, and reducing traffic along local routes that would emit even more carbon dioxide. Adding productivity gains and economic growth has a broader social benefit. So, the government would say it's a positive. But institutional investors would come to a different conclusion. Does the 'S' offset the 'E'? How is the materiality of different variables measured against one another?

Supportive policy, LP interest, government subsidies and demand for alternative energy sources are providing fertile ground for investment in renewables. What types of renewable energy infrastructure projects are promising and what are the challenges?

James: Most promising is wind, and particularly offshore wind, as the biggest challenges are regulatory and environmental. Renewable energy is one of the most attractive asset classes for investors in infrastructure. Renewables are driving down the price of electricity, especially offshore wind power that is shifting from smaller turbines to larger turbines. These projects can be done relatively quickly. Nuclear and coal are out, gas is so-so, and the problem with hydro is that you need to build a dam with a high capital cost, perhaps capitalised over 50 years, and predicated on a stable high tariff rate for electricity.

Sherena: Storage (batteries) is getting a lot of attention from an R&D perspective as a source of adding to a renewable portfolio. Smart energy campuses are another as a disruptor – transforming heating and cooling systems into a ring-fenced campus and selling the cashflow stream as a form of infrastructure investment. That's popped up a bit in the US as an emerging energy investment.

---

16 Devine, A. and N. Kok, 'Green Certification and Building Performance: Implications for Tangibles and Intangibles', *The Journal of Portfolio Management*, 2015, 41(5):151–163. https://www. researchgate.net/publication/282434130_Green_Certification_and_Building_Performance_ Implications_for_Tangibles_and_Intangibles.

I notice the topic of sustainable cities as it pertains to the challenges of urbanisation across the globe is one of James's areas of interest.[17] What would be good examples of cities that you consider sustainable?

James: Copenhagen, Stockholm and Malmo would be three examples – all in Scandinavia. All three have been in the sustainability game for a considerable period of time, have defined targets with effective policies in place, and can point to successes. All three are already reaping benefits in terms of economic growth. They've set very high targets for zero carbon emissions as an economic necessity. They have developed and embraced 'greentech' as an export. For example, Denmark is one of the largest manufacturers of wind turbines in the world. This commitment was the result of the economic downturn in the early 1990s. As port cities, they lost their maritime industries to Asia, and had to find new ways to rejuvenate their cities and attract and retain young workers. Improved quality of life was part of their economic model. Copenhagen launched into building transit from the proceeds of waterfront land sales, Malmo re-did their waterfront with highly sustainable redevelopment models, and Stockholm tackled traffic congestion with a congestion charge, the proceeds of which fund public transit. In these cities you see the results of firm environmental policies that have now been at work for more than several decades.

Do you have any views of the investment merits of economic versus social infrastructure (schools, prisons, hospitals) and PPPs? Is social infrastructure on its way to a 'core' status?[18]

James: No, it is not. Most large pension funds are not investing in PPP. They are looking to invest large sums – in the CAD$1bn to $3bn range. Unfortunately, PPPs as currently structured, certainly in Canada, have crowded out private capital and relied largely on public debt through sovereign-backed bond issues. This is a luxury when you have a strong debt rating and sufficient room to grow debt. It's a real constraint in emerging markets with no debt capacity and a non-investment-grade rating. This is where the multilateral development banks step in to help

---

17 Mercer has also published its own report on the topic: 'People First, Driving Growth in Megacities', Anderson D., and P. Siffel, 2018. Overpopulation, excessive consumption, pollution, and depletion of resources have presented environmental and health challenges in major cities.

18 There are challenges and opportunities in social infrastructure. An ageing population and proportionately fewer taxpayers will create challenges for government funding, but this opens up opportunities for the private sector and for investors.

launch PPPs, but typically with forms of debt financing and limited opportunities for equity participation.

Sherena: In mature markets, government debt is crowding out private capital. I wrote a paper on this. Ontario is one of the active social infrastructure locations, and seen as a gold standard around the world. So the challenge is that it becomes very similar to the return profile of bonds. Due diligence and asset management considerations make it far easier to invest in a government bond, rather than in a PPP for what is a minimal spread differential. Investments in social infrastructure imply the availability of a payment model that is akin to issuing government bonds. Concessions can arguably be seen as a form of PPP which investors are happy to invest in when the right risk/return conditions are present. In emerging markets where government debt ceilings are met, concessions or variations of PPPs that transfer greater degrees of risk onto private partners are being pursued. The question raised is whether the return to be received compensates for the additional risk being transferred.

James: If investors want bonds, they will go to the bond market which is far more liquid and not encumbered with complex legal agreements and unique risks. PPPs are not structured to accept large amounts of equity, have high transaction costs, and value for money is geared to drive down the cost of any capital and drive up the risk transfer to the private investor. One might claim that the PPP model has not managed to align the interests of government and private capital.

Over the last couple of years, banks globally have been pulling back from various forms of lending. That's left a gap for private real estate and infrastructure debt investors to step into. What do you make of this?

James: We had a financial meltdown in Ontario in 2008 and the banks withdrew from involvement in PPPs. The provincial government stepped up to the challenge, created the institutional environment to permit an infrastructure bond market, and offered to advance partial funding prior to an asset's substantial completion. Since then, the banks have not been big players and are in it for the short term, usually as construction lenders.

Sherena: There are roles for different types of banks. For example, in emerging markets there is a role for multilateral development banks to offer grants or low-cost debt capital to governments during an asset's origination stage to help structure business cases for political approval. In Canada, the idea of a federal infrastructure bank emerged and is now operational. At first, the idea of an infrastructure bank left many industry professionals scratching their heads as there is more than enough capital available in the market. Instead, this infrastructure bank is seen by the Canadian Government to be a mechanism that will use government funds to 'de-risk' certain infrastructure projects by offering feasibility funding or low-cost debt to permit projects to proceed to construction. Once those projects are operational, there can be a refinancing opportunity for private capital sources.

Since returns in brownfield space have fallen, investors have been forced to move into greenfield territory. As a consequence, more investors are taking on a higher level of risk and venturing into new technologies. What do you make of it?

James: The discussion must always come back to the risk/return profile of the asset and the portfolio of investments. Greenfield projects take time, can be fraught with political uncertainties, require a minimal infusion of private capital, and introduce new risks that investors may not be comfortable with. Investors want value-added opportunities. These may occur with new technologies but depend on the revenue prospects and the particular business model.

Sherena: Dipping their toes into emerging markets is something that is happening incrementally. Greenfield emerging-market infrastructure is becoming popular as large investors are gaining exposure in certain countries. This happens first through incremental or indirect exposure, such as through a specialty fund, then steadily increases through greater involvement with a local partner. This learning process can take years, and often occurs through investments in brownfield assets.

James: Greenfields may focus on technology like databanks or cell towers. Basically, investors invest in emerging technology they think holds promise. It could be energy related also or energy storage (batteries).

Let's talk about the Digital Age. What impact will AI and Big Data have for real estate and infrastructure investors?

James: I mention blockchain as the big unknown. It could drive down transactions costs and drive out the lucrative business of the many intermediaries. Both real estate and infrastructure have complex legal agreements, intermediaries and fees. So blockchain could help cut this down. We are already seeing the impact of AI in the real estate industry, particular with the emergence of new players offering the benefits of data management and new software systems.

Sherena: In connection with our upcoming book[19], James and I are writing about what those applications could look like. A lot of people are talking about blockchain and infrastructure, but the intersection has yet to be seen. The use of Big Data to optimise infrastructure assets is some-thing else that is overlooked. Consider the productivity gains that can emerge when more information is known about how and when infra-structure assets are used, by whom, and for what purpose. Convenience packages can be structured and third-party applications can be added onto the value proposition already offered by existing infrastructure assets. At the very least, Big Data can assist with the physical asset man-agement process. Major overhaul and rehabilitation processes can be better optimised with this information.

James: We are seeing some evolution on the real estate side where an old industry that puts everything in Excel spreadsheets (that seldom get read) is being replaced.

What new research projects are you currently working on? I note you are writing another book together – can you comment on that?

James: This June we launched the Sustainable Infrastructure Fellowship program.[20] We are bringing senior government officials from emerging economies on a six-week intensive program to better understand the role of private capital in infrastructure. This is followed by a two-week assignment to one of the 12 institutional investors supporting this initia-tive. It's a big challenge, but also a great opportunity to explore how the direct debt and equity investors are approaching emerging markets. The program was launched by 12 likeminded international pension funds with combined investments in excess of US$6 trillion. This program was announced to coincide with the G7 held in June 2018 in Canada. The sponsoring funds have established a new organisation called the

---

19 James and Sherena are co-authors of a forthcoming book provisionally titled *The Business of Infrastructure.*
20 https://www.investorleadershipnetwork.org/en/sustainable-infrastructure-fellowship-program.

Investors Leadership Network (ILN), to drive this program as one of three major initiatives.

Sherena: The ILN contains Canadian pension funds, but also others like CalPERS, PGGM, Generali, Allianz and Aviva Investors. What they know is that their future successes are tied to emerging markets. What they hope to achieve is to better prepare government leaders in those countries on the role of private capital in infrastructure capital provision. Participants from these countries will be senior decision makers at the executive level affecting the use of private capital to be deployed in infrastructure. Private capital and governments speak in different languages. This is a chance to create an ecosystem to share experience and knowledge.

This is in addition to research conducted on the role of private capital in infrastructure, from the perspective of finance, public management, economic geography, urban planning, and law and economies.

Is it therefore fair to say you parked your upcoming book for the moment?

James [laughs]: We have backed away for now, also because we have come a long way from what we thought two years ago. We've learned so much.

Sherena: We are connecting smaller research projects. But the book itself contains a lot of the global case study examples, which are now fleshed out quite a bit with the added perspectives of large direct investors in infrastructure.

What makes students get successful careers in real estate and infrastructure?

James: I guess we should be able to answer that one, since we have students! We offer both an MBA specialisation in real estate and infrastructure, and a one-year Master in Real Estate and Infrastructure.

Number one is always to attract the brightest and best from across the globe. We find that the students who do well come back to graduate studies with industry experience and are capable of contributing to the learning environment.

Second, they need to have a passion for and commitment to their chosen career. However, we have students who didn't know what infrastructure was, came in with a real estate background, and then switched to infrastructure. The challenges and career opportunities in this sector appealed to them.

Third, for infrastructure as distinct from real estate, you need to be an interdisciplinary thinker. Real estate is transaction driven. You do a building, then another. Infrastructure is driven from a portfolio perspective and is much more complex, so you need some soft skills. We're among the few people in the world teaching infrastructure from a development and finance perspective. Some universities pursue infrastructure under engineering or public policy. We're doing it within a business school, and we see this as a huge advantage.

Sherena: I would add to the soft skills, something our best students excel in. The ability to be persuasive, make a pitch, and engage with a variety of different stakeholders as to what an infrastructure asset means is critical and sets apart the successful student. Interdisciplinary thinking and critical assessment requires hard skill, but to become a leader, these must be combined with the soft skills. For example, the need to hone negotiating skills is essential to constructing shareholder agreements. This is something I teach under the rubric of experiential learning, where I carry out simulations. These workshops offer an opportunity to acquire substantive knowledge, but also assess how an individual performs. There is also the notion of lifelong learning and the understanding that education continues throughout one's career. Our new Fellowship program falls into this category.

What keeps you busy outside of office hours?

James: I am always trying to think how to get out of the office in time! [Laughs.] The last year has been all consuming and very challenging, but we're having fun. I haven't had much time to think of other things. I'm a reader, and always try to extend my understanding and ability to think laterally. As a professional and educator you've got to come to grips with what the future will offer, both positive and negative. This is especially relevant for infrastructure, as we are building for a long-term future. For example, understanding emerging technologies, social changes, demographic trends and the impacts of climate change are all important to forecasting our infrastructure needs. I want to see how other people think about some of these issues.

Sherena: I'm pursuing a charitable initiative called Shelter Bus which repurposes motor coaches once used to transport passengers between different regions, like hockey teams, into temporary shelters for our most vulnerable population.[21] In Canada, when it gets cold, it gets really cold, and people can face significant health challenges. The motor coaches used for Shelter Bus are at the end of their life and are often thrown away or scrapped by governments for very little value. This initiative hacks two items (transport and social issues) by placing them together to address a pressing social cause. The public transit industry and homeless advocates are excited about this project, which I hope to expand to other jurisdictions. In many ways this is an evolving form of social infrastructure using a new business model.

If you hadn't been doing this, what would you have been doing?

James: I've gone through a lot of careers in my time! I started out as an architect, then I built homes, then I launched MIT's real estate program. I've worked all over the world, so I've been very fortunate. And here I am still at university and continuing to learn new things.

Sherena: I practise law, and did so intensely for many years until I received a call from James one day stating the following: 'We're going to launch a Master in Real Estate and Infrastructure and need an ambitious infrastructure professional academic on our team. Are you interested?' There are always learning opportunities that are used as a launch pad for many different things. This is just one of those many opportunities.

How do you see the industry in 10 years' time?

James: I think this will be a fantastic industry. The opportunities are incredible. We've got a billion more urban dwellers in China and India between 2010 and 2050. The opportunities for really good thinking about new business models or the application of new technologies; we're just entering a golden era for infrastructure! How long can we live on 18th century infrastructure? I think a fantastic period is on the horizon. Look at who wants in: Google, IBM, Siemens, McKinsey – all these businesses want to extend their network. Everybody wants to be involved in shaping the future cities these days.

---

21 https://www.humanityfirstcanada.ca/shelter-bus and www.shelterbus.ca.

Sherena: A lot of creativity is coming. Not just technology but value creation and business models. These will be in emerging and established markets. We can't continue to build on what we've known in the past as our cities and populations evolve.

Finally – real estate and infrastructure investment: art, science or skill?

James: Well, I'm biased as I'm an architect. In architecture, you need to master the essential skills, then you transform into the creative thinker and artist. You first sit at that piano and master those black and white keys, and one day find yourself playing music, performing as an artist. You don't redesign the keyboard, you refine you creative skills. I'm a firm believer that you must first master the skills and then move forward.

On art and science, Steve Jobs once said, 'The future is at the nexus between art and science'. And I do believe that. A lot of the products he produced are art with an incredible understanding of science. You need to blend the two but you need the skills to do the blending.

Sherena: From the perspective of a lawyer, skills come into play, but the true value is about identifying and solving problems. So there's the art of creativity. You see the blending over time. The tools you need to be the artist is where the skills will take you.

Thank you for your time.

Conclusions

There are megatrends that will have a significant impact in both developed and emerging economies. North Americans represent around 5% of the world's population but consume approximately 30% of the world's resources. This is not sustainable, particularly when the rest of the world wants what we have. The 'infrastructure gap', however, may be a false claim. As James notes, 'there's all this money in the world looking for infrastructure opportunities. And yet there's all these governments bemoaning they don't have enough money to fund the gap.' Many greenfield projects don't have the profile once brownfield to attract institutional investors. What most governments do not understand is that investors are not bankers. Institutional investors prefer equity over debt, want value-added opportunities, and prefer to buy operating businesses, not assets. The 'Canadian pension fund model' of in-house management makes it clear that they buy businesses, not assets, and managing these businesses effectively is what sets them apart. As James notes, 'One only need look at the performance of an investor like Ontario Teachers to see returns over many years that might be similar to those achieved by Warren Buffett'. Most large Canadian pension funds are not investing in PPP. As Sherena notes, 'government debt is crowding out private capital'.

Compared to real estate, infrastructure is subject to major risks that set it apart from real estate, namely sovereign/regulatory risk, complexity risk and capital intensity. Real estate is a very transactional business. You build, you rent or you sell. It's almost a commodity today.

Finally, new technology creates new investment opportunities like in renewable energy, but can also drive out the lucrative business of the many intermediaries as both real estate and infrastructure have complex legal agreements, intermediaries and fees.

As James notes:

'I think this will be a fantastic industry. The opportunities for really good thinking, new business models, application of new technologies; we're just entering a golden era!'

— CHAPTER 11 —

ALPHA IN RESPONSIBLE INVESTMENTS

An interview with Professor Rob Bauer on optimising investment and social objectives

'That which is common to the greatest number has the least care bestowed upon it. Everyone thinks chiefly of his own, hardly at all of the common interest; and only when he himself is concerned as an individual.'
Aristotle (384 BC–322 BC)

The Global Financial Crisis highlighted the cost of unethical behaviour, especially in the financial services sector, which led to large-scale reforms and a focus on core business for banking. The Global Sustainable Investment Alliance estimates US$31 trillion is now invested in sustainable assets.[1] Responsible investing may be broadly classified as follows.

---

1   http://www.gsi-alliance.org/trends-report-2018/.

A framework for responsible investing

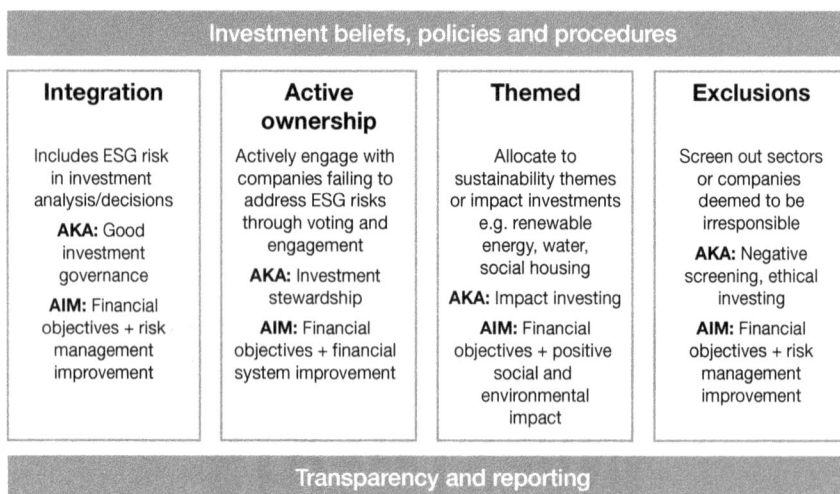

Investment beliefs, policies and procedures			
Integration	**Active ownership**	**Themed**	**Exclusions**
Includes ESG risk in investment analysis/decisions **AKA:** Good investment governance **AIM:** Financial objectives + risk management improvement	Actively engage with companies failing to address ESG risks through voting and engagement **AKA:** Investment stewardship **AIM:** Financial objectives + financial system improvement	Allocate to sustainability themes or impact investments e.g. renewable energy, water, social housing **AKA:** Impact investing **AIM:** Financial objectives + positive social and environmental impact	Screen out sectors or companies deemed to be irresponsible **AKA:** Negative screening, ethical investing **AIM:** Financial objectives + risk management improvement
Transparency and reporting			

Source: Mercer

More recently, engagement or *active ownership* has become more popular. Active ownership and shareholder advocacy are key elements in the adoption of proxy-voting guidelines, filing shareholder resolutions and engaging in dialogue with companies to promote social and environmental responsibility.

Institutional investors may also choose to *integrate* ESG risk into investment analysis and decisions and incorporate it as part of their investment beliefs. *Themed investing*, like renewables or water, has become more popular as climate change has become the focus of public attention and a major political issue in many parts of the world. To some, climate change represents just one issue, the 'E' as part of a large number of ESG issues. The CFA Institute suggests most investors (at least in the Americas) focus on the 'G', with the 'E' and the 'S' having a lower acceptance rate.[2] To others, the 'E' is the main issue that has caused many to rethink their approach to ESG. The World Economic Forum has classified environmental risk among the top five risks.[3] Does doing the right thing boost shareholder value? We examine what academic literature and empirical evidence have to offer on how to best combine investment and social objectives.

2 'ESG Integration in the Americas: Markets, practices and data', CFA Institute, 2018.
3 http://www3.weforum.org/docs/WEF_Global_Risks_Report_2019.pdf.

Introducing Professor Rob Bauer

Rob Bauer is Professor of Finance (chair: Institutional Investors) at Maastricht University School of Business and Economics in the Netherlands. His academic research is focused on pension funds, strategic investment policy, mutual fund performance, responsible investing, shareholder activism and corporate governance. Rob publishes regularly in professional and academic journals, and is a frequent speaker on national and international conferences.

Rob is Director of the European Centre for Corporate Engagement (ECCE) at Maastricht University, and Executive Director of the International Centre for Pension Management (ICPM) in Toronto. Rob is also founder and managing director of Rob Bauer Consultants, in which he advises and supports institutional investors on topics related to strategic investments.

Rob, thank you for participating in the book again. Can you compare and contrast for our readers how you see the difference between sustainability, responsible investment and ESG? There are a lot of workshops, conferences and buzzwords going around.

It's all semantics. The topic is sustainability. The question is: how can we translate this topic into investing? So you have to give that a name. Whether you call it ESG investing or responsible investing, I don't really care. ESG is just another way to frame the content into a nice three-letter abbreviation. It's still as confusing as when you wrote your first book 12 years ago! It's not what the name should be though. Responsible investing is not just about providing funds with ESG information. It should be mainstream. Mainstream MSCI All Country World Index (ACWI) investors should be looking at this, especially as asset managers and asset owners are investing on behalf of others. So they need to know what their clients' preferences are. It is important to communicate this to their clients. You cannot be as vague as saying: 'Do you like sustainability? Do you like ESG?' It has to be concrete if you want to manage products that clients really want.

What do you find to be the main reasons institutional investors go sustainable? Is it return enhancement, risk reduction, regulatory, client or societal pressure, or something else?

Out of these reasons you have to distinguish between asset owner and asset managers. For asset owners, all of them are relevant. This has grown hugely. Sustainable investing started with a small group of people with strong beliefs. Almost all of them started with a need for risk reduction. Then they started to talk about opportunities.

Societal pressure is huge now – although less so in the US – as well as regulatory pressure. A good example of regulatory pressure: in Europe, regulators are thinking about asking private investors to fill out a sustainability preference profile, similar to a risk profile, so that every bank has to deliver services in line with their sustainability profile. This puts pressure on asset managers, as otherwise you are in breach. This could be in effect in 2022.

So the frontrunners of sustainable institutional investors were those that were either very ethical or those that saw opportunities in risk reduction. Right now, large investors are looking at this, whether they want it or not, because they have to do this. So, it is a mix of all the reasons you mention now as sustainable investing has become mainstream.

'E', 'S' and 'G' – which one is the most important driver of investor interest?

'E', 'S' or 'G' are just three letters and very vague! You have to distinguish between sufficient conditions and necessary conditions, like in maths.

Governance is a necessary condition for a company to be good. If it's not good, it's not a good investment. In the context of sufficient conditions, climate change is a topic you cannot neglect any more as a company, whether you are a bank, a manufacturer or a service company. Big topics for humanity, like climate change, will trickle down in the way investors view companies. If these companies neglect big topics like climate change, they will face risks, competitive disadvantages, miss out on opportunities and be less prepared for regulation. It's way broader than climate change, and also relates to the Sustainable Development Goals (SDGs). The big pension funds especially take the SDGs very seriously and see a responsibility to contribute. Pooling all that money makes this a very important part of society. They are the ones determining investments into sustainable infrastructure. You see many examples of how investors are acting on this.

Last time we spoke, you mentioned the evidence was quite mixed and that you could find arguments in favour of and against a sustainability premium in shares. What is your view now that we have additional data? Do 'good' or 'bad' shares or sectors do better?

The problem is about what a premium is. It means that the stock price of a firm would be higher, so the expected return would be lower. If we all agree a company is really good, we will pay up for it. What is in the price? The really material information you can refer to from, for example, SASB is increasingly being clear what is material and what isn't.[4] That information is priced in. Only unexpected information leads to extra return. If investors know all the relevant information then it is priced so there is a higher price for better companies. If you know this and buy the good companies, you get lower returns and lower risk. If you can distinguish the bad from the good as they turn good, then you can collect a bit of a premium.

But to say that good shares have good returns, that is a really naïve thought!

Highly scoring companies or sectors on sustainability will have lower risk and therefore lower returns. Yes, companies that are sustainable may have lower risk and high ROE but a lot of that is already priced into the share price.[5]

Have you done any research on a sustainability premium for bonds?

Yes, I've done some myself.[6] There are a few others as well, like Chava.[7] Bond investors are also pricing the sustainability premium. Bonds that

---

4   https://www.sasb.org/.
5   Refer also 'ESG and Corporate Financial Performance: mapping the global landscape', Deutsche Bank, 2015, which investigated 2,250 studies, and 'From the stockholder to the stakeholder: how sustainability can drive financial outperformance', Oxford University/Arabesque Partners.
6   'Corporate Environmental Management and Credit Risk', Bauer R., and D. Hann, 2014. The findings suggest that firms with environmental concerns pay a premium on their cost of debt financing and are assigned lower credit ratings. https://papers.ssrn.com/sol3/papers.cfm?abstract_id=1660470.
7   'Environmental Externalities and Cost of Capital', Chava, S., 2014, *Journal of Management Science* 60(9). Investors demand significantly higher expected returns on stocks excluded by environmental screens (such as hazardous chemical, substantial emissions, and climate change concerns) compared to firms without such environmental concerns. Lenders also charge a significantly higher interest rate on the bank loans issued to firms with these environmental concerns.

are risky to climate change tend to pay higher interest for their bonds because the banks think the probability they will default is a bit higher. So, this is being priced as well. Whether it is fully priced I don't know, but it is being priced.

How do you see artificial intelligence and Big Data impacting ESG research?

I'm not a big expert on the topic. But I do see a lot of data coming out on ESG where there is a lot of uncertainty. If you have 600 criteria, then some are not easily measurable, like from employee surveys. So there you cannot use traditional methods, so AI could really help. AI and pattern recognition could also help in extracting the data. ESG data is less measurable and defined, and has a broader number of data points of different dimensions and different topics. It's hard to oversee all that as a human.

The number of dedicated sustainable funds remains quite small, compared to the amount of money flowing into mainstream index funds.[8] What do you make of this?

I think it shows that sustainability has become mainstream. Many traditional 'non-sustainable' investors are now integrating it anyway – although not labelling themselves as such – whether from a regulatory, societal or risk perspective. So only a few funds are left saying 'we are a typical sustainable fund'.

So I see it as a positive sign that this is happening. Most of the mainstream index funds have ESG-type index funds, with investors making customised index funds creating FTSE/MSCI data.

The reason money flowing into index funds has increased is that active funds are not producing excess returns. So investors want low-cost indices, but investors also want sustainability. All big index providers are now providing this. So, I wouldn't say the mainstream index providers are not doing sustainable investing.

---

8   As of end 2017 there were 235 US sustainable funds, with US$100bn in assets, according to Morningstar.

An increasing number of firms are providing ESG ratings.[9] What is the academic evidence? Do higher ratings outperform lower ratings?

Well, we sort of discussed this. Yes, sure, based on ESG ratings you can form a portfolio. So, for example, in 2004–10 higher rated firms did better as no-one paid attention to it. Now, people do pay attention and you pay a higher price, so you now get a lower expected return. Ratings agencies in general are increasingly making rating changes based on higher frequency information. But it's still a hunch. Look at the credit rating agencies. Did they predict the crisis? No. So you have to be very careful with ratings agencies.

Do you have any thoughts on sustainable hedge funds?

If it is the case that certain hedge funds use sustainable information in their decision making then I have no problem with that. Of course, as soon as such information is public it will not help with returns, and much of it is public. The problem with hedge funds though is their less transparent fee/pricing structure. I find those weird and not sustainable. But sure, if there was a hedge fund that could use sustainable information, then why not?

Dutch and Scandinavian pension funds seem particularly pioneering in the adoption of the UN Sustainable Development Goals (SDGs). Do you have any insights as to why?[10] How is sustainability best 'measured/scored' from an asset owner perspective?

I think the core reason why you see this in Northern Europe is related to legislation. The prudent person rule in the Netherlands is interpreted as 'you have to act as a fiduciary in the best interest'. In common law, like the US, it is 'in the best *financial* interest'. For a long time, sustainability was interpreted as not in the best financial interest.

So, the Dutch feel less pressure to focus on just this. In the context of SDG it's no longer just led by the Dutch and Scandinavians. I was at the

---

9   There are now over 120 ratings organisations offering over 500 products. Mainstreaming Sustainable Investing, CFA Institute, 2018. Research on the impact of ESG ratings remains quite limited, refer for example https://www.unpri.org/listed-equity/the-pris-esg-and-alpha-study-/2740. article.

10 https://top1000funds.cmail19.com/t/d-l-pjtlyjy-cjtlhdrkk-j/ Dutch pension fund Detailhandel (Retail trade) has created a new index for its global equity portfolio linked to four SDGs that reflect its key ESG priorities around labour rights, economic growth and mitigating climate change. The result is improved ESG scores, a reduction in the fund's carbon footprint, and a continued passive mandate. Refer also 'Get Real! Individuals prefer more sustainable investments', Bauer, R., Ruof, T., & Smeets, P., 2018.

ICPM in Toronto recently and they are all talking about it from all over the globe. It is a big topic.

The paper I wrote put the onus on plan participants. Funds wanted to involve their participants or clients. That is something, with the board committing to a survey ex-ante. Do members want to know more about integration of sustainability into their investments? We put this to their participants. They overwhelmingly said, 'let's do it!' Then the board had to do it. I wouldn't see this happen very soon in a UK or US context. Basically this is a member-driven outcome. This pension fund is way ahead of the curve.

As I said before, in two or three years' time private bankers in Europe will have to ask clients what they want. Pension funds, insurance companies and asset managers should ask their clients: what do they want in respect to sustainability?

How can investors best adjust portfolios for climate change, both from an investment and broader societal perspective? For example, by reducing carbon footprints, potential stranded assets, investments in renewables, or other?

I think that's a tough question. Is exclusion really the best strategy? Some investors like to claim in the press: 'We removed 50% of our carbon footprint by removing oil and coal companies'. But of course those companies are bought by someone else. So, only if a large group of people does it will it have an impact. Selling oil companies and buying green or renewable companies is not that easy either, as much of that is in the private space.

On the other hand, engagement with oil and gas companies is equally very difficult. It is their core business. It's just as difficult with tobacco companies, the difference being that we know tobacco is really bad and we don't have to smoke. Oil and gas, on the other hand, we still need during the energy transition and we need the oil companies to finance green and renewable energy initiatives. However, you could engage and keep on engaging forever.

Every investor is somewhere along this continuum of exclusion and engagement, but in the end it probably is the law that makes the difference rather than investor actions.

In your opinion, how useful are quantitative models to assist investors in dealing with potential outcomes of climate change?

Models are very important! As an academic, how could I say otherwise? The question should be 'models', not just 'quantitative models'. For example, Shell has had its scenario analysis since the late '60s. In 1969 they concluded that under certain scenarios crises could happen, like the OPEC crisis in 1973. They could then more easily adapt in 1973 than other companies.

There may be a parallel here with climate change. What are the scenarios we can investigate? What could happen? Then, what do you want to do? Do you want to model the average outcome, or do you want to prevent a certain scenario from happening and focus on that?

Scenario models make a lot of sense. If there is a 1% chance the whole world will be devastated because temperatures go up four or five degrees, then better to spend some money on it as insurance. In short, models help you frame the question correctly. Models can also be updated as data comes in, in a consistent and sophisticated way, to look at elevation and temperature changes.

The alternative would be endless unstructured debate, which may not be particularly useful!

What do you think will be the outcome and side effects of climate change over the next decade? For example, will it be more positive, such as a new technology and energy mix? Or more negative, like mass migration, global competition for increasingly limited resources, increased taxes, and reduced population and economic growth in emerging and developed markets?

Well, that is a Nostradamus-type question. I'm an optimist, so I think humanity will find ways to somehow invent new technology or change behaviour. I don't think we can afford to wait for the end of continued political procrastination. The stance towards doing something is increasing. This will lead to more R&D and new technologies. It's too early to look at the negative arguments as yet, at least not in the next 10 years.

When we caught up 12 years ago you had just started the European Centre for Corporate Engagement (ECCE) as a research platform.[11] Could you tell us a bit more about your recent activities there?

We changed our name to the European Centre for Sustainable Finance. Sustainable Finance is the term people use a lot. As a spinoff, ECCE was involved in setting up the Global Research Alliance of Sustainable Finance and Investment (GRASFI).[12] We had an inaugural conference in Maastricht last year, and have a program in Oxford in September. That is a program where large investors get together with the best researchers and best educators on sustainable finance from 25 universities. ECCE has also produced research and was involved in setting up the GRESB benchmark that pension funds use to measure greenness of real estate and infrastructure.[13]

More recently, you co-founded the Maastricht Graduate School of Business and Economics (GSBE) research Sustainable Development theme.[14] Can you expand on that initiative? What new research projects are you working on?

Yes, that is within Maastricht University. We came to the conclusion that sustainability should not be confined to one department. So we made it more multi-disciplinary. We are doing topics that vary from researching tobacco to health projects in Bangladesh. So we add psychology, law and development economics to finance and accounting. It helps also to get projects more easily financed by the EU or the national science foundations.

How do you see the investment industry in 10 years' time?

The industry was hit quite a bit by the Global Financial Crisis. To show that you have added value has become more and more difficult. The trend towards indexing shows that. Why spend fees if managers are playing a zero-sum game? Or negative-sum minus the cost? So, I don't think

---

11 ECCE is a joint initiative of Professor Kees Koedijk, affiliated with the Erasmus University/Rotterdam School of Management, Professor Rob Bauer of the University of Maastricht, and assistant professor Jeroen Derwall. In 2002 and 2005, their team received the US Social Investment Forum's prestigious Moskowitz Prize. Also in 2005, they obtained a large grant from the Swedish Foundation for Strategic Environmental Research (Mistra) to conduct research into the role of financial markets in promoting sustainable development.
12 https://www.sustainablefinancealliance.org.
13 https://gresb.com.
14 https://www.maastrichtuniversity.nl/research/sustainable-development.

we will go back to the same level of active management, but focus on long-term decisions and big topics like sustainability. That will continue.

For sustainability, you still have to engage. But the big nut to crack is investor collaboration to make it work effectively, so there are a lot of initiatives. If you pool together resources you will get better results, and more responsiveness from companies you invest in. That's a better strategy than just selling the stocks you don't like.

What keeps you busy outside of office hours?

I like to play the guitar and I collect vinyl records. Some records I still have from when I was 14. So both hobbies are nice in the context of sustainability!

Finally, investment: art, science or skill?

Science and skill are not mutually exclusive. You definitely need skill to be a good investor. That doesn't mean just skill in picking the right asset classes or stocks. It would also be skill in understanding your clients' preferences and creating consistent portfolios that meet their needs. You need models and science to do that. However, a lot of things are highly uncertain, so that is where the art comes into play. It's best to be humble when it comes to investing.

Thank you for your time.

Conclusions

We spoke to Rob again after 12 years, and now, sustainable investing has gone from niche to mainstream, whether due to investor beliefs, societal pressure or regulation. Despite it becoming mainstream, there are still a lot of buzzwords, and Rob notes it is 'still as confusing as when you wrote your first book 12 years ago!'

Rob notes governance is a necessary condition for a company to be good. If it's not good, it's not a good investment. In the context of sufficient conditions, climate change is a topic we cannot neglect any more.

He also notes that markets are becoming increasingly efficient in terms of pricing the sustainability premium. The really material information you can refer to is increasingly being clear. That information is priced in. Only unexpected information leads to extra return. He notes:

' … to say that good shares have good returns, that is a really naïve thought!' Companies that are sustainable may have lower risk and high ROE, but a lot of that is already priced into the share price. Companies that are risky to climate change tend to pay higher interest for their bonds because the banks think the probability they will default is a bit higher. So, this is being priced as well.

Rob mentions that AI and pattern recognition could help in extracting, as ESG data is less measurable and defined and has a broader number of data points of different dimensions and different topics. It's hard to oversee all that as a human.

The Netherlands remains a pioneer on sustainability, and a core reason for that he considers to be interpretation of the prudent person rule in the Netherlands. Asset owners there are leading the way with board members increasingly asking their members in surveys what they want, in essence giving member-driven outcomes on sustainability policies. He notes every investor is somewhere along the continuum of exclusion and engagement, but in the end it probably is the law that makes the difference rather than investor actions.

As an optimist, Rob thinks humanity will find ways to somehow invent new technology or change behaviour as the stance towards doing something is increasing towards climate change mitigation.

For sustainability, he notes you still have to engage. But the big nut to crack is investor collaboration to make it work effectively, so there are a lot of initiatives. As Rob concludes:

> ' … if you pool together resources you will get better results, and more responsiveness from companies you invest in. That's a better strategy than just selling the stocks you don't like.'

PART VI

LONG-TERM
INVESTING

— CHAPTER 12 —

INVESTMENT BELIEFS FOR THE FUTURE

An interview with Dr Cliff Asness

'Believe nothing just because a so-called wise person said it.
Believe nothing just because a belief is generally held.
Believe nothing just because it is said in ancient books.
Believe nothing just because it is said to be of divine origin.
Believe nothing just because someone else believes it.
Believe only what you yourself test and judge to be true.'

Buddha

Institutional investors, prior to making any investment, are first and primarily guided by their investment beliefs.[1] Surviving in the asset management industry requires not just a good organisation, a good staff and a well-defined mission. It also requires us to formulate our own investment beliefs and a clear view on how we perceive that capital markets work.

These may relate to our beliefs on market inefficiencies, how we can add value over different time horizons, and the best way of extracting

---

1 'Investment beliefs, every asset manager should have them', Koedijk, K., and A. Slager, *Journal of Portfolio Management*, 2007, vol. 33(3), pp.77–84.

this value. Various organisations may hold different beliefs.[2] They may be implicit or explicit, involving simple or comprehensive models of capital markets.

Investing, in the end, is about taking money out of cash earning the risk-free rate and investing in risky assets, with a belief we are rewarded for taking on that risk by being exposed to a certain risk premium.

While some beliefs are well accepted within the wider academic and professional community, such as the equity risk premium, there are others where various opinions remain.

Apart from the traditional 60/40 balanced fund, multiple approaches have evolved to put these risk premia together from a portfolio perspective.

In this chapter we confront some of the more common beliefs, and who better placed to do that than Cliff Asness, who deals with beliefs and risk premia on a daily basis.

Introducing Dr Cliff Asness

Cliff is a Founder, Managing Principal and Chief Investment Officer at AQR Capital Management. He is an active researcher and has authored articles on a variety of financial topics for many publications, including *The Journal of Portfolio Management, Financial Analysts Journal* and *The Journal of Finance*. He has received five Bernstein Fabozzi/Jacobs Levy Awards from *The Journal of Portfolio Management*, in 2002, 2004, 2005, 2014 and 2015. The *Financial Analysts Journal* has twice awarded him the Graham and Dodd Award for the year's best paper, as well as a Graham and Dodd Excellence Award, the award for the best perspectives piece, and the Graham and Dodd Readers' Choice Award.

In 2006, the CFA Institute presented Cliff with the James R. Vertin Award, which is periodically given to individuals who have produced a body of research notable for its relevance and enduring value to investment professionals. Prior to co-founding AQR Capital Management, he was a Managing Director and Director of Quantitative Research for the Asset Management Division of Goldman Sachs & Co. He is on the editorial board of *The Journal of Portfolio Management*, the governing board of the Courant Institute of Mathematical Finance at NYU, the

---

2 https://www.unpri.org/asset-owners/investment-beliefs-examples-from-practice/288.article.

board of directors of the Q-Group, the board of the International Rescue Committee, and the board of trustees of The National WWII Museum.

Cliff received a BS in economics from the Wharton School and a BS in engineering from the Moore School of Electrical Engineering at the University of Pennsylvania, graduating summa cum laude in both. He received an MBA with high honours and a PhD in finance from the University of Chicago, where he was Eugene Fama's student and teaching assistant for two years, so he still feels guilty when trying to beat the market. Cliff is fond of saying his secret sauce is not even close to secret, and made a very conscious decision to share his firm's research over time. He sees AQR as a bunch of academics who want to see theories work in the real world and make real money for real clients.

Cliff, thanks for your time. Do you have a current list of top peeves for investors regarding false beliefs?[3]

This may shock everyone, but I do not keep an ongoing list of peeves. But I can think of three off the top of my head.

The first is the mismatch in time horizon over which statistically you can reliably think a strategy will 'work', and the time horizon those same strategies are judged over. I admit I may be dating this interview, but it's been a tough year-and-change for a lot of quantitative factor strategies, so this is obviously on my mind. We absolutely expect to see periods like this occasionally and have seen them before, but they are astoundingly way more painful – even after 25 years of doing this and knowing they will happen – than they should be. So, I'm as guilty as everyone else and include myself in my peeve.

The second I actually just wrote a blog piece about.[4] The piece describes a made-up AQR fund – the S.M.O.O.T.H. fund – that does all the standard stuff we do but is unmarked for 10 years or marked at a tremendously slow-moving average. And I talked about how much better that is because drawdowns are much narrower, and it almost never shows losses. Of course, I'm really poking fun at private equity. Private equity absolutely has an economic purpose, but I do think the current institutional investor love affair with private equity is at least

---

3   In 'My top 10 Peeves', *Financial Analysts Journal*, 2014, v70(1), pp.22–30, Cliff discusses a list of peeves that share three characteristics: 1) They are about investing or finance in general, 2) they are about beliefs that are very commonly held and often repeated, and 3) they are wrong or misleading and they hurt investors.
4   https://www.aqr.com/Insights/Perspectives/Introducing-the-New-AQR-SMOOTH-Fund.

in large part about not marking to market. It may be rational – it may allow people to stick with it. But it is somewhat frustrating to those of us who manage strategies that people perceive as riskier just because we can tell you the prices.

A third peeve is the notion that risk factors can and should be timed, which I think is oversold. I don't think it's impossible – we talk about basic valuation and basic trend having some efficacy to time factors – but we emphasise that it is not the way you make most of your money. Most of what you do is hold them for the long term. We have to deal with people saying you should time, just like when the stock market drops people say you should guess those times. I don't think that's the way to do it.

In terms of research on investment beliefs, which areas do you think institutional investors should focus on?

I like to think of it as if you are in charge of an investment program – what do you need to have a view on, either mathematically or philo-sophically, explicitly or implicitly? I would start with having some view on what the equity risk premium (ERP) is, or even a range. The same goes for the risk premium of other major assets, but I focus on equities because for most investors that dominates the risk/return profile of their portfolios. Having a view on the ERP is important.

Going along with that is having a real understanding of the risk of the stock market. Not to say the past is always prologue, but we have a really long history on stocks, so look at what the worst drawdowns are. People are often shocked – and they should not be shocked – by their experience, especially given how good the last multiple years have been in stocks. Stocks are volatile beasts.

A third focus would be having a view on international diversification versus home bias. Our view is very pro-international, but some take the other side of that, particularly in the US.

A classic thing to have a view on is how tactical to be, if at all – an overall philosophy of whether you're going to time at all. It can range all the way from Jack Bogle – only rebalance for the rest of your life – but even he admitted to me, with a smile, that he did sell some stocks near the peak of the tech bubble. So even Jack would sin (time) a little.

The last one would be: what is your general view on active management? Do we believe in it, and that we can find it, and it pays off net of fees? People have very different views on that.

In terms of strategic research, which areas do you think institutional investors should emphasise? For example, strategic asset allocation, security selection, new asset classes, market timing, portfolio construction, risk management, principal–agency issues?

Strategic asset allocation (SAA) will determine most of your long-term returns. If you're 70/30 stocks bonds and I'm 30/70 stocks bonds, that is going to be a big source of our dispersion.

Having said that, that does not mean you should spend all day, every day on SAA. By its nature, SAA is a one-time decision. Maybe you update it occasionally if you have new research or a new view. One thing I think is kind of neat is that the most important thing is not the thing you should spend the most time on. It's some function of importance and your ability to move the dial. It could be a minor part of the portfolio that you're really good at. For example, if you think you can time the market, which I personally find less plausible, then go for it!

The lion's share of the day-to-day effort would probably be about portfolio construction, looking for diversifying sources of returns, risk management, and minimising principal-agent problems. For example, managers who, when they get really big, take much lower risks or managers taking in passive beta because it's a positive expected return, and they get paid for that over time. An investment management team can monitor these and make things better there.

Some of the key themes for institutional investors in relation to alternative assets are the increased allocation to more exotic assets, globalisation of portfolios, focus on ESG, changes driven by new technology and low-cost risk premia substitutes. Would you agree? Would there be any other themes you have identified?

There is one I would add: the general trend toward less liquidity. People are increasingly comfortable with illiquid investments. In theory, for many years, people have hypothesised and studied whether an illiquidity premium exists – that you should get paid more if something is illiquid. But we may be doing this backwards. If illiquidity actually makes you a better investor, since you can stick with it more because your hands are tied (you can't sell it and sometimes you don't even see the volatility), then people possibly desire it. This makes my brain go a little crazy, but you possibly could even accept a lower expected return because it is a desirable characteristic. Instead of *illiquidity* premium, there could be *liquidity* premium!

In terms of alternative assets, another current theme is that the ongoing US equity bull market is a headwind. If you asked any alternative manager or investor five years ago, 'if equity markets go mostly straight up, will alternatives keep up?' – they would have said of course not, and vice versa. It's the way of the world. The world likes three to five years' performance.

Why did you start AQR? Apart from the profit motive, was there something academic involved, like the search for the truth in the real world and sharing that knowledge?

I tend to shy away from highfalutin statements like this, but there is something like a search for the truth going on. Of the founders, three out of four of us were almost professors in finance. Trying to find out how markets really work and trying to prove that we could move the dial for real-life investors, that was and is still very exciting to us.

We almost left Goldman Sachs six months before we actually did. Goldman agreed to better economics for us, but we also wanted to focus only on our models and our trading. They had us doing other stuff as well – we were a support group. We wanted to separate those functions, but Goldman said no to that. I understand why, and it was actually quite lucky for me that they didn't do what I wanted!

So yes, it was the ability to focus on real research, to write what we believe in with no filter.

I'm not sure if you can call that heroic in hindsight! [Laughs.]

Campbell Harvey once said: 'Hundreds of papers and factors attempt to explain the cross-section of expected returns. We argue that most claimed research findings in financial economics are likely false.'[5] Do you have any comments on that? This seems like a complex agency problem due to the pressure to publish and/or promote products.

Cam and I go way back. He was a visiting professor at the University of Chicago when I was still a PhD student. My first paper he said was

---

5 ' ... and the Cross-Section of Expected Returns', Harvey, C.R., Liu, Y. and H.Q. Zhu, *The Review of Financial Studies*, v29(1), 2016, pp. 5–68.

'great on substance, but in need of some editing suggestions'. He then basically proceeded to rewrite the entire thing!

Data mining is a big danger, and it is somewhat prevalent in the industry. I would argue, however, a few things. First, academics are worse than practitioners. Academics focus on getting a paper published and that's it. In the industry, you have to live with the actual results. If we created a random number generator, that's not so good. So the industry has a bias too, but I would say it's not quite as bad as academia.

Second, applying this to current quantitative factor investing, Cam is right, but I think many other people go way too far in generalising these types of observations. Real-world quant practitioners – not just AQR, also Research Affiliates where Cam is a partner – actually believe in a relatively small handful of things, not hundreds of things. The ones we believe in are highly overlapping with the ones Cam believes in.

What most real-world quants work on is not this data-mined universe, but the small subset that passes the far more stringent battery of tests I have a lot of confidence in. Value, momentum, low risk, quality, carry – these are not hundreds of things. They work across all geographies and in many asset classes, without great exception, before and after publication, and in live trading. And they have some decent economic theory behind them. Of course, different quant firms always squabble over something – we're on the record about being very cynical about small cap. The original CRSP database didn't have the delisting returns negative enough, so it overstated the returns to small firms and understated the need to risk adjust and account for illiquidity – taking these into account, we find no small firm effect. And we believe in momentum maybe more than some others do. But overall, I agree with Cam that data mining is something to worry about and guard against, but it doesn't change our confidence in the far smaller subset of the things that we, he, and most other serious quants believe in.

A lot of cutting-edge research is led by the private sector, because of reduced public funding, but also because of the increased resources of private firms like yours, or say a Google. Does that concern you in terms of potential biases in the findings/barriers to innovation as firms protect IP? How do you see the IP discovery process going forward?

On the area of proprietary IP, much of what we do, we do share. We think long-term success is doing something that is good and reasonable, and then sticking with it through tough periods. The bad news is it's much harder to do than it might seem. The good news is the fact that it's hard to live with means you don't have to worry as much about others stealing your IP. Howard Aiken, a pioneer in computing, once said, 'Don't worry about people stealing an idea. If it's original, you will have to ram it down their throats!'

We will continue to produce new IP that will be private, but it is not the next small innovation that drives investment returns. It is the very basics of investing – doing something with common sense, a tremendous amount of evidence, and sticking with it like grim death – that makes up most of long-term success.

There seems to be increasing popular media considering the rise of machines and AI (thanks to super hero movies!) and folks citing defeat of humans in games like Go. What in your view are the practical implications of AI and Big Data for the general investment industry? How is this impacting long-term investors?

I should start out by saying we're certainly investing in this ourselves. Bryan Kelly, who is also a Yale professor, heads our effort in that area. With that said, we think of this stuff as evolutionary rather than revolutionary. AI at its core is still a way to extract truth from data. That's what quants have always done. And Big Data is still data. We've always looked for new data sets to analyse – a factor we added a number of years ago was ways to mimic informed investors, which required a tremendous amount of new data, such as filings and short positions.

While it may sound neat, new and cool, it is not all new. I'm fond of saying even our effort here is experimental. Over the next three to five years, will we have produced things that are really great? The thing about new research is that you can't actually promise it. It's all part of a big experiment. I don't think AI will have a big impact on the basic factors we believe in.

AI and Big Data applications can also be dangerous. AI is a bigger, stronger tool to extract patterns that may, or may not, be true! The industry is both worried about data mining and very excited about AI at the same time. That is a potential contradiction we all have to watch out for. Unstructured Big Data sets actually raise the need for AI and raise the validity of using it. The reason we have a problem with data mining is not that backtests don't tell us something, it's that they're not long enough – you only get to see history once. If you have much, much more data, data mining stops being a pejorative, and having a better technique for data mining, like machine learning, becomes important.

The characteristics of strategies that come out of AI merged with Big Data will be somewhat different. Say you are the first to find great new data sets and parse them well – you'll probably produce high Sharpe ratio strategies. But they won't last very long, as other people discover the data. It will be arbitraged down to low but positive Sharpe ratios. So you start to look for the next data set, and it becomes like an arms race.

Which areas of practitioner and academic research would you expect to be most impacted by new technology and Big Data developments?

Anything that is on the short-term side, anything with a lot of data, like high-frequency trading, will be impacted. That's not what we do at AQR, but it's a perfect place to apply machine learning and Big Data. There's not a lot of theory there, but a lot of data, and data mining becomes more permissible. Risk is a place where I think nonlinear relationships that can be found by AI might be really interesting. The more data and the less structured it is, the more you can use new technology.

On the other hand, it would be completely useless for long-term investing questions like: what is the ERP? This is a very key number to all of us in finance. We won't learn much about it from these new techniques. Some key questions are thus not impacted at all.

There is a wide dispersion among smart beta managers in terms of outcome, unlike regular beta. This comes down to choice of beta formula and effective implementation. Is this really 'beta' (like, say, S&P 500 beta), as you basically are dependent on manager skill again?

I had a multi-year campaign against using the phrase 'smart beta'. It is simple factor investing that a lot of people have been doing for a long time. I lost that battle as language is democratic – if you refuse to bend to that you end up a bitter old man no-one understands, so I have caved to that! Just calling something smart beta or factor investing doesn't matter, it is the same thing.

A criticism of smart beta/factor investing is indeed the return dispersion you mention. Another one is: you're all doing the same thing

– isn't it crowded? These are somewhat at odds. You can criticise for either one of the two, but not both at the same time.

I'll try to answer your question on dispersion directly. It's a very subtle topic. First, just calling two things smart beta doesn't mean they're the same. For instance, a smart beta fund that does fundamental indexing that is a pure simple value tilt will of course have different results than one doing another factor, like low volatility. Both are smart beta funds, but the tilts are uncorrelated with each other. So if you're just looking at a smart beta label and not looking at what they believe in, of course you will see different results.

Further, imagine building a smart beta fund tilting to two factors, value and momentum. I think it's better if you also use low risk, quality and carry, but I'm sticking with a simple example here. Assume we agree precisely on how to measure and trade value and momentum, except you believe the weights should be 60% value, 40% momentum, and I believe in 40% value, 60% momentum. In terms of outperformance, we are very correlated over the long term, about 0.65 using simple factors since 1990. But there are relatively long periods of gigantically different performance. During the technology bubble, the portfolio with more value got crushed, while the one with more momentum made a little money. Then it was the opposite when value came back. It's very easy for someone to say we're doing radically different things, but really, we're doing things that are long-term similar where short-term results can be very different. Taking it even further, to 75/25 versus 25/75, drives the average correlation to 0 even though we believe in precisely the same things and just disagree on optimal weights. If these things are true, we've both built good investment products. But we've also built uncorrelated investment products that will have vast periods of very large differentials. The bottom line is even when there is a shared philosophy, things can come out quite differently.

My basic advice is to go and find things you believe in, say four or five factors, and diversify across a handful of managers that you believe have strong implementation capabilities. In choosing those managers, balance between group think and manager diversification. You don't want managers that believe in precisely the same things, but having both value and anti-value managers is probably not a great idea. Decide which you believe in. And importantly, understand they won't look at all the same over the short term.

You said 'every few years I'm in a panic that everybody hates us.'[6] You describe this as the 'feast or famine' syndrome and recently wrote an article referring to a potential Ragnarok in liquid alts.

The investing world does over-lionise you when things have been good lately and over-demonise you when things have been bad lately. Many in the investing world are what I like to call 'momentum investors' but at a value time horizon. They want the winners – but not at a three- to five-month horizon, but at a three- to five-year horizon. That's mildly backwards at least, but that's a fact of life.

Can you comment on the trend towards 'dynamic asset allocation' and 'real return' strategies and the academic evidence that short-term market timing from tactical tilting adds value from an asset class or risk premia perspective?[7]

As I've already said, we don't think it's completely zero, so you can 'sin a little'. Antti Ilmanen and I wrote a paper by this name related to market timing, but we made the point that it also applies to factor timing. It's not without any power, but the power is quite weak. I think that dynamic asset allocation is just a form of timing and it is somewhat oversold.

Which of the following are the most likely reasons you think as to why premia may disappear or reduce half-life going forward:

1. **Institutional fund flows**
2. **Competition among investment firms**
3. **A change in social behaviour**
4. **Regulation**
5. **Evil robots!**
6. **Many never existed in the first place**
7. **Other: _____**

Let's start with the ones I don't worry about: 4) regulation could stifle our ability to exploit risk premia, but by making it harder to implement, regulation may make them bigger; 5) evil robots – that's a Schwarzenegger fantasy! 6) I do believe some of them never existed in the first place. The small firm effect is a good example.

---

6   Invest Spotlight, Cliff Asness. https://www.youtube.com/watch?v=qYPhvSJpTTc.
7   https://www.aqr.com/Insights/Research/White-Papers/Market-Timing-Sin-a-Little.

One that may reduce premia is: 1) fund flows are the ultimate way something gets arbitraged, as more money goes into it. I don't think this is happening right now – currently the spread in value is wide versus history, it is not expensive. Regarding 2), competition among investment firms leads to slightly better mouse traps. Most firms, like ours, DFA, RAFI, believe in the same four or five factor families. I don't think it makes the premium go away. And 3) is related to 1). Going forward, we expect the ERP is going to be lower because valuations are so much higher than historical average. It's possible the lower gross returns we expect going forward are going to lead to a similar net Sharpe ratio, because people now have much more efficient tools for getting equity exposure.

You once said 'hedge funds represent little alpha, lots of fees, lots of beta.'[8] How do you see the future of alpha and the hedge fund industry?[9]

I've been writing and talking about this for a while. Our first paper on this was in 2001. We only had seven years of data when we did the paper 'Do Hedge Funds Hedge'?[10] Even then – we have way more out-of-sample data now – we found exposures to the market were larger than people thought, and we didn't find giant alphas. They were mildly positive or even flat, after accounting for all the betas.

Returns can come from three sources: market risk premia (like the ERP, term, and so on), true alpha, and all the stuff in the middle like uncorrelated factors. The market risk premia are still the lion's share. And as we know, fees are getting close to zero for market risk premia due to near perfect competition. Alpha – we can all have a different opinion on how much is out there and whether we can find it. You'd pay a very high percentage of the alpha in fees, because it's uncorrelated, like a monopoly. Factors are somewhere in between, and fees should be somewhere in between. The problem with hedge funds is that, while gross of fees they are a pretty neat portfolio, they're also on average net-long and do tilt toward some of the common factors, so the canonical 2+20 fee means they're doing a portfolio of three different things but charging as

---

8 https://www.forbes.com/sites/nathanvardi/2017/03/20/how-cliff-asness-became-a-billionaire-by-building-the-vanguard-of-hedge-funds/#4f0f2d9f23a4.

9 The industry has now reached US$3.2tr in funds under management. https://www.hedgefundresearch.com/news/hedge-fund-assets-surge-on-hfri-1q-performance-gains.

10 https://www.aqr.com/Insights/Research/Journal-Article/Do-Hedge-Funds-Hedge.

if it's all alpha. So over time, I think we'll see a lowering of fees and more precision in what managers say they are doing.

You mentioned in an interview there was a set of core beliefs that most quant firms agree upon, and upon which the value and momentum premia are predicated:[11]

- Buy stocks at reasonable prices
- Buy good-quality companies
- Buy profitable companies
- With lower risk than alternatives
- Which are starting to get better in price and fundamentals

Do you still agree with this list?

This is still a pretty good list. Profitability I usually think of as a subset of quality, but that's probably semantic. Value, quality, profitability, low risk (beta, volatility, fundamental), and the last one is momentum, both price and fundamental. In the asset allocation world, like for currency and bond markets, we would add carry. Twenty-one years ago, when we started AQR, it was value and momentum. These things do evolve and grow, but they evolve and grow very slowly.

On the topic of the sustainability premium, you have mentioned 'it sucks that the virtuous have to accept a lower expected return to do good, and perhaps sucks even more that they have to accept the sinful getting a higher one.'[12] **What would it take to change that view?**

I would change it if God changes the basic rules of mathematics! Otherwise I'm going to stick to my view. In theory, a constrained portfolio can be as good – but not better than – the unconstrained portfolio. If the virtuous (constrained) portfolio were better, then the non-virtuous (unconstrained) should love it too.

That doesn't mean ESG isn't a wonderful idea. You may have a tactical view that capital will flow into ESG, but the non-virtuous people may also put on that same trade.

---

11 Momentum Investing Strategy, Cliff Asness, CWT Shorts. https://www.youtube.com/watch?v=TM3qYdb8lQo.

12 Refer https://www.aqr.com/Insights/Perspectives/Virtue-is-its-Own-Reward-Or-One-Mans-Ceiling-is-Another-Mans-Floor and https://www.aqr.com/Insights/Research/Journal-Article/Assessing-Risk-through-Environmental-Social-and-Governance-Exposures.

But there may also be non-pecuniary benefits?

That is true. For illustrative purposes, I measured investor utility only in the narrow risk and return sense.

'E', 'S' or 'G' – which one do you consider most important in terms of potentially differentiating investment returns?

I don't think this is too controversial. Most people focus on 'G' as the one that can possibly help with returns or maybe hurt the least. Largely it is because a large amount of 'G' looks like quality. 'E' and 'S' can be great things. If you believe in them, then do them. So far, there has been less evidence that they can help you on the return side.

What keeps you busy outside of office hours?

I wish I could be more interesting. My wife and I are raising four teenagers. The older ones are learning to drive. Between running AQR and that, I'm pretty busy. I don't have time to put wooden ships in little bottles. I don't golf. But I do hope to have hobbies one day. About 10 years ago, I gave the same boring answer as I had four toddlers. The woman next to me mentioned 'pre-Napoleonic British naval history' as her hobby. I said: 'Your hobby kicks the ass of my hobby!'

I don't think that's totally true as you're on the board of the International Rescue Committee and the board of trustees of The National WWII Museum?

I have joined a number of boards, but don't really like to brag about it. And yes, I try to help refugees, and I have an interest in history.

If you hadn't been doing this, what would you have been doing?

Well, there would have been a few possibilities. I could have been a professor of finance – I guess that would have been logical after my PhD.

I like history as well. I'm a bit of an amateur history buff, although being a history professor is a little less lucrative.

There are also many lawyers in my family – so I could have joined the dark side.

But I don't think money alone motivates you?

That's true. I could also have been a great stand-up comedian.

How do you see the industry in 10 years' time?

I do think systematic investing will continue to grow. Fees will continue to fall. The growth won't be close to linear.

I actually just wrote a blog post on that, called 'Quant Cassandra'.[13] Growth won't be linear of course, and we'll have good and bad periods. I think the move to passive is not over. Some say 'passive is akin to Marxism', but I think passive investing may be capitalism at its best. Even Jack Bogle said 'the whole market cannot be passive'.

Finally – investment: art, science or skill?

A science applied artfully: I wish it were a science, but it doesn't quite get there. For instance, it is not about simply building the best computer program and letting it run. There is human judgement required. We still need a good economic story. I don't think that part is pure science. Skill is also very important – you need to have the discipline necessary to stick with it. It's a mix of all three.

Thank you for your time.

Conclusions

It was a pleasure to speak to Cliff relating to beliefs on market inefficiencies, how investors can add value over different time horizons, and the best way of extracting this value.

Cliff's top peeves include the mismatch in time horizons when, statistically, you can reliably expect a strategy to work and the time horizon those same strategies are judged over, the appraisal-based nature of private equity, and investors' interest in the timing of risk premia.

He lists a series of beliefs every institutional investor should have, such as the range of the equity risk premium, the amount of risk they can tolerate, the home bias, their confidence in their ability to market time, and confidence in active management.

As Cliff notes, one of the reasons he started AQR was 'the ability to focus on real research, to write what we believe in with no filter'. As a real-world quant, he notes a small subset of factors passes a battery

---

13 https://www.aqr.com/Insights/Perspectives/Quant-Cassandra.

of tests. He is very cynical on the small-cap premium. He notes, 'there absolutely is no small cap effect and there never was'.

On the potential impact of AI, he notes: 'AI at its core is still a way to extract truth from data, and Big Data is still data. While it may sound neat, new and cool, it is not all new.'

Anything that is on the short term with a lot of data, like high-frequency trading, can be impacted. The more data and the less structured it is, the more you can use new technology.

On the other hand, AI he sees as completely useless for long-term investing questions like the range of the equity risk premium. Thus, some key questions are not impacted at all.

On the area of proprietary IP, Cliff notes that 'much of what we do, we do share'. He thinks long-term success is doing something that is good and reasonable, and then sticking with it through tough periods. The fact that it is hard to live with overwhelms the fear of loss of IP.

When discussing hedge funds, Cliff notes that they often have market and factor exposure as well as alpha, but the canonical 2+20 fee means they're charging like it is all alpha. Cliff foresees a lowering of hedge fund fees, and more precise delineation of what type of returns managers are providing.

He also thinks systematic investing will continue to grow, fees will continue to fall, and growth won't be linear. Investing in his view is science applied artfully. It's not simply aiming to build the best computer program. There is human judgement and an economic framework required, and from that perspective he does not consider AI taking over a real issue. Skill is very important as one needs the necessary discipline to stick with the rules. As Cliff notes:

'It is not the next small innovation that drives investment returns. It is the very basics of investing – doing something with common sense, a tremendous amount of evidence, and sticking with it like grim death – that is most of long-term success.'

— CHAPTER 13 —
VIEWS FROM THE IVORY TOWER

An interview with Professor Stephen Brown on developments in modern finance

'Ancora Imparo' ('I am still learning.')
Michelangelo (1475–1564)

Markowitz's work on modern portfolio theory (MPT) in 1952 and Sharpe's introduction of capital asset pricing theory (1964) are widely regarded as representing the beginning of the transformation of investment management from an art to a science. Trading on intuition and a feel for the market was replaced by an emphasis on risk-adjusted returns, correlations and diversification. A further major landmark work was the development of the Efficient Markets Hypothesis (EMH) as presented by Eugene Fama (1970). Proponents of the EMH argue that the make-up of the outperformers in any period being driven largely by luck. A key assumption of the EMH relates to 'Homo Economicus', the assumption that we all behave in a rational manner. Not too long after its introduction, evidence that markets may perhaps not be so efficient began to accumulate and anomalies began to emerge systematically. Well-known anomalies include value, size, momentum, quality and volatility. Behavioural finance, or the ability to profit from other investors' mistakes, emerged as one of the more intricate and controversial topics in modern finance, and as a significant challenge to the notion of market efficiency. Behavioural finance was for some time regarded as a collection of market anomalies that defy efficient markets, rather than being a coherent theory, although lately there have been attempts to bring it together into a more integrated framework.

From *Homo Economicus* to *Homo Digitalis*?

Loss aversion, overconfidence, overreaction, mental accounting and other behavioural biases are consistent with an evolutionary model of individuals adapting to a changing environment via simple heuristics. Many of the behavioural stories, while plausible by themselves, need to be shown to work together to explain asset prices. Many of the brightest people in the US are working to meet this challenge.

In this chapter we investigate the latest findings from academia and also how behavioural patterns and directions in academic research are expected to change with the introduction of increased machine learning, abundance of information and Big Data analytics in the Digital Age.

Introducing Professor Stephen Brown

Stephen Brown has been Professor at Monash Business School in Melbourne, Australia, since 2016 and Emeritus Professor of Finance at New York University Stern School of Business where he has been teaching courses since 1986. His research areas of interest include hedge funds, mutual funds, Japanese equity markets, empirical finance, and asset allocation and investment management.

He has served as President of the Western Finance Association and Secretary/Treasurer of that organisation, and has served on the Board of Directors of the American Finance Association. He was one of the founding editors of the *Review of Financial Studies*. Professor Brown has written numerous articles that have appeared in publications including the *Journal of Finance*, *Econometrica*, the *Journal of Financial Economics*, the *Review of Financial Studies*, the *Journal of Financial and Quantitative Analysis* and the *Journal of Business*. He has served on the editorial boards of the *Journal of Financial and Quantitative Analysis* and the *Journal of Finance*.

He is also on the board of the *Pacific-Basin Finance Journal* and currently the Executive Editor of the *Financial Analysts Journal*.

He is the author of five books, two of which have been translated into Japanese. In addition to his research, Professor Brown has been recognised for his excellence in teaching and received the NYU Stern Excellence in Teaching Award in 2000 and has served as an expert witness for the US Department of Justice. Professor Brown received his Bachelor of Economics from Monash University in Australia and his Master of Business Administration and Doctor of Philosophy in finance from the University of Chicago. He is a member of CFA Society of Melbourne and the CFA Society of New York.

Stephen is married and has two children. We discuss the current trends in modern finance with Professor Stephen Brown.

Stephen, many thanks for participating in our book again. As Executive Editor of the *Financial Analysts Journal*, can you introduce our readers to what you consider to be the most interesting and fertile topics of discussion in modern finance today?

It is common to point to machine learning and Big Data as the most obvious points along the intellectual frontier of work in the area of financial economics. What is interesting about these areas is that in both cases practice is far ahead of academic thought, and the problem is that much of this work is proprietary in nature. My concern is that shielding research from public view may encourage a triumph of mediocrity. In this context it's interesting to note that the concept of a blockchain, essential to cryptocurrencies, was developed at Bell Communications Research (Bellcore) by Haber and Stornetta in an article they published in 1991 in the *Journal of Cryptology*. Bellcore is an outgrowth of Bell Laboratories where I was first employed. Bellcore not only allowed their research scientists to publish their work; they required them to do so.

Since the financial crisis, one of the hot new areas of academic research lies at the intersection of macroeconomics and finance. One interesting question that arises is the macroeconomic determinants of the correlation between stocks and bonds. While practitioners concentrate on expected return inputs to asset allocation models, there is very limited attention paid to correlations. We do not even know at a point in time whether this correlation is positive or negative. Robert Engle at NYU Stern has been doing important work on the time series patterns of correlation structures, while John Campbell at Harvard has been working in this area analysing the macroeconomic determinants of these patterns. As it happens, Professor Campbell was a student of mine in the long distant past, and I asked him what it would take to bring this work to the point where it could be understood, and applied, by the reader-ship of *Financial Analysts Journal*. He acknowledged that this would be a very challenging intellectual task. My sense is that this area of research may yield new and surprising results in the next few years.

Which academic discussions are most likely to affect the way institutional investors behave in the future?

In disparate ways, much of the recent academic literature in finance is emphasising the fiduciary role of financial intermediaries. I was thinking about this recently in writing the obituary for a personal hero of mine, the late Jack Bogle. The issue of fiduciary responsibility was very important to him as evidenced in all of his writings from his Princeton undergraduate thesis in 1951 to his most recent contributions to the *Financial Analysts Journal*. His arguments against early concepts of unmanaged index-matching funds and his later innovation of the Vanguard 500 Index Fund were ultimately an issue of how to provide investors with access to a diversified fund of equities at the least cost. One of my favourite recent papers in the academic finance literature is the paper by Novy-Marx and Velikov that was published in the *Review of Financial Studies* in 2015, which draws attention to the costs of exe-cuting popular anomaly trading strategies. Concern about fiduciary responsibility lies at the heart of the principal–agent literature, as this is a particular issue in the context of delegated fund management. I would strongly recommend the work of my friend David Yermack, whose con-tributions on the responsibilities of directors and other fiduciaries are very important and are highly accessible.

A central focus of my own research in recent years has been the issue of operational risk and the importance of due diligence in a delegated fund context. Fiduciary rules emphasise the importance of due diligence in the context of public funds. However, for hedge funds and other limited investment partnerships, due diligence often starts and stops with the statement 'trust me'. In my research I have shown that operational due diligence can add as much as 2% per annum return to a diversified hedge fund strategy. This has begun to change with the Madoff disclosures, and fiduciary concerns have led to a substantial growth in operational due diligence consulting in the hedge fund context. However, there is still not complete agreement on what constitutes an effective hedge fund due diligence review. My own work has emphasised the importance of verification and truth telling and other behavioural characteristics of the manager as material in any due diligence review.

In terms of strategic research, which areas do you think institutional investors should focus on? For example, strategic asset allocation, security selection, new asset classes, market timing, portfolio construction, risk management, and principal–agency issues.

In the present environment, the emphasis very naturally is on return enhancement, particularly through new asset classes as well as factor tilts and smart beta strategies. This is understandable given that many public pension funds are struggling with unrealistically high required returns, and endowments are looking to fund spending requirements in the context of historically low fixed-income returns. My view is that the fiduciary responsibilities of institutional investors must compel them to pay attention to risk management, both in terms of operational as well as financial risk.

I remember in the 1970s Justice Posner, then a professor in the law school of the University of Chicago, was challenged in his advocacy of index benchmarks. Wasn't he condemning public funds to mediocrity? His response was that pension funds were not the venture capitalists of America. How prepared are public funds for any potential downturn in the markets over the next several years? There seems still to be much work done on measuring and controlling for the time variant nature of downside risk components.

As I mention above, we don't even know at a point in time whether the correlation between stocks and bonds is positive or negative. My own research has dealt with operational risk concerns in the alternative asset space; this is just one of the issues that should concern institutional trustees.

In the institutional world, there is currently a lot of focus on ESG, diversity and climate change. How does the academic world relate to those topics? Are there any strong views or is, for example,

the absence of reliable data or models a constraint to landmark publications or consensus on these matters?

In May 2015 I was invited by the Prince of Wales Accounting for Sustainability Project to a conference in London. Attending the meeting were all the editors of the leading finance and accounting research journals, as well as a number of business school deans from around the world. The Prince explained that the reason for calling the meeting was that in his perception, CEOs and other corporate leaders did not take environmental and climate issues seriously and that these issues were not taken seriously in business schools, particularly in the finance and accounting areas.

He believed that the reason for this was that professors in these areas could not publish on climate and environmental issues of concern to financial markets; the journals were not interested. We as editors were challenged to discuss why this might be the case. While we did discuss the lack of relevant data to address issues of this nature, the consensus was that there was lacking a critical mass of scholars working in this area. What were we as editors to do about this? I for my part assembled several papers on climate risk and wrote an editorial on this topic in the May/June 2016 issue of the *Financial Analysts Journal* with a view to encouraging further submissions on this topic. Andrew Karolyi, the Managing Editor of the *Review of Financial Studies*, was more creative. He instituted a call for research proposals, and in a competitive process selected a few for which he committed to publish the ultimate results of the research, positive or negative. By creating a special issue of the *Review of Financial Studies* devoted to new research in this area he hoped to jumpstart an interest in publishing more work in this field.

Can you comment on any interesting trends you see in the quantitative research field?

The most intriguing developments, in my view, have to do with the processing and interpretation of textual data. As I mentioned, one of the problems of assessing this literature is that much of it is proprietary and otherwise inaccessible. However, some very interesting work is being published. We published a wonderful paper on this topic in 2017 by Heston and Sinha, 'News vs Sentiment: Predicting Stock Returns from

News Stories'[1] which won a Graham and Dodd Scroll Award in 2018 for research published in the Journal. This is certainly a Big Data project and would not have been feasible even 10 years ago. However, this research is still at a formative stage, going little beyond simple dictionary searches to ascertain buy and sell signals. Unpublished work by Sinha's colleague Olesya Grishchenko at the Board of Governors at the Federal Reserve goes beyond this to consider the grammatical interpretation of public announcements.

Future work might consider the extent to which such announcements and public news items may contribute to our understanding and assessment of risk; the complexity of language in public announcements might provide a useful index of economic uncertainty. In another example, it was remarkable how prolix were the statements of investment objectives of all of the Madoff feeder funds; perhaps the reading level of such information releases might indicate operational risk exposure?

Is there any prospect that the increased use of machine learning and artificial intelligence finally results in a redemption of the Efficient Markets Hypothesis and rational investing at the expense of behavioural finance supporters? Programs do not suffer from human biases (although they may inherit their designer's biases).

I have never seen any conflict between EMH and behavioural finance. Behavioural finance explains how humans process information built into prices today. However, as Burt Malkiel explained in his book *A Random Walk Down Wall Street* many years ago, to make money from this view of the markets you have to explain how humans will process information built into prices tomorrow. Up to this point of time, behavioural finance has little to say on this topic. There is the hope and promise that machine learning and artificial intelligence might break the code that will allow us to interpret and understand this connection, but we are not there yet. Proponents are very alive to the problem of overfitting using complex nonlinear rules through many hidden layers.

This problem results from the fact that we are prisoners of history, and only have one history of data to work from. Can we trust the machine, following its recommendations without understanding why it makes the decisions? Is this consonant with our fiduciary responsibilities? On the

---

1   Heston, S.L., and N.R. Sinha, 'News vs. Sentiment: Predicting Stock Returns from News Stories', *Financial Analysts Journal*, 2017 v73(3), pp.67–83.

other hand, can we trust the decision maker not to overrule the machine? A friend of mine, one of the brightest people I have ever met, understood the behavioural literature very well and set up a very successful fund on a machine based on these premises. But then he failed, because at the depth of the recent financial crisis he overruled the machine. He was not immune from the behavioural biases that affect all of us at different points of time.

In 1945, the first issue of the *Financial Analysts Journal* (at that time, the *Analysts Journal*) was published by the New York Society of Security Analysts. These days, the Digital Age has caused an abundance of information and 'fake information', which increases the number of available papers and journals online and in print. In your opinion as Executive Editor of the *FAJ*, how has this affected the academic review process and acceptance rates?

The ability to critically assess information as it arrives will be the distinguishing characteristic of successful analysts as we go forward. There is so much information freely available on the web that lacks necessary balance and is provided on a self-interested basis. This is particularly an issue in the financial services area, and editors are very aware of the fact that research we publish might be motivated by a desire to promote particular products or services. At the *Financial Analysts Journal* we have taken several measures in response to this concern. As Executive Editor I read every submission to the Journal very carefully. If the paper passes initial review, we send it out for external review, typically to two reviewers who are high-level practitioners or academics with a keen interest in practice. This ensures that the work is both technically correct and maintains the appropriate balance. We ask that authors refrain from making specific references to products, services, individuals or firms unless this is absolutely necessary to advance knowledge or move the discussion forward. We follow the Best Practice Guidelines of the Committee on Publication Ethics, including its processes for addressing allegations of research and publication misconduct. Finally, we insist on transparency and frown upon results obtained using proprietary methods and procedures. We end up accepting about 5% of the papers submitted to us, in line with the acceptance rate at leading academic journals. This rigor comes at a cost however, a cost I would like to refer to as the Gresham's Law of academic publishing ('Bad money drives out good money'). We need to persuade authors that the credibility we bring to the process justifies the efforts they have to make to meet our standards, when they could instead publish their work to an online outlet that does not require such rigorous standards.

There seem to be credibility challenges (some suggest a crisis) regarding the non-replicability of theories in some major studies in the social sciences (and increasingly some of the 'hard' sciences).[2] These question the non-replicability, and suggest misrepresentation or even outright fraud. Do you have any views on that?

The critical difference between finance and other social science disciplines is that experiments in the finance area by very definition cannot be replicated except sequentially through time. Rarely are they as powerful on replication as they were on original publication, and this is often attributed to the market's attention to those studies and competing away the profits that were revealed. Or they may not have existed in the first place. I would here draw a critical distinction between *replication* and *reproduction*. I have made a habit of giving students the exercise of reproducing classic early studies. Some are robust; others are not reproducible, either because of database revisions or because of simple errors in coding or analysis.

Many years ago the leading publications in the area of finance stopped publishing comments on prior published work, perhaps in the desire to avoid publishing content that would be viewed as purely negative in content and tone. I think this was a mistake. At the *Financial Analysts Journal* we maintain a very robust tradition of publishing letters to the editor. These commentaries must be evidence-based rather than opinion-based in order to offer readers a constructive, respectful and to-the-point commentary that moves the discussion forward. We offer the author of the article an opportunity to respond to any letter that we publish on their research, and we find that in our experience, the resulting interchange represents the most widely read section of the Journal. In my view, this is a very healthy process that comes to some measure of truth.

In my previous book 12 years ago you wisely predicted 'the hedge fund industry will generate new dynasties that will last to the fifth generation. Silicon is the new steel, and the development and spread of information technology has at least as important a role to

2   http://knowledge.wharton.upenn.edu/article/research-replication-crisis/.

play in this financial innovation as has the profit opportunities that this innovation has given rise to.' What do you think of the state of the hedge fund industry now?

The hedge fund industry grew out of the 'safe harbor' 3(c)1 and (later) 3(c)7 provisions of the *Investment Company Act of 1940*, designed initially to protect family offices for the purpose of winning over an important constituency to support passage of the Act. The original purpose of this safe harbor provision was to provide liquidity for the markets as these entities are net suppliers of liquidity to the markets; they buy when no-one else is willing to buy and sell when no-one else is willing to sell. During the financial crisis it became evident that hedge funds were in many instances net demanders of liquidity as many unit holders rushed to liquidate their holdings, leading to the failure of many funds and particularly funds of hedge funds.

Hedge funds have underperformed the market since then, which is not surprising as they were set up and advertised as low-beta funds. At the same time, the passage of Dodd–Frank explicitly protected family offices, and as a result many of the best and brightest gravitated to the family office space. As a result, at this time hedge funds are more a brand than a concept, and a challenged brand at that.

What do you see as the hallmark of a successful long-term institutional investor?

As a disciple of Jack Bogle, I am increasingly convinced that the difference in performance among different long-term institutional investors is a matter of their asset allocation and how much risk they can bear. As Jack would argue, it would have to be the long-term institutional investor who has the patience to become rich slowly who ultimately will be successful. But at the same time, we have to acknowledge that investors differ in wealth and the risks they can support.

US foundations used to attract a lot of press coverage for their superior investment performance, much of which can be traced back to their early asset allocation decision to move into alternative assets. Would you still consider them among the top investors? Do you think their superior performance is due to a more innovative culture or access to thought leadership and alumni emanating from the academic world? Or does it have more to do with the fact that they are less constrained than other institutional investors such

as pension funds, and can afford a long time horizon and deep pockets?

I have very strong views on this. I believe that the wrong lesson was learned from the experience of David Swensen and the miracle of the Yale Endowment.

I taught at Yale in the years before the arrival of Swensen, and I learned something of the early history of the Yale Endowment. Up until the 1960s, the Yale Endowment had been run on a very conservative basis, largely invested in fixed income and real estate. The income from the endowment financed much of the New Haven educational enterprise. Kingman Brewster, the then President of Yale, sought release from the shackles of yield to invest in new areas of academic interest, particularly in the sciences. In 1967 McGeorge Bundy, President of the Ford Foundation, chastised university endowments for their overly conservative investment policies and a Ford Foundation report that advocated a total return basis for investments. As a result, Yale, along with many other endowments, adopted a much more risk-tolerant investment strategy, establishing the Endowment Management Research Corporation in 1967 to implement the Ford recommendations. In the same year the Yale Corporation adopted what they referred to as the 'University Equation', which in essence allowed the Corporation to spend the total return on the endowment. Unfortunately this was poorly timed, coinciding with the stock market decline in 1969–70, and the Yale Endowment along with other university endowments did not perform up to expectations. This was responsible for a very serious short-term financial crisis for the University, leading to significant budget cuts.

In 1974, Kingman Brewster initiated one of the first major capital campaigns for universities in the United States, the Campaign for Yale. This, together with more conservative spending rules, brought some financial equilibrium to the University, but it was not until the arrival of Swensen in 1985 as Chief Financial Officer that the financial health of the University began to take off. My interpretation of this history is that Swensen had to understand that the wealthy alumni who had contributed to the Campaign for Yale would never allow their beloved institution to fail, and that this, along with reasonably conservative spending rules, would allow him to take on far more risk than would be reasonably prudent for most other university endowments. This willingness to take risk may in part explain the outstanding success of the Yale Endowment over the past 30 years.

What are some of the more recent articles that you have authored or co-authored yourself? What new academic research projects are you working on at the moment?

My wife was very upset at me for having published a paper in the *Journal of Finance* in December of last year. At the age of 69 I should be slowing down, she argued. The paper – 'Sensation Seeking and Hedge Funds' with Yan Lu, Sugata Ray and Melvyn Teo – touches the central focus of my research interests. The issue this paper deals with is the question whether hedge fund managers take risks to benefit their clients or rather are interested in taking risk for its own sake. The latter is one attribute of what in the psychology literature is referred to as 'sensation seeking', a persistent personality trait associated with the seeking of varied, novel, complex, and intense sensations and experiences, and the willingness to take physical, social, legal and financial risks for the sake of such experiences. Hedge funds operating in a light-touch regulatory environment and characterised by high-stakes trading might be thought to be attractive to individuals who have this trait.

We argue that sportscar ownership might be a simple and verifiable measure of whether a particular manager is in fact a sensation seeker. This is not new. Sportscar ownership is often considered a red flag in operational due diligence reviews. We are able to provide some quantitative support for this practice. Using an extensive database of car purchases, we find that sportscar owners take more risk than those who purchase less powerful cars. This is not surprising.

What is surprising is that this risk taking is not rewarded. Sportscar owners have lower Sharpe ratios and alphas than other hedge fund managers. In other words, they take risk for its own sake. The funds these managers are associated with have a higher chance of failure than other funds, even after controlling for the risk of their investment strategies. They have more regulatory and legal issues than other funds, consistent with a view that sensation seeking leads to an increased operational risk exposure. Their pattern of trading is consistent with that which we would expect of a sensation seeker. In short, we find that sportscar ownership is material in an operational due diligence review of any hedge fund.

My current research has to do with macroeconomic uncertainty, how to measure this, and what role it should play in the context of investment management. In a new paper I am working on I find that disagreement about macroeconomic forecasts is a main determinant of the disagreement among analysts regarding the prospects of firms they cover. This work is very much at an early stage at the moment.

How do you consider the requirements for a finance graduate have changed over the decade? What would be the interesting fields that you would encourage students to pursue?

The increased importance of technology and Big Data has placed a premium on students who graduate with these skills. But this has been the case for at least the last two decades. A few years ago when I was advising students at NYU Stern who wanted a dual degree in finance and information sciences, I would ask them where they wanted to work. New Jersey or New York? Most of the back office facilities of major investment houses at that time were located in New Jersey, and while there was always a demand for technologically adept graduates, it was not necessarily those who would ultimately succeed. Rather, it was those who were comfortable with technology and could use it to advance their careers through their understanding of the markets.

In 1995 I had dinner with the head of a major investment bank asset management unit. He explained to me that his firm was not interested in hiring MBA students. Rather, all he was interested in were PhD graduates, or those undergraduates who showed a clear aptitude for PhD studies. My sense is that this is more true today than it was then. They are not interested in technicians. They are interested in people who can think and who can apply their knowledge to an understanding of the markets. These people are more likely to be found in a class of bright undergraduates or in a group of PhD students at a major research university. I have had the privilege of teaching in both settings, but in the last several years in Australia I have concentrated on teaching at the PhD level.

In the Digital Future, where technology and knowledge will become increasingly important, will book smart win over street smart?

Both will be needed. It is the ability to understand and apply the amazing technological advances that have occurred over the past several decades to the facts on the street. When I started my career at Bell Laboratories in 1976, it was explained to me that the idea is the easy part. It is the reduction to practice which is hard. The ideas of those who are only book smart can easily spin into irrelevance. This is what concerns me about much of what I read in the recent financial economics literature. There is a lack of groundedness, the groundedness that comes from the need to reduce these ideas to practice. It was for this reason that I accepted the invitation to become Executive Editor of the *Financial Analysts Journal*.

What keeps you busy outside of office hours?

I learned to sail when I was young, growing up in Australia. I have always wanted to own a boat, but due the pressures and the distractions of a high-power career in America, not to mention my family responsibilities, this has never been a practical option. In the last year I have discovered the joy of building and sailing radio controlled model yachts. I have just completed a wooden Marblehead class boat that is 1½ metres long and 2 metres tall. I have yet to sail it, and am looking forward to my return to New York for this purpose.

How do you see the investment industry in 10 years' time?

The financial crisis and coincident Madoff exposures have been a real challenge for the institutional investment industry. The pressure on costs and the demand for increased compliance is really challenging the business model of most funds. Jack Bogle, who just recently passed away, saw this with great clarity. He understood that ultimately it would be the lowest cost provider who would ultimately succeed, but even he acknowledged that in the early days it was not really clear whether the Vanguard business model would succeed.

The different flavours of factor investing will come and go, but low-cost index-type products and ETFs will be the ultimate survivors in the large public fund space. What this means is that there will be more opportunities for smaller boutique funds to arbitrage away the frictions which will develop. As Stephen Ross once observed, it only needs one rational player in a sea of irrationality to make the markets work.

Do you have any comments on Australia in particular?

I was at a conference in Sydney a few years ago where a representative from ASIC expressed concern about the systemic risk posed by investments in Australian hedge funds. I was confused. Many Australian hedge funds simply took positions in US funds as funds of hedge funds. What Australians should be concerned about is the much larger investments by family offices. Australia is a preferred domicile for these entities which fly under the regulatory radar screen and are very supple, and can take advantage of opportunities as they arise. I was then asked, 'What is a family office?' This is an example of where I see the investment industry in 10 years' time.

Finally – investment: art, science or skill?

All three. Science is central to the technological developments that are occurring, but without the skill to apply these developments in practice they are nothing. Ultimately the understanding of the markets has to be an art, but an art that is not informed by an appropriate application of the technology now available will not succeed.

Thank you for your time.

Conclusions

It was a privilege to speak to Stephen again after so many years, and be able to capture at least some of the knowledge of a great generation in modern finance prior to retirement. During the interview, Stephen lamented the recent passing of Jack Bogle, Stephen Ross and other seminal figures. In the *FAJ* he has now dedicated a section to their obituaries.

In the Digital Age, where information is widely available and increasingly dominated by self-interest, Stephen acknowledges practitioners at large, well-resourced corporations are increasingly far ahead of academic thought, and the problem is that much of this work remains proprietary in nature, although he also notes the existence of some firms that try to combine both the practitioner and academic angle, like the original Bellcore approach.

He also notes concern about fiduciary responsibility, which lies at the heart of the principal–agent literature. He concludes this is a particular issue in the context of delegated fund management. In essence, the conflict arises from the need to service shareholders and unitholders at the same time. The fiduciary responsibilities of institutional investors must compel them to pay attention to risk management, both in terms of operational as well as financial risk. In the present environment the emphasis instead lies on return enhancement, particularly through new asset classes as well as factor tilts and smart beta strategies.

He considers the difference in performance among long-term institutional investors to be a matter of their asset allocation and how much risk they can bear. Yale ended up as a risk taker in illiquid assets at the right time in 1985 at the start of a long bull market, but he also recalled a number of endowments which tried a similar approach in the 1970 stagflation years investing in illiquid (and real) assets and failed.

Hedge funds have underperformed the market, which he does not consider surprising. In his view, the passage of Dodd–Frank explicitly protected family offices, and as a result has caused many of the best and brightest to gravitate to the family office space. As a result, at this time he considers hedge funds more a brand than a concept, and a challenged brand at that. There will always be talented individuals in any area, as there will always be outliers that defy the average. On the other hand, the demise of S.A.C. Capital, and the corresponding TV series *Billions*, has not helped the reputation of the 'challenged brand' with the public and what really constitutes their 'trading edge'.[3]

As to the future and the Digital Age, there is hope and promise that machine learning and artificial intelligence might break the code, but we are not there yet. He suggests experiments in the finance area are rarely as powerful on replication as they were on original publication. In terms of skills for the future, he notes the interest is in people who can think and can apply their knowledge to an understanding of the markets. As he notes: 'the idea is the easy part. It is the reduction to practice which is hard.'

---

3   Refer also Kolhatkar, S., *Black Edge*, Random House 2017.

SUMMARY

'Alchemy may be compared to the man who told his sons
he had left the gold buried somewhere in his vineyard;
where they by digging found no gold, but by turning up the mould,
about the roots of their vines, procured a plentiful vintage.
So the search and endeavours to make gold have brought many
useful inventions and instructive experiments to light.'
Francis Bacon (1561–1626)

For the past chapters we have interviewed leading thinkers on many aspects of active management and engaged them on the alpha debate. Rather than seeking to cover all aspects of this broad topic, we focus on some of the central questions in the minds of many institutional investors.

Here I identify the top 10 themes that have emerged from the interviews.

1. Data science needs to be combined with a deep understanding of the markets.

'Most investors who try to use AI will fail because a strategy based on using AI to find the key relationships to bet on won't be able to compete with deep understanding. It's more likely to produce data mining that will be costly.'
Ray Dalio

'Rarely are studies as powerful on replication as they were on original publication, and this is often attributed to the market's attention to those studies and competing away the profits that were revealed. Or they may not have existed in the first place.'

Stephen Brown

2. Machine learning has the potential to disrupt, especially for short-term investors.

'For machine learning to have an impact, you need ample amounts of data, and effects that are not easily described using simpler models. This points towards the non-linear effects most prevalent at daily, intra-day and faster speeds.'

Anthony Ledford

'The main focus of a pension fund is long-term asset allocation and risk management. Most of these new techniques have a shorter term horizon, so are less relevant. The biggest impact for pension funds I would expect to be on risk mitigating, stress testing and scenario analysis.'

Stan Beckers

'We can learn to do uncomfortable things associated with behavioural finance anomalies. And certainly with the rise of AI, computers don't understand what uncomfortable is.'

Ben Inker

'AI will be completely useless for long-term investing questions like: what is the ERP? This is a very key number to all of us in finance.'

Cliff Asness

'AI and pattern recognition could really help in extracting ESG data as it is less measurable and defined, and has a broader number of data points of different dimensions and different topics. It's hard to oversee all that as a human.'

Rob Bauer

3. The potential for noise is overwhelming.

'Maybe there is a source somewhere that adds value, but in aggregate social media is one bunch of noise. I was at a New York conference recently where there was this oversupply of data scientists who knew everything about data science but nothing about economics of finance. That's a recipe for disaster!'

Stan Beckers

'It is not clear to me how useful this information is or how predictive it is. It becomes old hat very quickly. I believe there will be a trend back towards creating genuine, long-term wealth using fundamental analysis, rather than trading on the latest information craze.'

Deb Clarke

4. The investment environment: higher risks and lower returns.

A number of our experts are warning that investor expectations are not sustainable. Furthermore, the power of central banks to act as last-resort lender has greatly diminished.

'It strikes me there are two possibilities from here:

1. *The period of easy monetary policy unwinds and the tailwinds behind all sorts of long-duration assets – such as equity, bonds and real estate – turn into headwinds.*

2. *The second possibility is that central banks are never able to go back to the old world. If that is true, then that's not as bad in the short or medium term, but we are then faced with a long-term difficulty.'*

Ben Inker

'There is a lot of conflict between populists of the left and populists of the right because of the large wealth and opportunity gap, and there is a rising world power challenging the existing world power – both of which were also true in the 1930s.'

Ray Dalio

'Investors shouldn't allocate their entire portfolio to "risk on" assets, but take the time to understand how "risk off" assets can benefit the portfolio during times of market crises. Many investors are depending on central banks to protect them and bail them out, but that's not going to be as easy or as feasible in an increasingly populist world!'

Keith Black

'In the present environment the emphasis very naturally is on return enhancement, particularly through new asset classes as well as factor tilts and smart beta strategies. This is understandable given that many public pension funds are struggling with unrealistically high required returns. My view is that the fiduciary

responsibilities of institutional investors must compel them to pay attention to risk management, both in terms of operational as well as financial risk.'

Stephen Brown

5. Successful institutional investors focus on asset allocation, risk tolerance and an edge in private markets.

'As a disciple of Jack Bogle I am increasingly convinced that the difference in performance among different long-term institutional investors is a matter of their asset allocation and how much risk they can bear. This willingness to take risk may in part explain the outstanding success of the Yale Endowment.'

Stephen Brown

'Having a truly long-term view is really hard, no matter how desirable. Everybody wants to have the long-term view, but the most surprising part is how bad organisations are at creating any metric that would help them see whether they were still on track. I don't think most people are very good at timing things, if they are honest. But you can be more confident in the long run.'

Julia Hobart

'I think we will see highly specialised funds with better alignment. Markets will shift towards the large asset owners. LPs will become GPs. They will be empowered.'

Ludovic Phalippou

'At the end of the day the main drivers of the asset classes are pretty similar. But there is a way for private market investors to differentiate themselves. Private market managers with preferential deal flow will have a much higher ability to add value.'

Keith Black

'One only need look at the performance of Canada's large pension funds to see returns over many years similar to those achieved by Warren Buffett. They manage mostly in-house and have the advantage of size to acquire the technical specialities required. They buy businesses, not assets, and managing these businesses effectively is what sets these institutional investors apart.'

James McKellar

6. Hedge funds: the proof and the pudding.

While some of the larger and well-resourced hedge funds like Renaissance and Bridgewater continue to do well, a large part of the industry has struggled in recent years, as alpha waxes and wanes.

'One thing that did strike me is that the 1990s history of hedge funds looks so different from the recent history. So, if you segment hedge fund returns into the first 15 years and the last 15 years, the results are very different! Perhaps the database is maturing, or so much money has come into the space that alpha is being forced lower as markets are becoming more efficient. Strategy by strategy, the returns to liquid alts are highly correlated to hedge funds. The return differences are small, especially in the liquid strategies.'

Keith Black

'Hedge funds have underperformed the market, which is not surprising as they were set up and advertised as low-beta funds. The passage of Dodd–Frank explicitly protected family offices, and as a result many of the best and brightest gravitated to the family office space. At this time hedge funds are more a brand than a concept, and a challenged brand at that.'

Stephen Brown

7. Sustainable investing involves practical applications in an increasingly efficient market.

Responsible investing is going mainstream. Although the alpha benefit is eroded as markets become more efficient, with increasing concern on climate change, the sustainability theme is becoming more and more integrated into investment processes.

'Only unexpected information leads to extra return. If investors know all the relevant information then it is priced so there is a higher price for better companies. If you know this and buy the good companies, you get lower returns and lower risk. If you can distinguish the bad from the good as they turn good, then you can collect a bit of a premium. But to say that good shares have good returns, that is a really naïve thought!'

Rob Bauer

'From the standpoint of a responsible investor we don't know if there is a premium for being responsible, but there is some cyclicality.'

Ben Inker

'The best approach for ESG in emerging markets is in my opinion not negative screening but engagement.'

Mark Mobius

'Private equity is well suited for ESG. If you want to change the world, you have to be able to control the company.'

Ludovic Phalippou

'Renewable energy is one of the most attractive asset classes for investors in infrastructure. Renewables are driving down the price of electricity, especially offshore wind power that is shifting from smaller turbines to larger turbines. These projects can be done relatively quickly. Nuclear and coal are out, gas is so-so, and the problem with hydro is that you need to build a dam with a high capital cost, perhaps capitalised over 50 years, and predicated on a stable high tariff rate for electricity.'

James McKellar

'Storage (batteries) is getting a lot of attention from an R&D perspective as a source of adding to a renewable portfolio. Smart energy campuses are another as a disruptor – transforming heating and cooling systems into a ring-fenced campus and selling the cashflow stream as a form of infrastructure investment.'

Sherena Hussain

'Every ESG investor is somewhere along this continuum of exclusion and engagement, but in the end it probably is the law that makes the difference. For sustainability, you still have to engage. But the big nut to crack is investor collaboration to make it work effectively, so there are a lot of initiatives. If you pool together resources you will get better results, and more responsiveness from companies you invest in. That's a better strategy than just selling the stocks you don't like.'

Rob Bauer

8. Governments need to realign with investors to build infrastructure for a sustainable world.

'Most infrastructure projects are launched by governments, and the dilemma is they are launched with business models that are not attractive to investors. They decide on a solution to get from point A to point B, implement the solution through a highly structured proposal call, and then may discuss it with potential investors. Governments do not understand that investors are not bankers or lenders.

Institutional investors currently prefer equity over debt, want to invest large sums, seek value-added opportunities, and buy operating businesses, not assets. Investors need to be brought in early in the process, be involved in identifying possibilities, and prefer to see a pipeline or portfolio of projects to gain their attention.'
James McKellar

'In mature markets, government debt is crowding out private capital. I wrote a paper on this. Ontario is one of the active social infrastructure locations, and seen as a gold standard around the world. So the challenge is that it becomes very similar to the return profile of bonds. Due diligence and asset management considerations make it far easier to invest in a government bond, rather than in a PPP for what is a minimal spread differential.'
Sherena Hussain

9. In the absence of skill, fee pressure will accelerate in the investment industry.

'I don't think it is sustainable to have a business model which assumes you get a lot of money for doing something that can be done cheaply.'
Ben Inker

'Rather than cutting costs by 10%, how about cutting costs to 10% of what they currently are? We need to challenge ourselves more and move away from the incremental approach, which is unlikely to move the dial sufficiently.'
Julia Hobart

'We've only seen the start in the reduction of fees. We now see zero-fee ETFs emerging. I have also seen traditional active managers splitting alpha 50/50 after no (or even negative) management fee. I see fewer players and a more regulated industry with more passive players.'
Stan Beckers

10. Humans versus machines: humans win!

Despite all the emphasis on AI and machine learning, at the heart of superior performance lies human insight. Given the current available resources, the scope for sophisticated analysis is enormous. In that sense, science is a useful tool to help us develop ideas and make the most of them in the markets. Insight, focus and passion will continue to make the difference, however.

'I can't see humans being completely replaced by machines. We can still think more tangentially and relate things in a non-linear way. In a future world, there will most probably be some purely AI-driven managers, but I would like to think there will also be some 'bionic' managers where humans work with the machines, each doing what they do best.'

Julia Hobart

'Algorithms becoming aware and "taking over" is definitely in the domain of science fiction rather than science fact! That does not mean algorithms can't or won't exhibit destructive behaviour; however if they do, then it won't be because they've gained consciousness.'

Anthony Ledford

'We are now at the stage where hedge funds are launching their own satellites. We are now progressing into body language algorithms on films. But in the end technology is a means to an end. The intelligent/creative application is the differentiator.'

Stan Beckers

EVOLUTIONARY DYNAMICS IN THE DIGITAL AGE

'It is not from the benevolence of the butcher,
the brewer, or the baker that we expect our dinner,
but from their regard to their own interest.'
Adam Smith (1723–1790)

So far, in our book we have focused on how investors can add value across the different asset classes, styles, time horizons and instruments, or in the absence of value-adding ability are faced with fee erosion. In this section, we will examine some of the academic thinking into how evolutionary dynamics may help improve our understanding of the financial markets and the transformation of alpha and beta, or how investors can add value in the Digital Age.

As Stephen Brown mentioned:

'I have never seen any conflict between EMH and behavioural finance. Behavioural finance explains how humans process information built into prices today. However, as Burt Malkiel explained in his book A Random Walk Down Wall Street *many years ago, to make money from this view of the markets you have to explain how humans will process information built into prices tomorrow. Up to this point of time, behavioural finance has little to say on this topic.'*

The Adaptive Market Hypothesis

To bring it all together, leading academics such as Andrew Lo (2004, 2017)[1] have been working on theories of *evolutionary dynamics* to put together a more coherent paradigm. The Adaptive Market Hypothesis (AMH) is an attempt to reconcile economic theories based on the Efficient Market Hypothesis with behavioural economics, by applying the principles of evolution to financial interactions: competition, adaptation and natural selection. Much of what behavioural finance cites as counterexamples to economic rationality – for example, loss aversion, overconfidence, overreaction, mental accounting, and other behavioural biases – which can possibly offer superior investment opportunities are, in fact, consistent with an evolutionary model of individuals adapting to a changing environment via simple heuristics.[2] The AMH consists of the following components:

- Individuals act in their own self-interest.

- Individuals make mistakes.

- Individuals learn and adapt.

- Competition drives adaptation and innovation.

- Natural selection shapes market ecology.

- Evolution determines market dynamics.

Specifically, the adaptive markets hypothesis can be viewed as a new version of the EMH, derived from evolutionary principles.

> *'Prices reflect as much information as dictated by the combination of environmental conditions and the number and nature of species.'*[3]

If multiple species (or the members of a single highly populous species) are competing for rather scarce resources within a single market, that market is likely to be highly efficient; for example, the US stock market,

---

1   Lo, A., 'The Adaptive Market Hypothesis: Market Efficiency from an Evolutionary Perspective', *Journal of Portfolio Management*, 2004, volume 5(30), pp. 15–29 and *Adaptive Markets: Financial evolution at the speed of thought*, Princeton University Press, 2017.

2   This approach is heavily influenced by recent advances in the emerging discipline of evolutionary psychology, which builds on the seminal research of Wilson, E., Sociobiology: *The New Synthesis*, Harvard University Press, 1975.

3   Species may refer to a certain group of investors who share similar attributes; for example, portfolio managers, traders, arbitrageurs, central banks or pension funds.

as compared to, say, emerging markets or some of the more exotic private markets. The AMH also notes:

- *Innovation is the key to survival.* The classical EMH suggests that certain levels of expected returns can be achieved simply by bearing a sufficient degree of risk. The AMH implies that the risk/reward relation varies through time, and that a better way of achieving a consistent level of expected returns is to adapt to changing market conditions. With the advent of AI and Big Data, innovation and detection of new anomalies may increase beyond the speed of thought.

- *Survival is the only objective that matters.* While profit maximisation, utility maximisation and general equilibrium are certainly relevant aspects of market ecology, the organising principle in determining the evolution of markets and financial technology is simply survival. Even ideas are subject to 'survival of the fittest'.

'You have to work on the right problems and put in a lot of hours. If you put in the work, you deserve to win. It is important for anybody who wants to outperform to understand what the underlying driver is of the performance and why it's sustainable. If it is mainly for effort, you must damn well put in plenty of effort!'

Ben Inker

The persistence of risk premia in the Digital Age

One of the conclusions that can be reasonably drawn from the AMH is that the existence of behavioural risk premia is to at least some extent cyclical in nature, and in some cases can entirely disappear in the Digital Age, through the increased use of technology. This view is supported by some of our participants.

'Whether there is a permanent premium to value is a much harder one to solve. The basic argument why value wins is a behavioural one. While I think some of the behavioural finance people would say human beings don't change, I think human beings do change, and the prospect of profits is a pretty good incentive to change. We can learn to do uncomfortable things, and certainly with the rise of AI, computers won't have that issue. They don't understand what uncomfortable is. On the other hand, for

cyclicality to not remain, volatility would have to completely disappear. As long as prices remain more volatile than the underlying cashflows, the market can remain inefficient.'

Ben Inker

Cyclicality does not imply that alpha from market timing will be easy to achieve in the Digital Age.

'For those that can do it, obviously it's a source of value add. However, it is virtually impossible to demonstrate or prove this skill as it is a binary decision at any point in time, and the number of times that people make market timing decisions is not large enough to gather enough data points. So in theory it's possible to be a successful market or factor-timer; in practice it's hard to demonstrate. Often the skill is more in the storytelling rather than in the results!'

Stan Beckers

An argument for the *persistence of alpha* may trace its origins to Simon (1955)[4], who introduced the concept of bounded rationality, suggesting that individuals are incapable of the rational behaviour and optimisation that neoclassical economics assumes. As optimisation is costly and humans are limited in their computational abilities, they engage in 'satisficing', an alternative to optimising in which individuals make choices that are satisfactory, but not necessarily optimal. Individuals make choices based on past experience and their best guess as to what might be optimal, and they learn by receiving positive or negative reinforcement from the outcomes. If they receive no such reinforcement, they do not learn.

'So the real question is: will the Digital Age increase rationality? I don't think so. For example, take populism, which is certainly not rational from an economic perspective, but nevertheless is on the rise. Look also at the amount of noise in social media. So I believe the amount of alpha will not change as investors continue to behave irrationally.'

Stan Beckers

It is no surprise that many fund managers and even institutional asset owners are in fact not optimising investment returns, but rather are

---

4   Simon, H., 1955, 'A Behavioural Model of Rational Choice', *Quarterly Journal of Economics*, 69, 99-118.

maximising asset gathering while minimising career risk, as a result of the competitive short-term environment they operate in. Rather than labelling such behaviour as irrational, it should be recognised that sub-optimal behaviour is not unlikely when we take heuristics out of their evolutionary context. A more accurate term for such behaviour might be 'maladaptive'.

As Andrew Lo puts it, 'the flopping of a fish on dry land may seem strange and unproductive, but under water, the same motions are capable of propelling the fish away from its predators'.

From an agency perspective, therefore, without a proper alignment of incentives these agents will not optimise investment returns or behave as rational investors.

> *'I don't think many people are very good at timing markets. But I believe you can be more confident about long-run trends. Most organisations are taking a much shorter view due to external pressures, so if you think on a different timescale you are more likely to be able to see value.'*
> Julia Hobart

In addition, while the amount of information has increased, the amount of noise these agents face in the Digital Age has also increased. Market efficiency is context-dependent and dynamic, depending on the seasons, the number of predators and prey, and the ability to adapt to an ever-changing environment. The increased availability of AI and Big Data in the Digital Age suggests the half-life of alpha strategies will continue to shorten.

> *'The characteristics of strategies that come out of AI merged with Big Data will be somewhat different. Say you are the first to find great new datasets and parse them well – you'll probably produce high Sharpe ratio strategies. But they won't last very long, as other people discover the data. It will be arbitraged down to low but positive Sharpe ratios. So you start to look for the next dataset, and it becomes like an arms race.'*
> Cliff Asness

AFTERWORD

'The only thing that is constant is change itself.'
Heraclitus (535 BC – 475 BC)

In a world of constant change, the academic and industry leaders who have contributed to this book have raised different perspectives on the megatrends and investment issues that will possibly affect us and generations to come. But of course there is one perspective missing from the book, which is the view of time. Evolution and life are all about change. Similarly, institutional investing is a dynamic process, and it is very likely that the questions in this book will produce very different answers if posed in a few years' time, even if the interviewees are the same. The book is therefore not meant to provide definitive answers, but can be used as a tool for deliberating upon what may happen to the industry based on the wisdom of a great generation.

Nevertheless, a number of common themes recurred during the interviews which, coming from leading thinkers, provide us with important guidance for the investment industry in the decade ahead:

- In the low-yield environment, investors' market return expectations will need to reduce.

- We will keep finding new betas (market exposure) that explain what was once presumed to be skill (alpha), and even newfound betas will be subject to 'survival of the fittest' as behavioural biases adapt.

- Institutional assets will be held by fewer, larger and better resourced investment decision makers driving down alpha opportunities in especially the larger liquid markets. Conversely, this might mean additional alpha opportunities for smaller niche investors.

- The constantly changing nature of the demand and supply of alpha will increase the complexity of active management and technology required.

- With no reduction in investment risk on the horizon, and expected returns reducing, more emphasis will be placed on managing risks.

- The increasing cost of regulation and compliance will disadvantage smaller firms.

- Fees and transaction costs will continue to come down as technology improves.

- There will likely be a disruptor that comes along, like a 'Google' or 'Amazon' asset management.

- Asset owners will start to disintermediate from agents to become business owners, rather than asset traders, similar to the Canadian or Warren Buffett model of patient long-term investing.

- Institutional investors will evolve from shareholders to stakeholders as sustainability becomes mainstream.

As the level of institutional investor education rises and investors better understand the factor exposures underlying their investment portfolios, alpha and beta will in due course be rewarded at their relevant pricing as institutional investors continue to evolve their processes.

As a final word, in nature successful evolution is the exception, and extinction is the norm: something worth pondering when considering the alpha-producing capabilities of the *average* (hedge) fund manager.

The investment industry has always been in a state of evolution. The increase in available data, processing power, as well as the constant search for new return sources in the low-yield environment has increased the speed of that evolution as we enter the *Digital Age*.

ABOUT THE AUTHOR

Dr Harry Liem is Director of Strategic Research and Head of Capital Markets for Mercer in the Pacific region. He consults to a variety of clients on strategic issues and is based in Sydney. Prior to joining Mercer in November 2004, Harry gained 10 years of international experience in the investment management industry working as a portfolio manager and strategist for a number of reputable companies, including ING, Perennial and Rabobank/Stroeve Investment Bank in Amsterdam, Singapore and Sydney.

He regularly presents at conferences and is also author of the book *2020 Vision: Investment Wisdom for Tomorrow*. His work has been published in professional and academic journals, including the *Journal of Portfolio Management* and *European Financial Management*. He has received awards from the Australian government, corporations and industry bodies such as the CFA Institute, the Alternative Investment Management Association (AIMA) and Kaplan. He has extensive experience teaching CFA, CIMA and MBA programs.

Harry holds a Doctor of Philosophy (Finance) from the University of Technology Sydney, and a Master of Business Administration from Stirling University (UK). He also holds a Master of Science (Computing Science) and a Bachelor of Science, both from Delft University of Technology (The Netherlands). Harry is a holder of the right to use the Chartered Financial Analyst designation, and also holds the Chartered Alternative Investment Analyst designation.

He can be contacted at:

harry.liem@mercer.com
www.linkedin.com/in/harry-liem-581aba3a
www.mercer.com.au/investmentwisdombook

www.ingramcontent.com/pod-product-compliance
Lightning Source LLC
Chambersburg PA
CBHW071159210326
41597CB00016B/1598